DESIGNING WEB & MOBILE GRAPHICS

FUNDAMENTAL CONCEPTS FOR WEB AND INTERACTIVE PROJECTS

Christopher Schmitt

New Riders

VOICES THAT MATTER™

DESIGNING WEB AND MOBILE GRAPHICS:

Fundamental concepts for web and interactive projects

Christopher Schmitt

New Riders
www.newriders.com

New Riders is an imprint of Peachpit, a division of Pearson Education.

To report errors, please send a note to errata@peachpit.com

Senior Acquisitions Editor: Michael J. Nolan
Associate Development Editor: Margaret Anderson/Stellarvisions
Version Wrangler: Rose Weisburd
Production Editor: Becky Chapman Winter
Copyeditor: Gretchen Dykstra
Indexer: James Minkin
Proofreader: Jan Seymour
Cover and Interior Designer: Charlene Charles-Will
Compositor: Kim Scott/Bumpy Design
Illustrator: Richard Sheppard

Page 105, Figure 5.13: Engraving by G.J. Stodart after a photo by Fergus of Greenack, before 1890; Figure 5.15: Autochrome photograph by Louis Lumiere, 1910. Page 128, Figure 6.3: Photo courtesy of Flickr user FaceMePLS, under a Creative Commons - Attribution license.

ISBN 13: 978-0-321-85854-2
ISBN 10: 0-321-85854-9

9 8 7 6 5 4 3 2 1

Printed and bound in the United States of America

For Nick, Elisabeth, Matt, Mary Rose, Michael,
Ryan, Megan, Meredith, Gianna

Acknowledgments

A book such as this is blessed to have been touched by many skilled and talented folks.

Thanks to Molly Holzschlag and Estelle Weyl for some last minute edits, and to Christina Ramey for figure and example development.

New Riders is an integral part of the web design community, having published groundbreaking books and continuing to push the industry today. Thanks to Michael Nolan for giving me this opportunity to be part of their legacy.

Special thanks to Rose Weisburd, who remained polite and cool as the whooshing sound of deadlines grew louder and louder. I have profound appreciation for the dedication and resourcefulness of the crew at Peachpit: Becky Winter, Tracey Croom, Margaret Anderson, Gretchen Dykstra, Jan Seymour, Kim Scott, James Minkin, Claudia Smelser, Richard Sheppard. You could not find a finer team anywhere.

From speaking at conferences and helping students to writing books, web education is more than a second job to me. So, a very special thanks to Ari Stiles for understanding how much I love what I do and realizing it's an integral part of who I am. I love her for that.

CONTENTS

INTRODUCTION

In the beginning, print designers created web designs in Photoshop and exported them as one enormous image, declaring that a web site. It wasn't pretty.

Designers started to change their ways after realizing that text and multiple images can not only make designs with HTML and CSS, but make *great* designs. But a part of that process often meant designs would be at least 960 pixels wide or some fixed width.

With the increased adoption of mobile devices like smartphones and tablets that can present a rich web experience in portrait or landscape mode, the desktop browser window width is no longer the standard for which to design. This new mobile component to web design has led us to re-examine our best practices and adopt new techniques.

Designing Web and Mobile Graphics is intended to give the beginner or intermediate web designer a look into how to create and build up visuals that meet current web and mobile standards.

In this beautiful web, all these tasks can be done by one person. Each person like yourself, dear reader, has the power to be an independent content producer.

Designing Web & Mobile Graphics provides a foundation in HTML and CSS in the context of development. Building on quick successes from techniques and tips, we move from chapter to chapter to more advanced or unique web design solutions.

GET READY,... GO!

In web design, things are constantly changing. *Designing Web and Mobile Graphics* is the book intended to give you the foundation you need to work with images and much, much more.

Menu 1 (View menu):

View | Bookmarks | Tools | Window | Help

- Toolbars ▶
- Zoom ▶
- Images ▶
- Style ▶
- Encoding ▶
- Presentation view ⇧⌘F
- Full Screen ^⌘F
- Fit to Width ⌘F11
- Developer Tools ▶
  - Source ⌥⌘U
  - Frame Source ⇧⌘U
  - Validate ⌥⇧⌘U
  - Reload From Cache
  - Opera Dragonfly ⌥⌘I
  - Page Information
  - Page Security Info ⌥⌘I
  - Plug-Ins
  - Cache
  - Error Console ⇧⌘O

Menu 2:

: Designer, Web Developer, Author, Project

christopherschmitt.com/

Page ▾ | Safety ▾ | Tools ▾ | ⑦ ▾ | ✦

- New window Ctrl+N
- Add site to Start menu
- Cut Ctrl+X
- Copy Ctrl+C
- Paste Ctrl+V
- E-mail with Windows Live
- Translate with Bing
- All Accelerators ▶
- Save as... Ctrl+S
- Send page by e-mail...
- Send link by e-mail...
- Compatibility View
- Compatibility View settings
- Zoom (100%) ▶
- Text size ▶
- Style ▶
- Encoding ▶
- Caret browsing F7
- Properties
- View source

Menu 3 (Tools menu):

Tools | Window | Help

- Web Search ⌘K
- Downloads ⌘J
- Add-ons ⇧⌘A
- Set Up Sync...
- Zotero ⇧⌘Z
- Greasemonkey ▶
- Gmail Manager ▶
- Charles ▶
- SEO For Firefox ▶
- Web Developer ▶
- Web Developer Extension ▶
- Page Info ⌘I
- ColorZilla ▶
- Alert Config Panel ⇧⌘Z
- Start Private Browsing ⇧⌘P
- Clear Recent History... ⇧⌘⌫
- Delicious Options
- Make Web Video
- FireUploader
- DownloadHelper ▶
- Adblock Plus ▶

Submenu (Web Developer):

- Firebug ▶
- FireFTP
- Web Console ⌥⌘K
- Inspect ⌥⌘I
- Responsive Design View ⌥⌘M
- Debugger ⌥⌘S
- Scratchpad ⇧F4
- Style Editor ⇧F7
- Page Source ⌘U
- Error Console ⇧⌘J
- Tilt ⇧⌘M
- Get More Tools

Menu 5 (Develop menu):

Develop | Window | He

- Open Page With
- User Agent
- Use WebKit Web Inspe
- Show Web Inspector
- Show Error Console
- Show Page Source
- Show Page Resources
- Show Snippet Editor
- Show Extension Builde
- Start Profiling JavaScri
- Start Timeline Recordi
- Empty Caches
- Disable Caches
- Disable Images
- Disable Styles
- Disable JavaScript
- Disable Site-specific H
- Enable WebGL

"Getting information off the Internet
is like taking a drink from a fire hydrant."
—*Mitchell Kapor*

Chapter 1 UNDERSTANDING HTML

The Internet is full of content. Pretty much everything you can think of is waiting for you to see, and it was all put there by people like you and me. You too can take an active role in creating content for the web. HTML is the key to getting your ideas out there for others to see.

HTML stands for *hypertext markup language*. While it sounds like a computer language, it wasn't created to make the average person annoyed when using it. The best way to think of HTML is as a set of descriptions wrapped around your words and images to make them appear in a web browser.

WHY LEARN HTML?

HTML is the most complete system for allowing people to exchange information all over the world, with greater speed and efficiency than ever before.

HTML Made the Internet Popular

While the *Internet* made it possible for computers to network with one another, it was a choppy experience through the command line and rudimentary programs that had names like Gopher (**FIGURE 1.1**) or Archie. *Web browsers* changed all that.

The World Wide Web's HTML-created pages and links made it easier for Internet users to navigate content. With the adoption of images in the browser to go along with basic text formatting, this quick, addictive publishing and sharing of content opened the door to more people.

FIGURE 1.1 *Using text-display of Gopher to access the Internet. Notice the lack of ad banners.*

```
─────────────────  INTERNET  ─────────────────

              Your Internet ID: monopoly@host.yab.com

            Getting Files                     Finding Information
   [A]  Find Files on the Net (Archie)  [G]  Search for Information (Gopher)
   [F]  Get Files from the Net (FTP)    [W]  Hypertext Search (WWW)
   [Y]  File Transfers for Net Account  [Q]  Query About Someone (Finger)
            Entertainment                          Messages
   [M]  MUDs (Games)                    [E]  Internet E-Mail
   [I]  Internet Teleconference (IRC)   [U]  Internet Message Areas (Usenet)
   [J]  Tintin Interface for MUDs                   Help
            Miscellaneous               [D]  Detailed Reference Text
   [B]  Unix Shell Access (BASH)        [H]  Help Using Internet Functions
   [T]  Connect to Other Sites (Telnet) [K]  If You're Stuck at "Password"
                 SLIP Access (Mosaic, NetScape, etc)
   [S]  SLIP - Graphical Interface      [C]  How To Configure SLIP Access
   [P]  PPP - Point-to-Point Protocol


   Your Choice (A,B,C,D,E,F,G,H,I,J,K,M,P,Q,S,T,U,W,Y or X)? :
 (N)onstop, (Q)uit, or (C)ontinue?
 Menu: <Ctrl R-Shift>              2400 8N1            VT100      Online
```

HAND-CODING COMPLETE WEBSITES

Some argue that the days of hand-coding entire websites are all but gone. Thanks to content management packages like WordPress, Drupal, and ExpressionEngine, you can create sites where the work of building navigation menus and organizing blog entries is done for you. Those blogging applications assemble the header, footer, and sidebars of a site from stored HTML snippets and templates.

While it's easy to automate the repetitive components of a website, a blogging solution isn't up to the task of assembling the main part of each page, where everyone's needs and goals are unique. That's where an understanding of HTML will help you succeed.

Knowing HTML Gives You a Better Understanding of Web Design

Knowing the basics of HTML makes you a better web designer. It helps you more quickly make your pages look the way you intend, and when they don't, it gives you an idea why and what you can do about it. Many *real* programming languages integrate with HTML to create the web's bells and whistles.

Learning HTML Is Easy

Many designers have taught themselves HTML to become more complete professionals. With the industry constantly evolving, even seasoned web designers find themselves learning more from others about what HTML can do.

It's really simple to examine the code behind a web page compared to the code behind desktop and mobile applications. That code transparency makes it easy to quickly learn HTML and the other particulars of web design. To find out how HTML is used in a web page, select the equivalent of the View Source command on your browser (usually found under the File or View menu), and you can see exactly what the code looks like (**FIGURES 1.2–1.5**). Through this method many beginners and professionals copy examples of code—a practice that is not frowned upon, but rather encouraged!

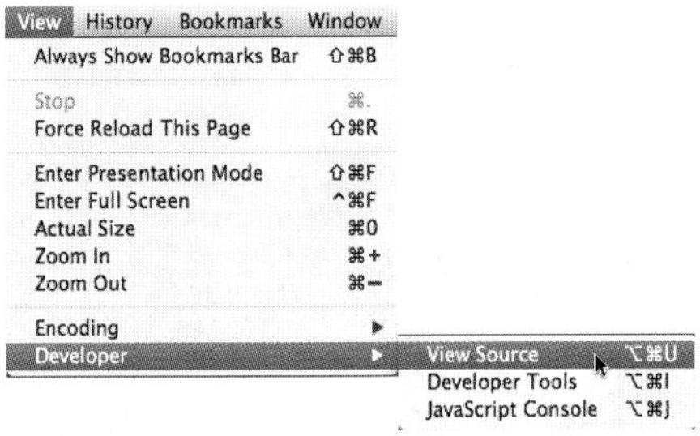

FIGURE 1.2 *Viewing source code in Chrome.*

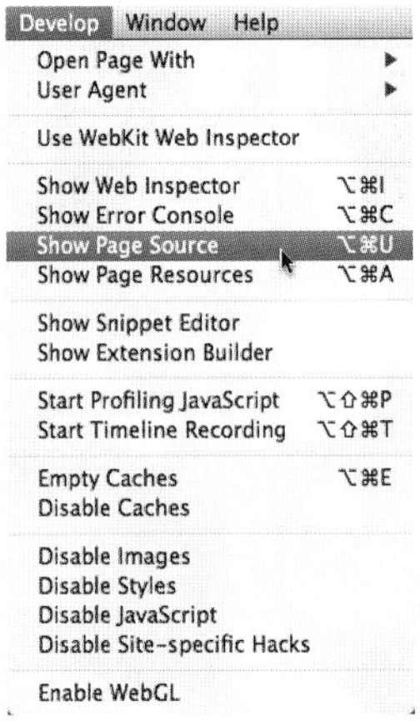

FIGURE 1.3 *Viewing source code in Safari.*

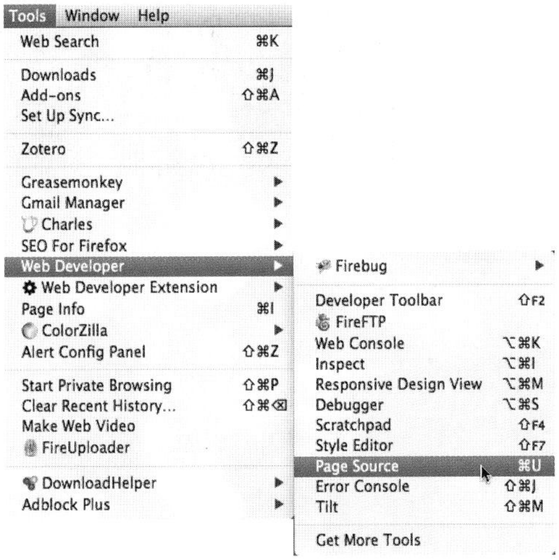

FIGURE 1.4 *Viewing source code in Firefox.*

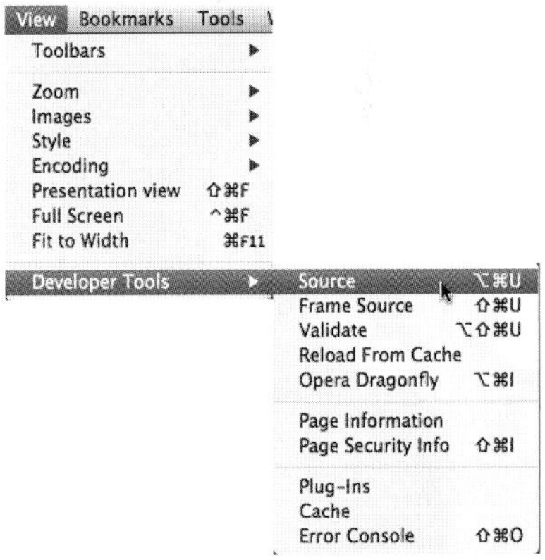

FIGURE 1.5 *Viewing source code in Opera.*

There are numerous sites that focus on web design and development:

- A Beginner's Guide to HTML & CSS
  (http://learn.shayhowe.com/html-css/)

- HTML Dog
  (http://htmldog.com)

- HTML Goodies
  (http://www.htmlgoodies.com/primers/html/
  article.php/3478151/web-Developer-Class-
  Learn-the-Basic-HTML-Tags.htm)

- Smashing Magazine
  (http://www.smashingmagazine.com)

Check out these web design books, too:

- *Bulletproof Web Design, 3rd Edition* by Dan Cederholm, (New Riders)

- *HTML & CSS: Design and Build Websites* by Jon Duckett, (Wiley)

- *Learning Web Design, 4th Edition* by Jennifer Niederst Robbins, (O'Reilly)

PROGRAMMING VS. MARKUP   If programming is telling a piece of software what to do with some bits of information, then HTML could be considered a *programming language*. However, computer programming in languages like Java, C++, Python, and countless others requires more specialized expertise and software for more complex tasks than HTML could ever do. So, while "language" is in HTML's name, it might not be as daunting as other languages.

SHARE WHAT YOU LEARN

A great aspect of working in the web design and development industry is the openness. Share what you learn with others through blog posts, blog comments, and coding on GitHub, Dribbble, or any number of spots. Our industry changes at a lightning pace. Help others that help you along the way.

WEB LEXICON

To get the most out of this book, you'll need to know the following terms and facts about designing for the web:

- The **web** consists of millions of sites, each of which has a unique web address called a uniform resource locator, or **URL** (for example, `http://www.google.com`).

- Each **site** consists of many pages with related content.

- Each **page** on a website can be viewed in a browser (such as Chrome, Internet Explorer, Firefox, Safari, or Opera) on a desktop computer or on a mobile device (such as a smartphone or tablet).

- Web users navigate from one page to another via web links, also called **hyperlinks**.

! COPY TO MASTER, NOT TO PASS OFF

Copying examples of code you like is a great way to learn the tricks of the trade. One caveat: don't blindly copy and paste code or graphics as your own. You wouldn't copy a paper you found on the web and submit it to your teacher as your own work—the same goes for web design (and, really, any industry).

HTML CODING BASICS

There are a few basic terms to learn before you start to code in HTML.

The Text Editor

In order to write code, you need a **text editor**. Look on your desktop computer for a basic editing application such as Notepad if you're using Windows, or TextEdit if you're on a Mac. Every PC worth its salt has a text editor on it, no matter how whizbang or decrepit its features are.

PROFESSIONAL TEXT EDITORS I recommend using a professional text-editing tool like TextPad for PC (http://www.textpad.com) or BBEdit for Mac (http://www.barebones.com/products/bbedit/). Sublime Text 2 is a great option that's available for Mac or PC (http://www.sublimetext.com/2).

First, it's important to note that HTML must be saved in text-only mode and include the file extension `.html` or `.htm`, preferably in Unicode format (see sidebar below).

Word Processors Aren't Text Editors

Microsoft Word and Apple Pages are word processing programs, not text editors. These programs add formatting to your text that messes up your code.

Apple's built in text editor, TextEdit, is a hybrid that can do a lot of the formatting that word processors do, but it also has a plain text mode, so you can use it for editing web pages (and, hey, it's free!).

You'll need to take steps to prevent TextEdit from stripping out your HTML when you save your files. Choose Preferences. In the New Document section; under the Format subheading, check "Plain text." Then click the Open and Save section, and check "Ignore rich text commands in HTML files."

UNICODE

Popular operating systems like Mac and Windows that are used all over the world have to display text in different languages and different alphabets. The underlying digital descriptions that computers use to display text were originally written in a very limited, localized way that didn't account for other character sets like Spanish accents and Chinese ideographs.

Back in the old days, visitors to web pages from other parts of the world often saw a jumble of substituted characters. The browser tried to render the text, but it couldn't call up the right letters from the local user's fonts, as shown in **FIGURE 1.6**.

Working towards solving that problem is the Unicode standard, which encapsulates over one hundred thousand characters, including icons and most of the world's writing systems. Saving HTML pages with Unicode gives you a good platform to have your page reach a wide audience.

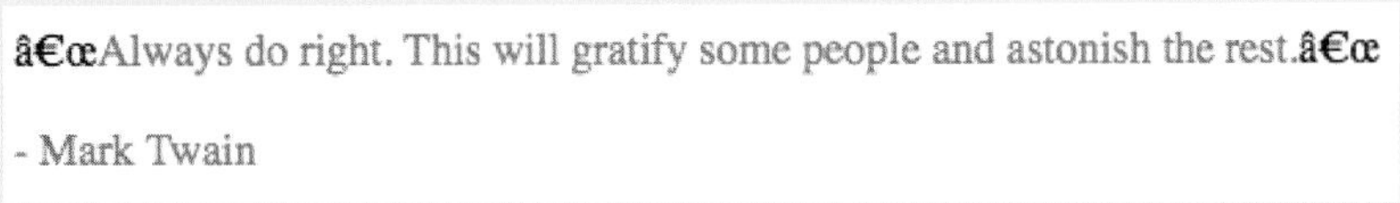

â€œAlways do right. This will gratify some people and astonish the rest.â€œ

- Mark Twain

FIGURE 1.6 *Translating between character encoding causes weird text display.*

Coding with HTML

Right, so let's look at a quote from a US author that's typed into a file called **twain.html** (**FIGURE 1.7**):

"Always do right. This will gratify some people and astonish the rest."

—Mark Twain

HTML's **p element** (**FIGURE 1.8**) instructs the browser that you want the quote and the author to be recognized as being two *paragraphs*.

```
<p>"Always do right. This will gratify some
people and astonish the rest."</p>
<p>- Mark Twain</p>
```

A **p** element is made up of **tags** wrapping around **content**. With a few exceptions, HTML elements come in pairs of **opening** and **closing tags** like **<p>** and **</p>** that surround content (**FIGURE 1.9**).

Elements that don't come in pairs are said to be **self-closing**.

For example, the horizontal rule tag (**hr**) never actually encloses or wraps around any text; it simply specifies the presence of a horizontal line as shown in **FIGURE 1.10**.

```
<p>"Always do right. This will gratify some
people and astonish the rest."</p>
<p>- Mark Twain</p>
<hr />
```

FIGURE 1.9 *A schematic of opening and closing tags.*

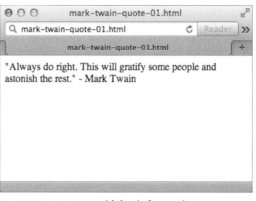

FIGURE 1.7 *A page with basic formatting.*

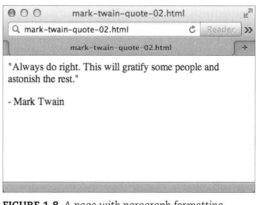

FIGURE 1.8 *A page with paragraph formatting.*

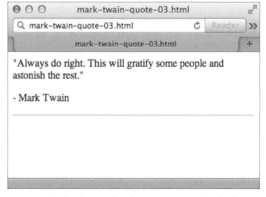

FIGURE 1.10 *How an hr element appears in the browser.*

It would be tedious to immediately follow every opening horizontal rule tag with a closing one, like this: `<hr></hr>`. Instead, it's much easier to add a **trailing slash** to the single tag: `<hr />`. This trailing slash isn't necessary, but it helps make the code look a little better.

STRUCTURING A WEB PAGE

Through elements, HTML provides **structure** to a web page or document. This structure is established by headings, paragraphs, blockquotes, hyperlinks, and major sections. Let's start marking up a text file to create an HTML document.

Specifying the DOCTYPE

In your favorite text editor, add the following tag to the very first line:

```
<!DOCTYPE html>
```

The first line in the HTML document is the **DOCTYPE**, or document type declaration. The DOCTYPE tells the browser which version of HTML you're using, and thus determines how the browser renders the page. For this document and for examples throughout the book, I'll be using the HTML5 DOCTYPE unless otherwise specified. At the time of this writing, HTML5 is the latest version of HTML and it opens up a great number of new features.

If you omit the DOCTYPE or declare the wrong DOCTYPE, the browser still displays the page, but the document won't validate properly, and the page may look and behave differently than expected.

! HTML VALIDATION

Be sure to include the DOCTYPE declaration tag at the beginning of your document. We'll discuss validation in more detail later in the book.

! HTML ISN'T FOR DESIGNING

HTML was never intended to control the look or design of a web page by specifying fonts, colors, and the position of elements. It's about semantics and making sure every bit of content uses the correct corresponding HTML element.

XHTML   There was a time when HTML was wrapped up in XML, which stands for eXtensible Markup Language. XHTML was more stringent in terms of coding practices. As a result, very few sites on the web were built with valid XHTML. Now, we embrace nonprogrammers' easygoing markup style as a part of HTML5.

TO MARK UP THE HEAD, BODY, AND TITLE, FOLLOW THESE ⑤ STEPS:

① Wrap your document in opening and closing **html** tags. Place the opening tag below the DOCTYPE and the closing tag at the end of the document:

```
<!DOCTYPE html>
<html>
</html>
```

② Now add tags to divide the document into two parts: the **head** and the **body**. The **head** element of the page contains important information about the document, such as its title, author, and keywords (to improve its results in search engines) as well as any other required metadata. Place this at the top, before the text begins.

```
<!DOCTYPE html>
<html>
  <head>
  </head>
</html>
```

③ The body of the page contains the meat of the document: the content, or what's actually displayed in the browser window. Wrap the entirety of your page content in **‹body›** tags:

```
<!DOCTYPE html>
<html>
  <head>
  </head>
  <body>
  </body>
</html>
```

④ The title element is placed within the head tag pair. While most of the elements within the head of the page are optional, all HTML documents must have a title. This is displayed to the web user in the title bar of the browser. (This is the only part of the head information that is displayed.) Enter your **title** element like so:

```
<!DOCTYPE html>
<html>
  <head>
    <title>Mark Twain Quote</title>
  </head>
  <body>
  </body>
</html>
```

(5) All HTML documents must have a DOCTYPE, head, and body; this is the basic skeleton of the document. Now, since we know that the content we see in a web browser goes in the **body** element, let's add the Mark Twain quote into this page:

```
<!DOCTYPE html>
<html>
  <head>
    <title>Mark Twain Quote</title>
  </head>
  <body>

<p>"Always do right. This will gratify some people and astonish the rest."
</p>
<p>- Mark Twain</p>
<hr />

  </body>
</html>
```

Saving and Viewing the Page

Now save the file as an HTML document. Go to Save As in your text editor's File menu and save the file with the extension **.html** (as **twain.html**).

Once your page is properly saved as an HTML document, the file displays with the icon of your default web browser. Simply double-click the page to view it in your browser, or go to File > Open in your browser (**FIGURE 1.11**):

Huzzah! We've officially created an HTML web page!

! BE MINDFUL OF HOW YOU SAVE YOUR FILES

If you're using TextEdit for Mac OS X, make sure to select Make Plain Text from the Format menu, and save it under Unicode (UTF-8) plain text encoding. On a PC, make sure All Files and Unicode (UTF-8) are selected.

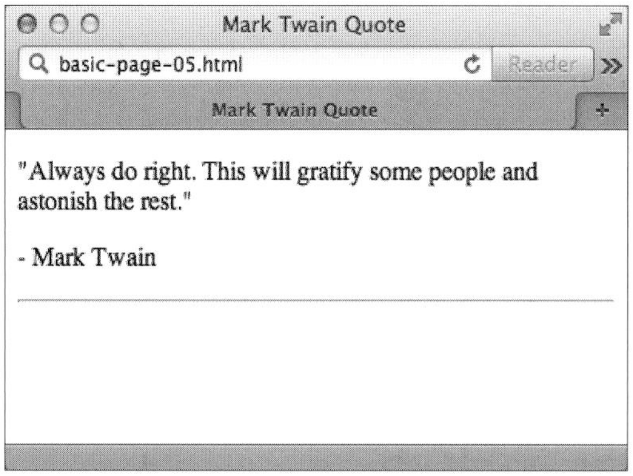

Note that if we removed those **p** elements and left the text as is, the browser would render the text without paragraph breaks, as shown in **FIGURE 1.12**.

If you want line breaks, extra spaces, or paragraphs, you'll have to specify those elements within the document by adding markup tags. So let's make the web page a bit more presentable by providing some structure.

STRUCTURING PAGE CONTENT

Now that we have a bit of content on the web page, let's add some headings and typographic treatments.

HTML Headings

First, use **h1** tags to bring in a heading (**FIGURE 1.13**) to the web page:

```
<!DOCTYPE html>
<html>
  <head>
    <title>Mark Twain Quote</title>
  </head>
  <body>
    <h1>Mark Twain Quote</h1>
    <p>"Always do right. This will gratify some people
and astonish the rest."</p>
    <p>- Mark Twain</p>
    <hr />
  </body>
</html>
```

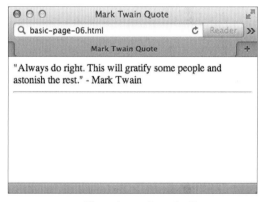

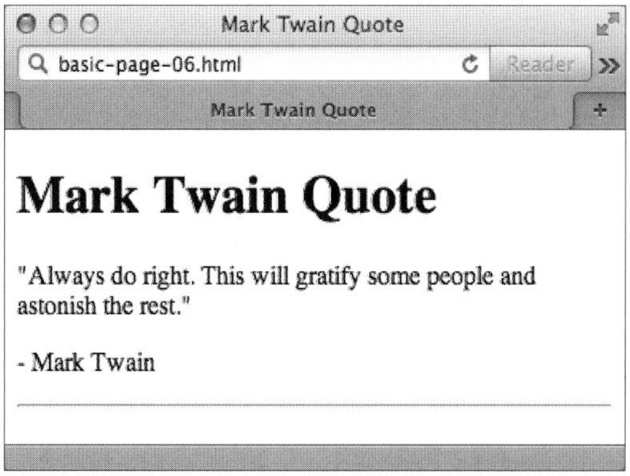

FIGURE 1.11 *How the page looks in a browser.*

FIGURE 1.12 *Without the markup, the lines start to run into each other.*

FIGURE 1.13 *Applying the heading to the page.*

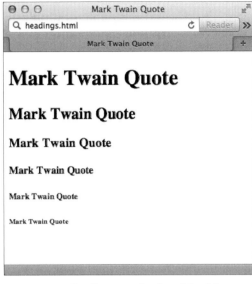

FIGURE 1.14 *Heading examples from* **h1** *to* **h6**.

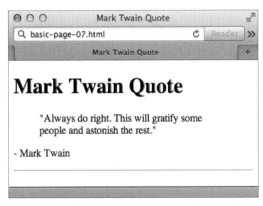

FIGURE 1.15 *The* **blockquote** *element is applied to the quotation.*

Heading tags can range from **h1**, the top-level heading, down the line to **h6**, the lowest-level heading (**FIGURE 1.14**).

Use headings to organize your web page and break your content into manageable chunks. This makes it much easier for users to scan the page and find the information they're looking for.

HTML Text Markup

Now let's add some semantic markup to the text. Since we have a quotation in the page, let's use the **blockquote** element (**FIGURE 1.15**):

```
<!DOCTYPE html>
<html>
  <head>
    <title>Mark Twain Quote</title>
  </head>
  <body>
    <h1>Mark Twain Quote</h1>
    <blockquote>
    <p>"Always do right. This will gratify some people
and astonish the rest."</p>
    </blockquote>
    <p>-Mark Twain</p>
    <hr />
  </body>
</html>
```

MARK UP HEADINGS THE RIGHT WAY

It's good practice to implement your tags in the right order. If you use a subhead below the **h2** tag, for example, the subhead should be wrapped in the **h3** tag (not **h4** or **h5**). Wrap the title of the page in the **h1** tag, not the **h2** tag. In short, don't skip heading levels!

Using heading tags in the right order is semantically correct and aids results from search engines, which rank information in order of importance according to headings. Don't worry if the size or look of a particular heading bothers you—you'll learn how to change it to suit with CSS in Chapter 3, "Web Typography."

Next, let's add some bold and italics to the document (**FIGURE 1.16**) by using **strong** and **em** elements, respectively:

```
<!DOCTYPE html>
<html>
  <head>
    <title>Mark Twain Quote</title>
  </head>
  <body>
    <h1>Mark Twain Quote</h1>
    <blockquote>
    <p>"<strong>Always do right</strong>. This will gratify some people and
<em>astonish</em> the rest."
</p>
    </blockquote>
    <p>-Mark Twain</p>
    <hr />
  </body>
</html>
```

Note that the default rendering of **strong** is bold and **em** is italics. Also, you could use **b** and **i** elements to get the same visual effects in the browser. In other words, you can use either pair of elements to achieve these effects.

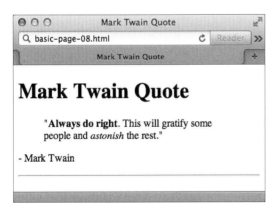

FIGURE 1.16 *Adding emphasis to words within the quotation.*

ng to People magazine, Lennox, wl
down the aisle in a long white gowr
-inspired headpiece.

FIGURE 1.17 *The cursor hovering over a link.*

Creating a Link to a Website

Arguably the most defining feature of the web page is the link. If we weren't able to interconnect our web pages together using **hyperlinks** (**FIGURE 1.17**), the World Wide Web would be much less, well, web-like.

We define hyperlinks using the **anchor tag**. The **a** element is used to label some text or mark an image as a pathway (**FIGURE 1.18**) to another document or a different part of the current document.

```
<!DOCTYPE html>
<html>
  <head>
    <title>Mark Twain Quote</title>
  </head>
  <body>
    <h1>Mark Twain Quote</h1>
    <blockquote>
    <p>"<strong>Always do right</strong>. This will gratify some
people and <em>astonish</em> the rest."</p>
    </blockquote>
    <p>-<a href="http://en.wikipedia.org/wiki/Mark_Twain">Mark Twain
</a></p>
    <hr>
  </body>
</html>
```

SAYING YOU ARE AN ATTRIBUTE IS ALL THAT'S NEEDED

Sometimes in HTML, just having an attribute is all that's needed to get the browser to render an element.

The starting anchor tag is *expanded* by the addition of **attributes** and **values**. An attribute is an additional bit of information included in the starting tag that provides contextual information about the element. Each attribute may have a quoted value that's enclosed in quotation marks.

FIGURE 1.18 *The cursor hovering over a link in our example.*

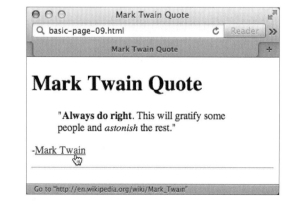

Adding a Title Attribute

Use the **title attribute** to provide additional information about a link (or any other element, for that matter). When a user hovers over a link (or another element) with a title attribute, the browser displays a **tooltip** with the title's content.

```
<!DOCTYPE html>
<html>
  <head>
  <title>Mark Twain Quote</title>
  </head>
  <body>
    <h1>Mark Twain Quote</h1>
    <blockquote>
    <p>"<strong>Always do right</strong>. This
will gratify some people and <em>astonish</em>
the rest."</p>
    </blockquote>
    <p>-<a href="http://en.wikipedia.org/wiki/
Mark_Twain" title="Information on Mark
Twain">Mark Twain
</a></p>
    <hr>
  </body>
</html>
```

The result would look like **FIGURE 1.19** in a browser.

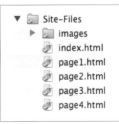

FIGURE 1.19 *How the page looks in a browser.*

! TITLE VS. TITLE

A title *attribute* is different than the title *element*. The title element is placed inside the head element and is used only once to name the page.

Linking within a Site

Let's take a look again at the first link we made:

```
<a href="http://en.wikipedia.org/wiki/
Mark_Twain" title="Information on Mark
Twain">Mark Twain</a>
```

The type of address above is known as an **absolute link**. Because the link is a complete URL or page address, it can be visited regardless of where the user is on the Internet.

Using Relative Links

When creating links within a site or collection of similar pages, you sometimes want to use **relative links**. Relative links are addresses that are valid only if you are surfing to another page on the same site. For example, let's say we have a site composed of four pages: `index.html`, `page1.html`, `page2.html`, and `page3.html`. And suppose they are all located within the same **root folder**, a folder that contains the site's HTML files along with any images and supporting files (**FIGURE 1.20**).

FIGURE 1.20 *The site's folder structure.*

```
▼ 🗀 Site-Files
  ▶ 🗀 images
    📄 index.html
    📄 page1.html
    📄 page2.html
    📄 page3.html
    📄 page4.html
```

ROOT FOLDER BY ANY OTHER NAME

A root folder is essentially the entire website. It contains all the files and resources for your site to work.

If you want to create a link from the index page to another page on the same website, instead of creating a link with an absolute path like this:

```
<a href="http://example.com/page1.html">Page 1</a>
```

You can instead use a relative link, such as this:

```
<a href="page1.html">Page 1</a>
```

Relative links contain neither the full **http://** protocol nor the domain name. When a browser navigates to a relative link, it looks for the page relative to the page the user is currently on. Try adding a relative link from the **index.html** document to **page1.html** (**FIGURE 1.21**). You could add a link back to the index page, too!

Navigating Folders

Just as there are numerous folders containing numerous files on your personal computer, sites are also composed of many folder sets and files. To link from a folder to another document in a different folder *within the same site*, use relative links. For example, let's say there's a main page within a folder called "subfolder." The following code example links to **page1.html** in a folder called **subfolder**:

```
<a href="subfolder/page1.html">page1.html<a>
```

The folder must be in the same directory as the page you're navigating from.

This next code example links to **page1.html** when the current page is in a folder that's in the same directory as **page1.html**. That is, the browser navigates outside the current folder and looks for the file in the directory above it (**FIGURE 1.22**). The two dots and slash tell the browser to go up one folder level.

```
<a href="../page1.html">Page 1</a>
```

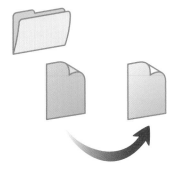

FIGURE 1.21 *Both source and destination are in the same folder.*

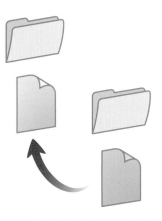

FIGURE 1.22 *The link's destination is a level above the link's source in the folder structure.*

If you want to go up two levels, the link would repeat the two-dot-and-slash combination (**FIGURE 1.23**).

```
<a href="../../page1.html">Page 1</a>
```

Using Root Relative Links

Using relative links to move between folders of a website can be tricky for large sites. Imagine having to type all those dot-dot-slashes to set up navigation between folders on a massive site!

Another linking method is to use a **root relative link**, which tells the browser to go right to the top of the folder stack and work its way down from there as indicated by the path. Let's say **page1.html** is in a folder called **products**, but the page currently being viewed is in some other folder (**FIGURE 1.24**). We use a slash to tell the browser to get to the top of the folder stack, and then look in the products folder for **page1.html**.

```
<a href="/products/page1.html">Products Page 1</a>
```

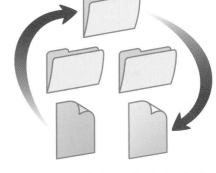

FIGURE 1.24 *The browser looks for the destination in a specified folder relative to the root folder.*

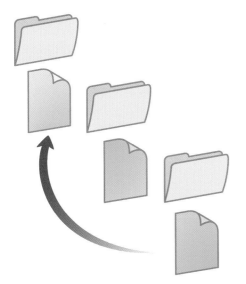

FIGURE 1.23 *The link's destination is two levels above the link's source in the folder structure.*

WORKS ON A WEB SERVER

Root relative links work when you have your pages uploaded onto a web server. Contact your local site administrator or your web host's tech support for how to do that.

Also, you can set up a local web environment. Local means that it's only visible to you, but it's a great way to test how your site should work and leverage unique server features like root relative links. Check out how to set up a local web server on a Mac (http://www.macinstruct.com/node/112) and for a PC (http://www.labnol.org/internet/turn-home-computer-into-web-server/9111/).

Personally, I use a Mac as my main operating system and recommend using MAMP PRO (http://www.mamp.info/).

Every site has a root directory—the main directory that contains the home page and the first set of subfolders. If you're in a subfolder of this root folder and you want to refer to a page in the root directory or one of its subfolders, then precede the path with a forward slash ("/").

Here's a quick recap of different types of links:

- Use absolute links when referring to pages that are external to your site.

- Use relative links when linking to a page within your site. This saves you the pain of renaming your links if you move your pages to another site.

ADVANCED HTML   Now that you know some HTML basics, you might want to take a spin with a mature, professional template. Check out the HTML5 Boilerplate (http://html5boilerplate.com), which is filled with tips and techniques for leveraging HTML and working around quirky browser behaviors. We'll talk more about HTML5 Boilerplate in Chapter 2, "Styling with CSS." And don't forget to check the Boilerplate documentation (https://github.com/h5bp/html5-boilerplate/blob/v4.0.0/doc/README.md).

If you go to that documentation file, you'll find a file extension that might be new to you. A .md file is a Markdown file (http://daringfireball.net/projects/markdown/), which is a text file and can be opened with any text editor you use for HTML. Markdown is a rethinking of HTML as a simpler markup language. It's used by code repository sites like GitHub to help programmers write software documentation.

You can read a Markdown file straight from the Chrome browser with the TextDown extension available at http://joaocolombo.com/textdown. If you're on a Mac or use an iOS device, Byword (http://bywordapp.com) is a great app for writing and reading content in Markdown.

IN CONCLUSION

We've looked at the basics of creating a web page with the fundamentals of HTML. In the next chapter, we take what we've learned and start using Cascading Style Sheets to set the presentational characteristics.

Chapter **2** STYLING WITH CSS

When we get ready each day, we don't change our internal organs to get ready for the day. No, we just change our clothes. Changing a website design should be as easy as changing a set of clothes.

Imagine you're designing a website that consists of twenty pages, and you want to change design elements such as the colors, fonts, sizing, and alignment. Using traditional HTML coding, you'd have to mark up every single element for its specific color, font, alignment, and layout—an extremely tedious and error-prone process. The site's HTML documents would quickly get bogged down with additional code, making both the content and the code nearly unmanageable.

CSS TO THE RESCUE

The development of Cascading Style Sheets (CSS) relieved HTML of the burden of presenting content (**FIGURE 2.1**). HTML was still used to mark up structure (to indicate "this is a paragraph" and "this is a header"), but CSS could now tell the browser what each component looked like ("paragraphs look like this" and "headers look like this").

In addition, multiple HTML documents could be linked to one style sheet, letting the designer control the look of an entire site with one piece of code. This made HTML documents much easier to work with: HTML code had less bloat and designers could make site-wide adjustments quickly and easily just by changing the one style sheet, rather than hundreds of individual pages.

There was just one catch in CSS's rise to prominence. For years HTML and CSS depended on the support of the makers of web browsers and other devices that let people view pages on the internet. When CSS was first developed, competing browser companies (Microsoft and Netscape) disagreed about which features to support. Since "browser support" was spotty, CSS could not be guaranteed to work on all computers, which slowed adoption.

As web designers began to catch on to CSS's potential, however, and the web standards movement gained momentum, browser support became more reliable. Today CSS is the standard for styling web pages.

FIGURE 2.1 *The home page of CSS at the W3C.*

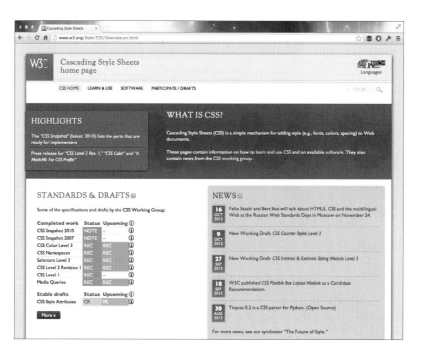

GETTING TO KNOW STYLE

CSS allows one or more rules to dictate how a web page's HTML elements should look. But what does CSS look like? A CSS rule has two parts: a **selector** and a **declaration** (**FIGURE 2.2**). A set of declarations grouped under one selector is a declaration block. **A declaration contains a property and the property's value:**

```
p {
  background-color: #ccff00;
}
```

Declarations

In the example shown in Figure 2.2, **p** is the selector. Located between the brackets is a single declaration: **background-color: #ccff00;**. If applied to a web document with multiple paragraphs of copy marked with the **<p>** tag, the color behind the paragraphs is set to gray **#ccff00**.

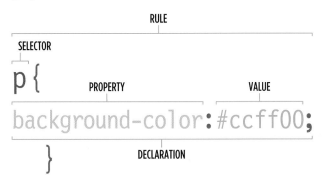

FIGURE 2.2 *Anatomy of a CSS rule.*

Selectors

A selector tells the style rules where to apply their magic: it lets you join styles to a specific element or a class of elements. The following example contains what is called a **generic** or **element selector,** in that it's named after and applies rules to an HTML element:

```
p {
  background-color: #666666;
}
h2 {
  color: #cc0000;
}
td {
  background-color: red;
}
```

A **class selector** builds off an *attribute* with an HTML element. That attribute is always **class** and it is set to a value related to the meaning of the content:

```
<p class="source">Hoc est insanit. Voca me
dent. Fortasse.</p>
<p>This is crazy. Call me sometime. Perhaps.<p>
```

To write the CSS for a class selector, start with a period (.), then write out the value of that **class** attribute:

```
.source {
  background-color: #666666; /* grey */
}
```

For an **ID selector**, insert an **id** attribute in the HTML element:

```
<p class="source">Hoc est insanit. Voca me
dent. Fortasse.</p>
<p id="translation">This is crazy. Call me
sometime. Perhaps. <p>
```

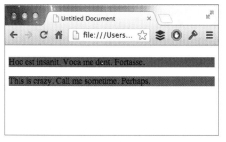

FIGURE 2.3 *Applying an ID selector to the second paragraph.*

Then add an ID selector into the CSS to achieve a change in the web page (**FIGURE 2.3**):

```
.source {
 background-color: #666666; /* grey */
}
#translation {
 background-color: #ff0000; /* red */
}
```

More CSS Hooks

There are other, more complex selectors that build on a generic selector (**TABLE 2.1**) . The generic selector along with the **class** and **id** selectors are probably reasonably familiar, but there's more detail about the others after the table.

TABLE 2.1 *Selectors and Syntax*

Type of Selector	Syntax	Examples
Generic or element	a	p { color: #000; }
Universal	*	* (color: #000; }
Descendant	a b c	footer blockquote p { color: #000; }
Child	a > b	p > blockquote { color: #000; }
Adjacent sibling	a + b	p + p { text-indent: 2.5em; }
General sibling	a ~ b	h1 ~ blockquote { font-weight: bold; }
Attribute	a[attr] a[attr="value"] a[attr~="value"]	Img[title] { color: #000; }
Class	a.class .class	.production { color: #000; }
ID	a#id #id	#header { color: #000; }

- A **universal selector** applies a style rule to every HTML element in a page:

```
* {
  font-size: 110%;
}
```

- A **descendant selector** applies a style to an element that's a descendant of another element. For example, if you want to apply a text color of black to a paragraph that's inside a **blockquote** and that **blockquote** is inside a footer, the CSS rule looks like this:

```
footer blockquote p {
  color: #000;
}
```

- A **child selector** applies a style to an element that's a direct descendant of a parent element. For example, the unordered list element has **li** elements within it. So, this CSS rule sets the link text *only* in list items to bold.

```
ul > a {
  font-weight: bold;
}
```

- An **adjacent sibling selector** needs two selectors: an originator and a target separated by a plus sign (+). In this example, the CSS rule says "apply a text indent to a paragraph *only if* there is a paragraph element immediately before it":

```
p + p {
  text-indent: 2.5em;
}
```

- A **general sibling selector** is similar to an adjacent sibling selector in that it needs two selectors: an originator and a target. The selectors are separated by a tilde (~) and can apply to one or more target elements, unlike an adjacent sibling selector. In this example, if there is more than one blockquote after an **h1** element, each **blockquote** displays text as bold:

```
h1~blockquote {
  font-weight: bold;
}
```

- An **attribute selector** uses an attribute and an attribute value to determine where a CSS rule gets applied. In this example, only form input set to a value of **text** gets a yellow background:

```
input[type="text"] {
  background-color: yellow;
}
```

MORE ATTRIBUTE SELECTORS

Element and attribute selectors let you deliver CSS design rules without having to insert attributes like ID or class selectors. You can read more about CSS attribute selectors at Dev.Opera (http://dev.opera.com/articles/view/css-3-attribute-selectors/).

ANATOMY OF A LINK ELEMENT

A link element is composed of four parts:

1. The **link** element instructs the browser that there is a resource it can pull into the document. While link is an *empty* element that doesn't need a closing tag, you may close it with a forward slash at the end of the element if you want to.

2. The **href** attribute instructs the browser on *where* the file is located.

3. The **type** attribute tells the browser *what kind* of media is being referenced. Since the file being referenced is a text-based style sheet, the value is **text/css**.

4. The **rel** attribute defines the kind of relationship or link the file has to the web page for the browser. Since the file is being pulled in, the value is **stylesheet** (one word).

ADDING CSS FORMATTING

You can use linking and internal styles within a web page. Both are needed to fully understand how to best design a web page with CSS.

Linking to CSS

Using the following CSS code, create a file using a text editor and save it as **style.css** into a folder on your computer (or download the file from http://dwmgbook.com):

```css
body {
  background-color: #96B45A;
  width: 600px;
  margin: 15px;
}
p {
  font-family: Arial, Helvetica, sans-serif;
  font-size: 14px;
  color: #000000;
  text-indent: 10pt;
}
h1 {
  font-family: Verdana, Arial, Helvetica, sans-serif;
  font-size: 36px;
  color: #FFEEB8;
  letter-spacing: 1px;
  background-color: #336600;
  padding: 15px;
  border: 1px dashed #666600;
}
h2 {
  color: #FFEEB8;
  font-family: Verdana, Arial, Helvetica, sans-serif;
  font-size: 18px;
  text-indent: 5pt;
}
img {
  padding: 3px;
  background-color: #669900;
  margin: 3px;
  color: #336600;
  float: right;
}
```

```
ul {
  font-family: Arial, Helvetica, sans-serif;
  font-size: 14px;
  color: #000000;
}
a {
  color: #003300;
  text-decoration: underline;
}
```

Look for the **head** element at the top of the HTML code for the page. The page title is located there within the **title** element, and we'll add a **link** element, like this:

```
<head>
<title>Author Quotes</title>
<link rel="stylesheet" type="text/css"
href="style.css" />
</head>
```

Add the emphasized line from the above block in its proper place above the closing **</head>** tag, save the page, then open it in a browser (**FIGURE 2.4**).

The attached or associated CSS has formatted the HTML beyond the basic styles built into the browser.

FIGURE 2.4 *A web page with styles applied.*

ADDITIONAL STYLES   A web document can contain more than one link element and therefore can pull in more than one style sheet.

```
<link rel="stylesheet" type="text/css" href="style-basic.css" />
<link rel="stylesheet" type="text/css" href="style-typography.css" />
<link rel="stylesheet" type="text/css" href="style-color.css" />
<link rel="stylesheet" type="text/css" href="style-pages.css" />
```

Separating styles like this is an approach you might want to take when modularizing or separating out many, many CSS rules into their respective applications.

! **BE MINDFUL OF TYPOS AND FILE PLACEMENT**

If you have trouble seeing the formatted version, make sure you've entered the code exactly as shown above, and that your HTML file is saved to the correct folder.

Internal Styles

CSS rules can be placed within the web page itself. Begin by including starting and closing **style** elements:

```
<!doctype html>
<html>
<head>
 <title>Inline CSS Example</title>
 <style>
 </style>
</head>
```

Then add a **type** attribute with the **text/css** value to let the browser know the composition of rules:

```
<!doctype html>
<html>
<head>
 <title>Inline CSS Example</title>
 <style type="text/css">
 </style>
</head>
```

Add new CSS rules or take the same CSS rules from the **style.css** file. Place them in the **head** element and wrap an HTML style element:

```
<!doctype html>
<html>
<head>
 <title>Inline CSS Example</title>
 <style type="text/css">
body {
 background-color: #96B45A;
 width: 600px;
 margin: 15px;
}
p {
 font-family: Arial, Helvetica, sans-serif;
 font-size: 14px;
 color: #000000;
 text-indent: 10pt;
}
h1 {
 font-family: Verdana, Arial, Helvetica,
sans-serif;
 font-size: 36px;
 color: #FFEEB8;
 letter-spacing: 1px;
 background-color: #336600;
 padding: 15px;
 border: 1px dashed #666600;
}
h2 {
 color: #FFEEB8;
 font-family: Verdana, Arial, Helvetica,
sans-serif;
 font-size: 18px;
 text-indent: 5pt;
}
img {
 padding: 3px;
 background-color: #669900;
 margin: 3px;
 color: #336600;
 float: right;
}
ul {
 font-family: Arial, Helvetica, sans-serif;
 font-size: 14px;
 color: #000000;
}
a {
 color: #003300;
 text-decoration: underline;
}
 </style>
</head>
```

This internal method of adding styles is perfect for getting started or experimenting with a page design.

INLINE STYLES AS A STARTING POINT When you're ready to go from testing to building a solid website, move the files to an external style sheet. This separation of design from content is at the heart of CSS, allowing you to control dozens or even hundreds of web pages with one file.

BLOCK AND INLINE FORMATTING

The way content is structured with HTML underpins how its appearance can be modified by CSS. HTML5 has several content models. The ones we'll make the most use of are *phrasing content* and *flow content*, which are similar to what we used to call block-level and inline content, respectively. CSS, being presentational, still uses the display values *block* and *inline*. A **block element** creates its own space, forcing a line break before the content that follows it. In this way it defines a portion of a web document for itself horizontally across a browser viewport. In **FIGURE 2.5**, the heading and paragraph are separated from the inline image element:

```
<h1>Of Friendship</h2>
<img src="Francis_Bacon.jpg" alt="Portrait of Francis
Bacon" title="Francis Bacon">
<p>It had been hard for him that spake it to have put
more truth and untruth together in few words, than in
that speech, Whatsoever is delighted in solitude, is
either a wild beast or a god.<p>
```

An **inline element** such as **em** or **img** doesn't force a line break and typically focuses on text within a block element. The control that CSS gives you over the outside areas of block elements is not possible with inline elements. Inline elements still allow for visual control of fonts and colors.

IMAGES ARE INLINE-BLOCK Figure 2.5 may look like a block-level element because it's separate from the heading and paragraph. But it's not a block-level element: it's an **inline-block** element. The heading and paragraph draw their own boundaries, leaving the image isolated.

In **FIGURE 2.6**, an image is added into the flow of text inside a **p** element. The paragraph text is aligned with the bottom of the image; the image doesn't start a new line for itself:

```
<h1>Of Friendship<h2>
<p>It had been hard for him that spake it to have put
more truth and untruth together in few words, than
in that speech, <img src="francis-bacon.gif" alt=""
title="Francis Bacon">
Whatsoever is delighted in solitude, is either a wild
beast or a god.<p>
```

FIGURE 2.5 *Block elements are separated to define their own portions of a web page.*

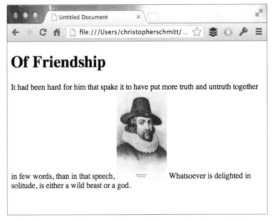

FIGURE 2.6 *An image placed inline with the text in the paragraph.*

HTML's Generic Elements

When none of the standard methods of use for HTML tags match up with your content, HTML's generic **div** and **span** elements can help. These nonsemantic elements let you mark up any content as either a block-level element (**div**) or an inline element (**span**) and add a **class** or **id** attribute as a CSS styling hook (**FIGURE 2.7**):

```
<div class="post" id="post-1595">
 <h2><a class="title" href="http://christopherschmitt.com/2007/10/23/
 css-floats-to-display-columns-in-any-order/" rel="bookmark">CSS Floats to
 Display Columns in Any Order</a></h2>
 <div class="info">
  <span class="date">Saturday; September 29, 2012</span>
 </div>
</div>
```

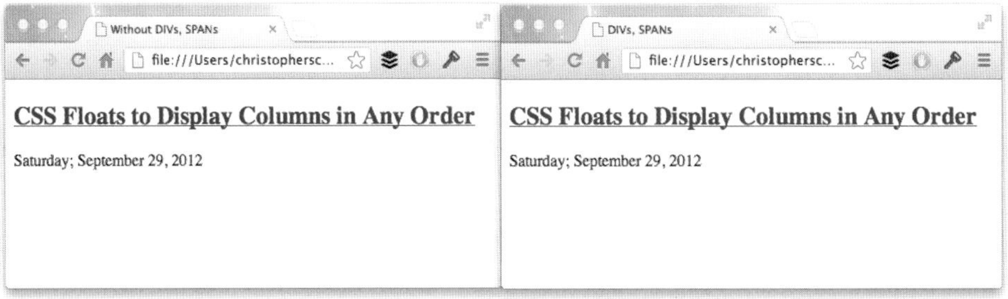

FIGURE 2.7 *The content is rendered the same in both browsers, but generic HTML elements let us graft a more semantic approach onto the content.*

MICROFORMATS

HTML elements describe the kinds of content surrounded by their tags. But there are many kinds of content, and only about a hundred HTML elements. So, there are situations where there's no appropriate HTML element for a piece of content or group of related pieces of information.

This is where Microformats comes in (http://microformats.org). Microformats is a design library that offers time-saving markup patterns for content like business cards, recipes, reviews, resumes, and more. Google understands a few of the microformats; if Google understands your content and can deliver it in the proper context, that can mean a potentially higher Google page or site rank. For more information, read Emily Lewis's *Microformats Made Simple*.

Pseudo-classes and Pseudo-elements

Special classes and elements called **pseudo-classes** and **pseudo-elements** let you style sections of a page dynamically without even wrapping HTML around them. For example, to set the first line of a paragraph to bold, use the following CSS rule (**FIGURE 2.8**):

```
p:first-line {
  font-weight: bold;
}
```

As you adjust the browser window and the first line changes, it stays bold no matter its length or how many words land on the first line (**FIGURE 2.9**).

FIGURE 2.8 *Styling the first line of a paragraph.*

FIGURE 2.9 *The browser at different lengths; the first line is always bold.*

We can't replicate that effect with HTML elements because we can't know where the first line ends when a browser window can be almost any length. For example, we might look at our page in a browser and decide to first place a span element where the first line ends as we are seeing it.

```
<p><span>In compliance with the request of a friend of mine, who wrote me
from the</span> East, I called on good-natured, garrulous old Simon Wheeler,
and inquired after my friend's friend, Leonidas W. Smiley, as requested
to do, and I hereunto append the result. I have a lurking suspicion that
Leonidas W. Smiley is a myth; that my friend never knew such a personage;
and that he only conjectured that, if I asked old Wheeler about him, it
would remind him of his infamous Jim Smiley, and he would go to work and
bore me nearly to death with some infernal reminiscence of him as long and
tedious as it should be useless to me. If that was the design, it certainly
succeeded.</p>
```

We could assign bold text style to that span element, and it would look right so long as we never make the browser window a different size. But if we resized the browser, the end of that span element would no longer correspond to the end of the first line (see **FIGURE 2.10**):

```
p span {
  font-weight: bold;
}
```

FIGURE 2.10 *Hard-coding the effect with actual HTML elements fails to reproduce the effect of bolding just the words on the first line of the paragraph.*

Pseudo-classes are used to produce changes that happen as a user interacts with a page, such as clicking on a link. As shown in **TABLE 2.2**, each state of an action can have a style applied. Pseudo-elements (**TABLE 2.3**) become available for CSS depending on their position in the text flow, such as being the first line or the first letter.

TABLE 2.2 *Pseudo-Classes*

Pseudo-class	Description
`:first-child`	Applies to the first element within a string of common elements
`:link`	Applies to unvisited links
`:visit`	Applies to visited links
`:hover`	Applies to the mouse-over effect on links
`:active`	Applies to clicking links
`:focus`	Applies to an interactive HTML element such as a text field

TABLE 2.3 *Pseudo-Elements*

Pseudo-element	Description
`:first-letter`	Applies to the first letter of an element
`:first-line`	Applies to the first line
`:before`	Generates content before an element
`:after`	Generates content after an element

DELIVERING CSS JUST TO IE

Internet Explorer (IE) has enjoyed widespread popularity over the years, and old versions are still in use. There are times when you'll need to create custom styles for these old browsers to make sure they're delivered to IE.

For example, IE8 does not handle the `:nth-child(n)` selector. A common use for this selector is to create zebra table rows, that is, rows in alternating colors (**FIGURE 2.11**):

FIGURE 2.11 *Making every other table row gray increases legibility.*

Type of Test	Cost	Date
Buying Microwave Popcorn	$100.00	October 9th
Bad Popcorn Protocols	$299.00	October 12th
Microwave Popcorn Certification	$599.00	October 13th
Bad Popcorn Anger management	$799.00	October 14th

The CSS rule that applies this color change is fairly straightforward:

```
ul li:nth-child(even) {
   background-color: #ccc;
}
```

However, older versions of IE don't understand that rule and skip over it. To work around that limitation, you can insert a **class** attribute into the HTML:

```
<ul>
<li>Harper Lee </li>
<li class="even">Mark Twain</li>
<li>F. Scott Fitzgerald </li>
<li class="even">J.D. Salinger </li>
</ul>
```

And then deliver a custom style sheet with the filename **ie8.css**, with the following line:

```
.even {
   background-color: #ccc;
}
```

! **CLASS SELECTORS DON'T CHANGE DYNAMICALLY**

To work around the lack of advanced CSS selector support in older versions of Internet Explorer, we can inject class attributes into the HTML. The drawback is that, unlike the **nth-child** pseudo-class, the class attributes don't dynamically reapply to content. This means if you insert one table row, you'll have to get back to the right sequence by moving the class attributes in the rest of the table below the insertion.

Then insert the following conditional comment:

```
<!--[if IE 8]>
<link rel="stylesheet" type="text/css"
href="ie8.css">
<!--<![endif]-->
```

Based on the HTML5 Boilerplate (**FIGURE 2.12**), the conditional block is a great way to be smart with coding.

Supporting many old versions of IE would result in multiple, separate IE files that need to be inserted with conditional comments:

```
<!--[if IE 7]>
<link rel="stylesheet" type="text/css"
href="ie7.css">
<![endif]-->
<!--[if IE 8]>
<link rel="stylesheet" type="text/css"
href="ie8.css">
<![endif]-->
<!--[if IE 9]>
<link rel="stylesheet" type="text/css"
href="ie9.css">
<![endif]-->
```

HTML5 BOILERPLATE

The HTML5 Boilerplate is a collection of snippets and techniques rolled into one template. It's a great starting point for making your own web template. For more information, see http://html5boilerplate.com/

FIGURE 2.12 *HTML5 Boilerplate*

Instead of creating *separate* CSS files for older versions of IE and then inserting them into a web page with a new **link** element, you can apply conditional comments to output different iterations of the **html** element with specialized **class** attributes:

```
<!DOCTYPE html>
  <!--[if lt IE 7]>
    <html class="no-js lt-ie9 lt-ie8 lt-ie7">
  <![endif]-->
  <!--[if IE 7]>
    <html class="no-js lt-ie9 lt-ie8">
  <![endif]-->
  <!--[if IE 8]>
    <html class="no-js lt-ie9">
  <![endif]-->
  <!--[if gt IE 8]><!-->
    <html class="no-js">
  <!--<![endif]-->
<title>Author Quotes</title>
<link rel="stylesheet" type="text/css"
href="style.css">
</head>
```

Then use class selectors to deliver specific rules for each older version of IE. In this example, both of these CSS rules could be left in one **style.css** file:

```
ul li:nth-child(3n+3) {
  background-color: #ccc;
}
.lt-ie9 .third {
  background-color: #ccc;
}
```

These conditional CSS rules for IE demonstrate how powerful CSS is for controlling the look and feel of not only dozens or hundreds of pages, but also for tailoring rules for specific browsers.

NORMAL FLOW AND POSITIONING

The CSS position property lets you move elements precisely on a page. The position property takes one of four values: **static**, **fixed**, **relative**, or **absolute**.

Each technique comes with distinct pros and cons. Before getting into the details of positioning, let's look at the basics of browser rendering.

Static Positioning

When a browser renders the content of a web page, it lays out each element in its unstyled place on the page from top to bottom. This is known as having a *static* position.

In essence, it means the first block-level element within an HTML page gets placed vertically on top of the next block-level element and so on. Inline elements like **em** and **strong** are arrayed along the *horizontal* text flow within a block (**FIGURE 2.13**):

FIGURE 2.13 *An unstyled web page revealing the normal flow.*

This default positioning of elements is known as the *normal flow* of the document.

Fixed Positioning

When an element is given a fixed position, it always stays in the same position relative to the browser window or viewport, at the offset properties entered in the rule. Even when the user scrolls to the bottom of a long page, and element with fixed position will remain visible exactly as it is at the top of the window.

Relative Positioning

When an element is relatively positioned, it is initially placed within normal flow, and then adjusted according to its offset properties.

Let's say you have a document with three paragraphs, the second of which you assign an **id** value of "positioned" and style like so:

```
#positioned {
    position: relative;
    top: 30px;
    right: 30px;
    background-color: #eee;
}
```

The resulting page would look something like **FIGURE 2.14**.

The browser first lays out the paragraphs according to normal flow, and then offsets the positioned paragraph 30px from the top, and 30px from the right of its default or static position.

Other position properties are **bottom** and **left**. You can use one or two pairs of values at a time, such as bottom and left, or just one at a time, like left.

FIGURE 2.14 *The element is moved from its location in the normal flow, but the space it left is untouched.*

! CONFLICTS IN POSITIONING PROPERTIES

If you use bottom and top, you're telling the browser to move an element both up and down at the same time. Which one wins? With all things being equal, the last property in the declaration block wins.

Absolute Positioning

When an element is absolutely positioned, it's taken out of normal flow and placed *relative to the edges of its containing box,* according to its offset properties.

Containing Boxes

You can place other elements inside block level elements. For example, take a look at the following markup:

```
<!DOCTYPE html>
<html>
 <head>
 <title>Francis Bacon's Of Beauty</title>
 <link rel="stylesheet" type="text/css"
href="style.css">
 </head>
<body>
<div id="content">
    <div id="main">
        <h2>Of Beauty</h2>
        <p>Virtue is like a rich stone, best
plain set; and surely virtue is best, in a
body that is comely, though not of delicate
features; and that hath rather dignity of
presence, than beauty of aspect.</p>
        <p> Neither is it almost seen, that
very beautiful persons are otherwise of great
virtue; as if nature were rather busy, not to
err, than in labor to produce excellency. </p>
        <p>And therefore they prove
accomplished, but not of great spirit; and
study rather behavior, than virtue.</p>
        <img src="Francis_Bacon.jpg"
alt="Portrait of Francis Bacon" title="Francis
Bacon">
        <p><i>Francis Bacon (1561-1626)</i></p>
    </div>
</div>
</body>
</html>
```

The head and the paragraph both are contained within the "main" **div**, while the "main" **div** is contained in the "content" **div**. You can think of these elements as boxes nested inside one another—every element is placed within a *parent* element. In this example, the "main" **div** is the *child* of the "content" **div**.

The containing block of an element that is absolutely positioned is the nearest block-level ancestor that is positioned. If no block-level ancestor is positioned, then the root element, which is visually expressed as the browser viewport, serves as the containing block (**FIGURE 2.15**). The primary ancestor, or root, element in any HTML document is the HTML element.

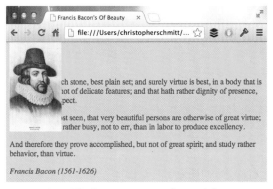

FIGURE 2.15 *The image moves to the top-left corner of the browser's viewport.*

ABSOLUTELY POSITIONED ELEMENTS HAVE NO FOOTPRINT IN THE NORMAL FLOW

Absolutely positioned elements lead a solitary life. They're ignored by elements in the normal flow, and have their original land taken from them. The original location of a newly absolute positioned element is quickly taken up by the other page elements that are still in normal flow.

BLOCK ELEMENTS REMAIN OUTSIDE OF INLINE ELEMENTS—USUALLY

Ordinarily, block level elements cannot go into inline elements. For example, don't try to place a **div** element inside a **strong** or **em** element. But this practice is OK for allowing an anchor ("**a href**") element around a **div** element or some other block level element.

```
<a href="http://http://www.authorama.com/
essays-of-francis-bacon-43.html">
<h2>Of Beauty</h2>
<p>Virtue is like a rich stone, best plain
set; and surely virtue is best, in a body
that is comely, though not of delicate
features; and that hath rather dignity of
presence, than beauty of aspect.</p>
</a>
```

This is easier than repeatedly adding links to block level elements:

```
<h2><a href="http://http://www.authorama.
com/essays-of-francis-bacon-43.html">
Of Beauty</a></h2>
<p><a href="http://http://www.authorama.
com/essays-of-francis-bacon-43.
html">Virtue is like a rich stone, best
plain set; and surely virtue is best,
in a body that is comely, though not of
delicate features; and that hath rather
dignity of presence, than beauty of
aspect.</a></p>
```

An absolutely positioned element usually uses the upper left-hand corner of the browser viewport as the starting point. However, this starting point can be reassigned:

```
<!DOCTYPE html>
<html>
 <head>
 <title>Francis Bacon's Of Beauty</title>
 <style type="text/css">
 img {
  position: absolute;
  top: 0;
 }
 </style>
 </head>
<body>
<div id="content">
    <div id="main">
        <h2>Of Beauty</h2>
        <p>Virtue is like a rich stone, best
plain set; and surely virtue is best, in a
body that is comely, though not of delicate
features; and that hath rather dignity of
presence, than beauty of aspect.</p>
        <p>Neither is it almost seen, that very
beautiful persons are otherwise of great
virtue; as if nature were rather busy, not to
err, than in labor to produce excellency. </p>
        <img src="Francis_Bacon.jpg "
alt="Francis Bacon">
    </div>
</div>
</body>
</html>
```

Moving Elements with Positioning

Let's break down a container block element with an example (**FIGURE 2.16**):

Notice that initially the center of the White House is sitting off to the upper left:

```
#whitehouse {
  width: 700px;
  height: 525px;
  margin: 10% auto;
  background: #2942c4 url(wh.jpg) no-repeat;
}

#wh_top {
  position: absolute;
  top: 0;
  left: 0;
  background-image: url(wh_top.png);
}
```

FIGURE 2.16 *The center of the building is separated from the photo.*

Absolute positioning takes **#wh_top**, which is the center portion of the White House, and places it at the top left corner of the browser. Adding **position:relative** to **div#white house** places this chunk inside its parent, the photo (**FIGURE 2.17**):

```
#whitehouse {
  position: relative;
  width: 700px;
  height: 525px;
  margin: 10% auto;
  background: #2942c4 url(wh.jpg) no-repeat;
}

#wh_top {
  position: absolute;
  top: 0;
  left: 0;
  background-image: url(wh_top.png);
}
```

FIGURE 2.17 *The center of the building is now at the top left corner of its parent element.*

We've changed the *positioning context of the parent element.* Since the parent element now has explicitly said it's positioned relatively, this overrides the `html` element as the go-to element for the absolutely positioned element.

Using offset properties slides, we can slide **#wh_top** into place (**FIGURE 2.18**):

```
#whitehouse {
  position: relative;
  width: 700px;
  height: 525px;
  margin: 10% auto;
  background: #2942c4 url(wh.jpg) no-repeat;
}

#wh_top {
  position: absolute;
  top: 88px;
  left: 226px;
  background-image: url(wh_top.png);

}
```

IN CONCLUSION

In this chapter, we set the stage by discussing some basic methods for formatting a web page with CSS. In the next chapter, we'll take a closer look at how we can apply CSS to web typography.

FIGURE 2.18 *The building is put back together.*

POSITIONING NOTHING FOR THE WIN   We didn't set any offset properties for the main White House photo. Merely stating that an element is relatively positioned is enough for the browser to change the location of the positioning context from the `html` element. The bonus is that since we don't have to assign a value to the relatively positioned element, the White House photo stays in its normal flow location.

The difference between the almost-right word and the right word is the difference between the lightning bug and the lightning!"

—*Mark Twain*

Chapter **3** WEB TYPOGRAPHY

Communication is emotional. Words written by authors such as Upton Sinclair, Harriet Beecher Stowe, and Thomas Paine have moved people to tears, sparked movements, and changed the course of nations.

How words are presented visually affects how readers perceive them. Matching the right font with the right message is the role of the designer. When conveying a serious message, for example, a designer should obviously avoid using an informal font like Comic Sans.

Text is used throughout a page for different purposes: headings, subheadings, navigation menu labels, main content, figure captions, small print in the footer, and so on. CSS allows designers to make compelling type for all of these purposes.

WORKING WITH WEB TYPE

Superior typography is one of the main benefits of using CSS (**FIGURE 3.1**, facing page), so let's look at different parameters for designing type on a page.

It's a good idea to begin any project by exploring basic options for paragraph and header styling. To specify the font in a certain element, use the **font-family** property.

Create these rules in your text editor, save the document as **style.css**, and associate it to the HTML, then view your HTML page in a browser.

```
h1 {
  font-family: Verdana, Arial, sans-serif;
}
p {
  font-family: Georgia, "Times New Roman",
serif;
}
```

If you've done this, your file should look like **FIGURE 3.2**.

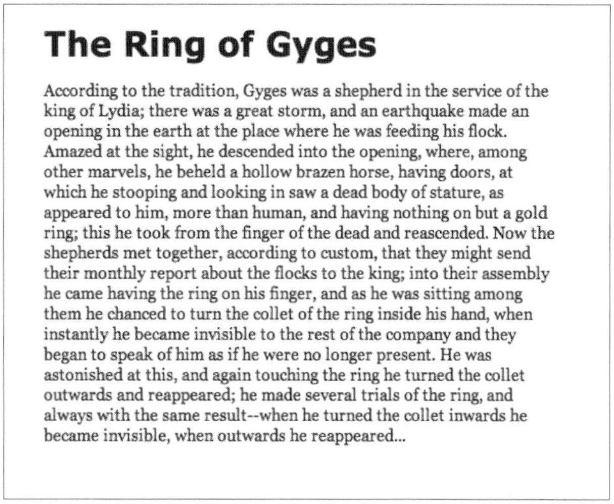

The Ring of Gyges

According to the tradition, Gyges was a shepherd in the service of the king of Lydia; there was a great storm, and an earthquake made an opening in the earth at the place where he was feeding his flock. Amazed at the sight, he descended into the opening, where, among other marvels, he beheld a hollow brazen horse, having doors, at which he stooping and looking in saw a dead body of stature, as appeared to him, more than human, and having nothing on but a gold ring; this he took from the finger of the dead and reascended. Now the shepherds met together, according to custom, that they might send their monthly report about the flocks to the king; into their assembly he came having the ring on his finger, and as he was sitting among them he chanced to turn the collet of the ring inside his hand, when instantly he became invisible to the rest of the company and they began to speak of him as if he were no longer present. He was astonished at this, and again touching the ring he turned the collet outwards and reappeared; he made several trials of the ring, and always with the same result--when he turned the collet inwards he became invisible, when outwards he reappeared...

FIGURE 3.2 *Setting fonts in a web page is easy with CSS.*

FONT STACKING   The practice of listing fonts in order of preference within the value of the **font-family** is called font stacking.

You'll note that we can specify more than one font family here. How does the browser know which font to display? Macintosh, Windows, and Unix operating systems come installed with different fonts. A font that's on a system you develop a site on and readily see in your web pages might not be installed on a site visitor's computer.

That's the reason we create a list of similar fonts for a property. If the first font is installed in the user's operating system, then that font is used. If the first font is not installed, then the browser moves on down the line until it finds a font that is installed.

The last font listed is a generic font family. In the example, the **p** element is set to use serif fonts so the generic font type is serif, which displays the system's default serif font. It's advisable to include a generic font family like serif or sans serif at the end of the value list just in case the user doesn't have one of the specific fonts in your style rule.

!   **NEVER COUNT ON USER'S FONTS**

While certain standard fonts are installed on Windows, Mac OS X, and Unix, users have the option of uninstalling these, so you can never be sure which fonts any particular user has installed.

SIGN UP FOR NEWS ABOUT FUTURE SEED CONFERENCES

* A ONE-DAY CONFERENCE *on* DESIGN, ENTREPRENEURSHIP *and* INSPIRATION *

On Friday, June the 6th 2008 in Chicago

Learn about *taking control of your own work* by seeking out methods to

INSPIRE NEW THINKING AND ADOPT UNCONVENTIONAL IDEAS ABOUT COLLABORATION AND BUSINESS VIA
SIX PRESENTATIONS AND DISCUSSIONS LED BY 37SIGNALS, SEGURA INC, COUDAL PARTNERS AND FRIENDS

The 3rd SEED CONFERENCE

WILL FILL YOUR HEAD WITH KNOWLEDGE YOU CAN USE. THIS ISN'T ABOUT THEORY, IT'S ABOUT PRACTICE
*You should attend if you're a designer (print, web or video) or a business-minded soul who is looking to take creative
ideas and turn them into something SATISFYING & BANKABLE. Anyone creative with an open mind will take away
something useful. This is a day of active learning, not just idle listening. Only 270 seats available.* **REGISTER NOW**

THE VENUE WILL INFORM THE DISCUSSION TOO, SEED WILL BE HELD IN THE "CATHEDRAL OF MODERNISM"

CROWN HALL *by* Mies van der Rohe

*Painstakingly renovated in 2005, Crown Hall stands as one of the most important buildings of the modern age and it
was also held in the highest regard by Mies himself who said it best represented his "architecture of almost nothing."*

* THE DAY'S SCHEDULE *and* INVITED GUESTS *

CARLOS SEGURA is the founder of Segura, Inc. an internationally recognized visual communications company and the creator of T.26 the web's original digital type foundry as well as the 5" retail brand and the Cartype weblog.

EDWARD LIFSON is a National Public Radio correspondent, architecture critic, blogger and Loeb Fellow at the Graduate School of Design at Harvard. He'll talk during lunch about the Crown Hall, the IIT Campus and Mies.

JASON FRIED is the founder of 37signals, influential creators of web-based communication and collaboration tools Basecamp, Highrise, Backpack & Campfire and authors of the book *Getting Real* and the popular weblog Signal vs. Noise.

JIM COUDAL is the founder of Coudal Partners, a design and advertising consultancy that has created numerous brands and concepts such as The Deck Advertising Network, Jewelboxing, Layer Tennis and Field Notes.

JAKE NICKELL is the Founder and **JEFFREY KALMIKOFF** is the Creative Director of skinnyCorp, the force behind the unstoppable community-based tee shirt design concept Threadless and a steady stream of other great ideas.

GARY VAYNERCHUK is the proprietor of Wine Library TV and a perfect example of someone who has used the web and his own ingenuity to harness the power of his passion. Check him on Conan, Nightline and Ellen.

An **OPEN PANEL DISCUSSION** will follow the presentations and the day will conclude with a
RECEPTION *on the* LAWN *of* CROWN HALL featuring wines selected by Mr. Vaynerchuk.

* SIX CONCISE INTENSE PRESENTATIONS *and* AN OPEN PANEL *to* ALLOW FOR *

Much DISCUSSION *and* INTERACTION

An amazing setting, great food all day catered by Big Delicious Planet and a reception on the lawn afterwards. SEED
promises to be an amazing Friday, which will leave you with an entire summer weekend in Chicago & take our word
for it, a summer weekend in Chicago is pretty tough to beat. Regarding SEED, you can take other people's word for it
too. Here are a few reviews of SEEDS 1 & 2: Mike Rohde, Jameson Watts, Anthony Zinni, Bud Caddell, Chad Udell
DK Design, Scott Dierdorf, Larry Wright, Wake Interactive, Matt Jankowski, plus search Google for more comments

SEED *is* SOLD OUT

Add your email address here and we'll let you know the date and location of the next SEED

Any questions?

VARIOUS DETAILS: Registration opens at 8a and the conference will conclude around 5p, followed by the reception. Breakfast, a
buffet lunch, including vegetarian options, and appetizers at the reception will be served. WIFI is free. Parking is included and IIT
is easily accessible by public transportation. In fact, the CTA Green Line runs right through the Campus Center. From downtown a
taxi should be around $10. Directions. Google Map. We don't have any hotel affiliations but we dig The Burnham, The Amalfi and
The James. The Sox host the Twins SEED weekend. REM is at The UC, Blues Fest is on, as is The Printer's Row Book Fair. Peace.

SEE)

FIGURE 3.1 *Typography is rich on the web, as seen in this example of text-based design.*

Specifying a generic font family ensures that your site will display in a font that is at least similar to the font you really want to use in your design. There are five different generic font family types:

- **Serif fonts** have small, finishing strokes (called serifs) and are generally considered more traditional typefaces. Times New Roman is a classic example of a serif font. Georgia is a font made specifically for screen legibility, so it's a great choice for web use (**FIGURE 3.3**).

- **Sans serif** fonts are fonts that lack serifs. Arial is a typical sans serif font, and Verdana is a sans serif font made specifically for the screen (**FIGURE 3.4**).

- **Cursive fonts** have handwriting-like letters. Comic Sans is an example of a cursive font (**FIGURE 3.5**).

- **Fantasy fonts** are typefaces used primarily for decorative purposes. These can work well for display type or highlights, but it's generally not a good idea to use them for long blocks of text. Impact is an example of a fantasy font (**FIGURE 3.6**).

- **Monospace fonts** are fonts whose characters all have the same width, like a typewriter typeface. Courier and Monaco are examples of monotype fonts. They are often used to represent samples of computer code (**FIGURE 3.7**).

Experiment with different values for the font-family property, viewing the changes in your browser, before you continue.

FIGURE 3.3 *A sample of Georgia.*

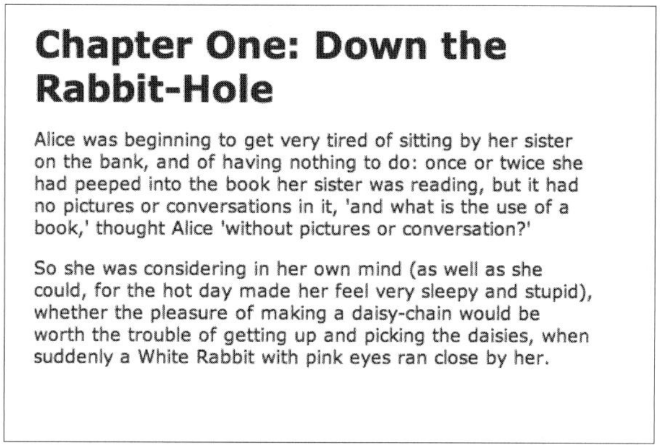

FIGURE 3.4 *A sample of Verdana.*

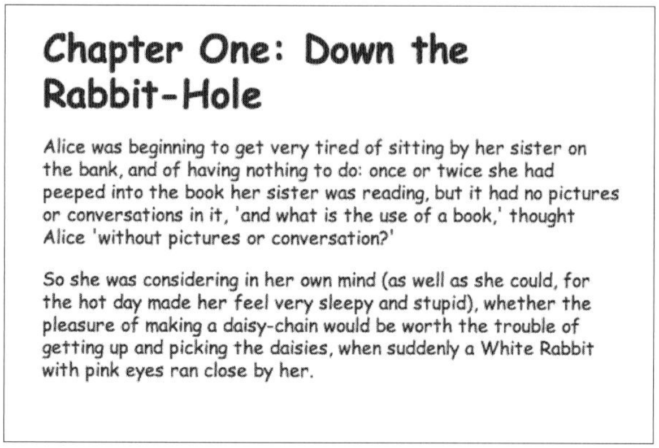

FIGURE 3.5 *A sample of Comic Sans.*

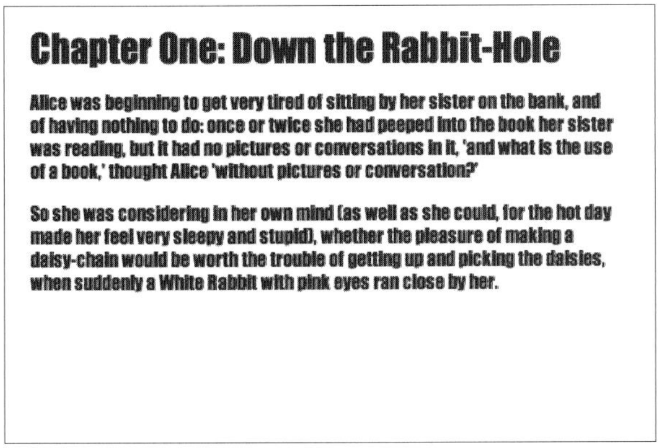

Chapter One: Down the Rabbit-Hole

Alice was beginning to get very tired of sitting by her sister on the bank, and of having nothing to do: once or twice she had peeped into the book her sister was reading, but it had no pictures or conversations in it, 'and what is the use of a book,' thought Alice 'without pictures or conversation?'

So she was considering in her own mind (as well as she could, for the hot day made her feel very sleepy and stupid), whether the pleasure of making a daisy-chain would be worth the trouble of getting up and picking the daisies, when suddenly a White Rabbit with pink eyes ran close by her.

FIGURE 3.6 *A sample of Impact.*

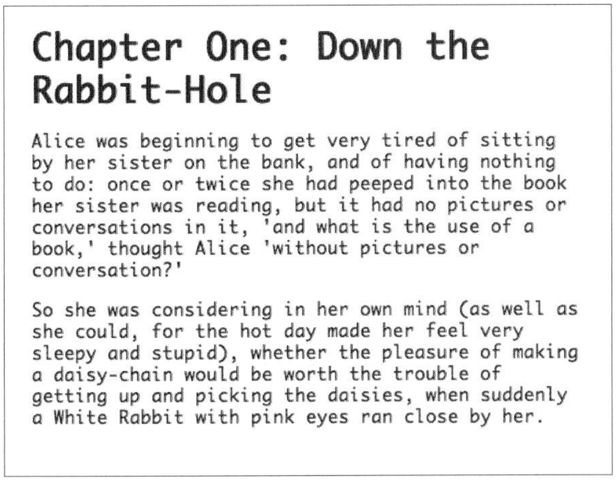

Chapter One: Down the Rabbit-Hole

Alice was beginning to get very tired of sitting by her sister on the bank, and of having nothing to do: once or twice she had peeped into the book her sister was reading, but it had no pictures or conversations in it, 'and what is the use of a book,' thought Alice 'without pictures or conversation?'

So she was considering in her own mind (as well as she could, for the hot day made her feel very sleepy and stupid), whether the pleasure of making a daisy-chain would be worth the trouble of getting up and picking the daisies, when suddenly a White Rabbit with pink eyes ran close by her.

FIGURE 3.7 *A sample of a monospace font.*

Size Properties and Values

You can set the size of a font using the **font-size** property. This example uses a font measurement unit called an em (see the definition on the following page), as shown in **FIGURE 3.8**:

```
h1 {
    font-family: Verdana, Arial, sans-serif;
    font-size: 1.8em;
}
p {
    font-family: Georgia, "Times New Roman",
serif;
    font-size: .9em;
}
```

Various units of measurement are available to set the size. You can set the size using absolute units, which represent a static height. These include:

- **cm** (centimeters)
- **mm** (millimeters)
- **in** (inches)
- **pt** (points—1/72nd of an inch)
- **px** (pixels—1/96th of an inch traditionally, but technically varies depending on the device and distance to the user)
- **pc** (picas—12 points)

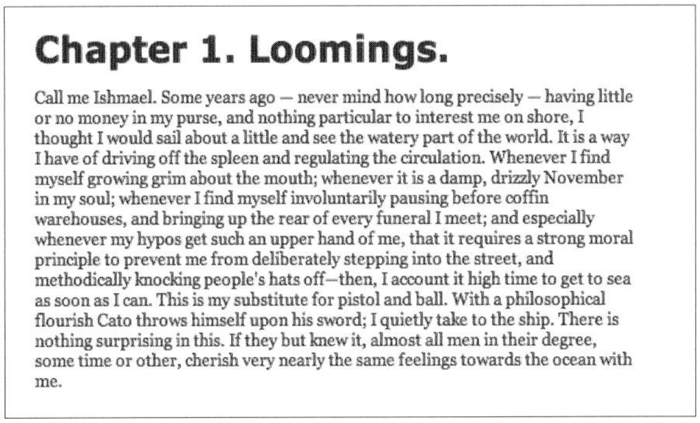

Chapter 1. Loomings.

Call me Ishmael. Some years ago — never mind how long precisely — having little or no money in my purse, and nothing particular to interest me on shore, I thought I would sail about a little and see the watery part of the world. It is a way I have of driving off the spleen and regulating the circulation. Whenever I find myself growing grim about the mouth; whenever it is a damp, drizzly November in my soul; whenever I find myself involuntarily pausing before coffin warehouses, and bringing up the rear of every funeral I meet; and especially whenever my hypos get such an upper hand of me, that it requires a strong moral principle to prevent me from deliberately stepping into the street, and methodically knocking people's hats off—then, I account it high time to get to sea as soon as I can. This is my substitute for pistol and ball. With a philosophical flourish Cato throws himself upon his sword; I quietly take to the ship. There is nothing surprising in this. If they but knew it, almost all men in their degree, some time or other, cherish very nearly the same feelings towards the ocean with me.

FIGURE 3.8 *Setting the type size.*

Or, you can use relative units, which represent measurements that vary in relation to the user's *viewing context*. These include:

- **em** (1 em is the width of an upper case "M" in any given font at any given size. For screen typography, it's a base measure that maps to a browser's default font size.)

- **rem** (equal to the root element's default value)

- **ex** (the *x-height* is equal to the height of the font's lowercase "x")

- **%** (percent)

- You can also set the size using one of the following keywords (**FIGURE 3.9**):

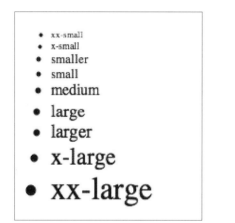

FIGURE 3.9 *Each size keyword is rendered in its own respective sizes.*

> **!** **PIXELS PAST**
>
> Pixels give you more precise control over the design of the page, particularly when you measure other elements in pixels. However, pixels aren't consistent and, if you're supporting older versions of IE, they have terrible effects on layout when you're resizing type.

So, What Measurement Should You Use?

Designers tend to use either ems or rems. Ems, which are a relative unit, are a bit more friendly and more adaptive to different devices and screen readers. As more and more devices, such as smartphones and tablets, are being brought to market, the desktop's share of the browsing experience is shrinking. So, our font choices need to be able to scale. Using ems is a good way to meet that challenge (**FIGURE 3.10**):

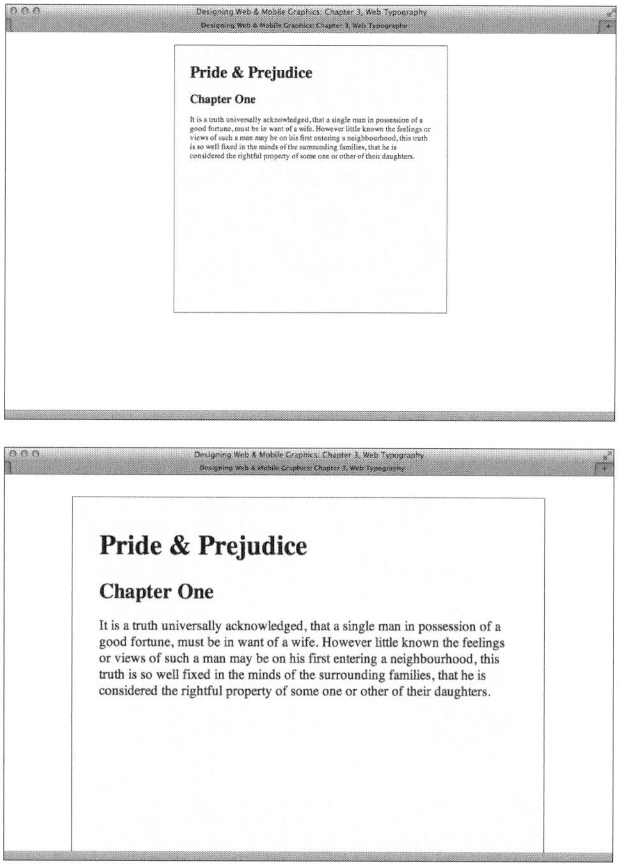

FIGURE 3.10 *Scaling fonts with ems makes content scale.*

Problem with Ems

The problem with em units is that their values can compound, as seen in the font size of the nested list items in **FIGURE 3.11**:

```
body {
 font-size:62.5%;
}
h1 {
 font-size: 2.4em;
 }
p {
 font-size: 1.4em;
}
li {
 font-size: 1.4em;
}
```

To work around this problem, we could reset the font size property for nested list items with a descendant property:

```
li li {
 font-size: 1em;
}
```

However, that would mean adding more and more resets as more and more typography elements get nested. The rem units work around this problem by using the default size and only the default size of the root element. So, there's no need to go back into the code to patch things up (**FIGURE 3.12**):

```
html {
 font-size: 62.5%;
}
body {
 font-size: 1.4rem;
}
h1   {
 font-size: 2.4rem;
}
p  {
 font-size: 1.4em;
}
li {
 font-size: 1.4rem;
}
```

The only problem with rem units is that they aren't supported in IE8 and lesser versions.

FIGURE 3.11
Nested list items get compounded font sizes.

FIGURE 3.12 *Using rem units alleviates the compounding font size issue.*

lighter	100 (thin)
normal	200
bold	300
bolder	400 (normal)
	500
	600
	700 (bold)
	800
	900 (black)

FIGURE 3.13 *Font weights in text set in their respective values.*

Normal	
The reports of my death have been greatly exaggerated. –Mark Twain	
Oblique	
The reports of my death have been greatly exaggerated. –Mark Twain	
Italic	
The reports of my death have been greatly exaggerated. –Mark Twain	
Oblique	*in my of*
Italic	*in my of*

FIGURE 3.14 *Georgia normal tilted to make an oblique style, and Georgia italic.*

Weights, Styles, Variants, and Decorations

If you like typography, you'll be excited to learn that further options exist beyond selecting **font-family** and size. Weights, styles, variants, and decorations can each be modified to give you more precision.

Font-Weight

The **font-weight** property controls the weight (or thickness) of a font (**FIGURE 3.13**):

```
p {
  font-weight: bold;
}
```

Possible values include lighter (than the parent), normal, bold, bolder (than the parent), 100 (thin), 200, 300, 400 (normal), 500, 600, 700 (bold), 800 , 900 (black).

Font-Style

You can set the style of a font using the **font-style** property:

```
p {
  font-style: oblique;
}
```

There are three possible values: normal, oblique, and italic. Oblique fonts are the normal font, but tilted a bit forward. Italic fonts are also tilted, but they are actually a separate typeface (notice the difference in how the f's, i's, m's, and n's are formed) as shown in **FIGURE 3.14**. Most modern browsers render italic and oblique fonts the same, so at this point it doesn't much matter what you specify.

As mentioned in Chapter 1, "Understanding HTML," **em** and **strong** are HTML elements that *appear* to perform the same function as the **font-weight** and **font-style** tags. The **em** element indicates emphasized text. By default, it is rendered as italic text. The **strong** element indicates more strongly emphasized text, and, by default, it is rendered as bold text. However, unlike the CSS properties, these elements are not really meant to control the *presentation* of the text. Rather, they are intended to point out the *function* of certain text—to point out that text is emphasized rather than italicized. You may decide that you'd rather emphasize your text by making it red. You could easily do that by styling the **em** tag:

```
em {
  font-style: normal;
  color: red;
}
```

Then, this HTML:

```
<p>I was <em>very, very</em> upset by the
disheartening news.</p>
```

would look like this **FIGURE 3.15**:

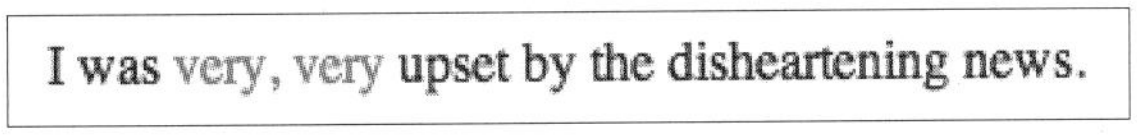

I was very, very upset by the disheartening news.

FIGURE 3.15 *Using other styles for emphasized text.*

Furthermore, remember that not all *italicized* text is really *emphasized* text. Take a book title, for example. Conventionally, titles are italicized, but we're not *putting emphasis* on them by italicizing them. In fact, it would be semantically inappropriate to wrap them in **<em>** tags. Rather, we would probably want to mark them up with their own class:

```
<span class="book">The Lion, the Witch, and the
Wardrobe</span> by C.S. Lewis
```

and then style that class as italicized:

```
.book {
  font-style: italic;
}
```

That way, we don't rely on HTML for presentation, but leave that up to CSS.

Text-Decoration

You can add various effects to text by using the text-decoration property.

```
p {
  text-decoration: line-through;
}
```

It takes the following values (**FIGURE 3.16**):

- none
- underline (puts a line under the text)
- overline (puts a line over the text)
- line-through (puts a line through the text)

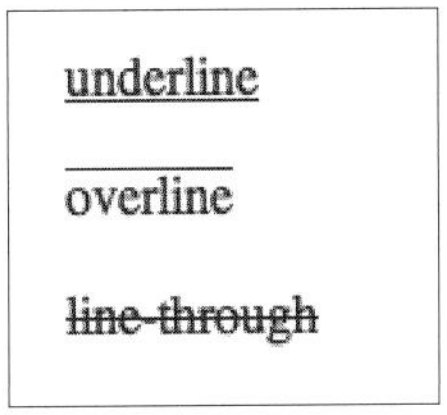

<u>underline</u>

<span style="text-decoration: overline">overline</span>

~~line-through~~

FIGURE 3.16 *Examples of text decoration options.*

Line through is, of course, a classic style to use for the omnipresent online price discount! (No one should ever pay regular price.) It's also perfect for showing text that has been changed or fixed so the viewer can see the old version. Couple the CSS value with the **del** element for that case:

```
del {
  text-decoration: line-through;
}
```

Alignment

Here's a technique you can apply to a section of a page. You can align text in a block-level element using the text-align property.

```
body {
  text-align: justify;
}
```

It takes one of four values: left, right, center, and justify (spreads the text to fit the line width) (**FIGURE 3.17**).

CHAPTER I. Down the Rabbit-Hole

Alice was beginning to get very tired of sitting by her sister on the bank, and of having nothing to do: once or twice she had peeped into the book her sister was reading, but it had no pictures or conversations in it, 'and what is the use of a book,' thought Alice 'without pictures or conversation?'

So she was considering in her own mind (as well as she could, for the hot day made her feel very sleepy and stupid), whether the pleasure of making a daisy-chain would be worth the trouble of getting up and picking the daisies, when suddenly a White Rabbit with pink eyes ran close by her.

There was nothing so VERY remarkable in that; nor did Alice think it so VERY much out of the way to hear the Rabbit say to itself, 'Oh dear! Oh dear! I shall be late!'

FIGURE 3.17 *The four values of the text-align property.*

Letter Spacing and Line Height

In print, there are two ways to adjust text spacing: tracking alters the spacing between the letters, while leading changes the spacing between the lines.

Using CSS, you can adjust the horizontal spacing between the letters using the letter-spacing property. It takes as its value some length:

```
h1 {
  letter-spacing: .1em;
}
```

You can assign a negative length (such as −.2em) to squeeze the letters more tightly together. Use a positive number to spread them farther apart. This level of control is particularly helpful for headings (**FIGURE 3.18**):

A Tale of Two Cities

A Tale of Two Cities

A T a l e o f T w o C i t i e s

FIGURE 3.18
Adjusting letter spacing between characters.

The line height is the distance from one baseline (the invisible line on which the text rests) to the next. If you assign a line height using no units of measurement, then the browser derives the value of the line height from the font size. So, if you use pixels as the unit of measure for your font, and you have a 10-pixel font and specify a line height of 1.25, the line height would be 12 pixels. If you specify your font as 1 em, that same line height would become 1.25 em. For the web, a good line height to use is 1.5 (**FIGURE 3.19**).

I hope you'll agree that the text is much easier to read with these rules applied.

Default line-height:
It was the best of times, it was the worst of times, it was the age of wisdom, it was the age of foolishness, it was the epoch of belief, it was the epoch of incredulity, it was the season of Light, it was the season of Darkness, it was the spring of hope, it was the winter of despair, we had everything before us, we had nothing before us, we were all going direct to Heaven, we were all going direct the other way— in short, the period was so far like the present period, that some of its noisiest authorities insisted on its being received, for good or for evil, in the superlative degree of comparison only.

Line-height adjusted to 1.5:
It was the best of times, it was the worst of times, it was the age of wisdom, it was the age of foolishness, it was the epoch of belief, it was the epoch of incredulity, it was the season of Light, it was the season of Darkness, it was the spring of hope, it was the winter of despair, we had everything before us, we had nothing before us, we were all going direct to Heaven, we were all going direct the other way— in short, the period was so far like the present period, that some of its noisiest authorities insisted on its being received, for good or for evil, in the superlative degree of comparison only.

FIGURE 3.19 *Adjusting the distance between lines with line height.*

PRACTICING SAFE TYPOGRAPHY

The ability to send content through the web from a server and leverage assets on the reader's computer, like type and cached assets, is genius. It makes pages speedy. But this efficiency comes at a cost as not all computers have the same fonts.

Web-Safe Fonts

There is an overlap of fonts that are installed on most desktop computers (**FIGURE 3.20**). The common or shared fonts across operating systems, called **web-safe fonts**, are shown in **TABLE 3.1**.

With the usage of common software applications like Microsoft Office and Apple's iWork suites, the number of potential web-safe fonts has increased.

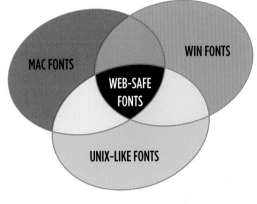

FIGURE 3.20 *Venn diagram of fonts.*

TABLE 3.1 *Desktop Web-safe Fonts*

Windows/Mac OS Font	Font Family	Example
Arial	Sans serif	Blowzy night-frumps vex'd Jack Q.
Arial Black	Sans serif	**Blowzy night-frumps vex'd Jack Q.**
Comic Sans MS	Cursive	Blowzy night-frumps vex'd Jack Q.
Courier New	Monospace	Blowzy night-frumps vex'd Jack Q.
Georgia	Serif	Blowzy night-frumps vex'd Jack Q.
Helvetica	Sans serif	Blowzy night-frumps vex'd Jack Q.
Impact	Sans serif	**Blowzy night-frumps vex'd Jack Q.**
Tahoma	Sans serif	Blowzy night-frumps vex'd Jack Q.
Times	Serif	Blowzy night-frumps vex'd Jack Q.
Times New Roman	Serif	Blowzy night-frumps vex'd Jack Q.
Trebuchet MS	Sans serif	Blowzy night-frumps vex'd Jack Q.
Verdana	Sans serif	Blowzy night-frumps vex'd Jack Q.
Wingdings	(Symbol)	✎●□◆⌘⊠ ■✴♈♍♒♦✑▨✗□◆○□◆

Mobile-Safe Fonts

With smartphones and tablet devices relatively new compared to personal desktop computing, the list of **mobile-safe fonts** is even smaller than web-safe fonts as can be seen in **TABLE 3.2**.

TABLE 3.2 *Mobile Web-safe Fonts*

Windows/Mac OS Font	Font Family	Example
Arial	Sans serif	Blowzy night-frumps vex'd Jack Q.
Helvetica	Sans serif	Blowzy night-frumps vex'd Jack Q.
Courier/Courier New	Monospace	Blowzy night-frumps vex'd Jack Q.
Georgia	Serif	Blowzy night-frumps vex'd Jack Q.
Times	Serif	Blowzy night-frumps vex'd Jack Q.
Times New Roman	Serif	Blowzy night-frumps vex'd Jack Q.
Verdana	Sans serif	Blowzy night-frumps vex'd Jack Q.

iOS FONTS

For a complete listing of fonts on iOS and its different versions (**FIGURE 3.21**), check out http://iosfonts.com.

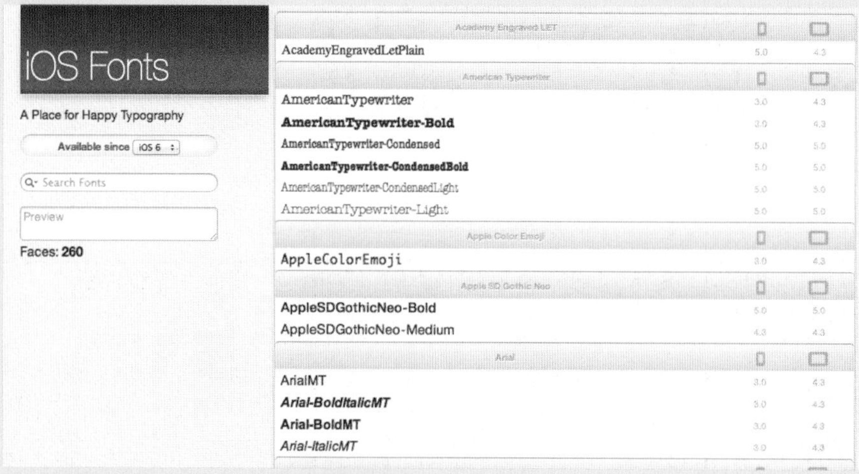

FIGURE 3.21 *Review font options available on iOS devices.*

MAKING BETTER FONT STACKS

We can use web-safe fonts as a starting point. Let's reexamine the humble font stack with a web-safe font and a generic font family (**FIGURE 3.22**):

```
font-family: Arial, sans-serif;
```

With all the options before us, our strategy should be to first select a font name that, ideally, would be installed on the user's machine:

```
font-family: "FF Meta Web Pro", Arial,
sans-serif;
```

If the font is installed, then the font will be seen instead of a web-safe font or generic font family. But let's not stop there. Let's apply other, more desirable web-safe fonts *before* the basic fonts for a stronger font stack (**FIGURE 3.23**):

```
font-family: "FF Meta Web Pro", Tahoma,
Verdana, Arial, sans-serif;
```

FONT NAMES WITH SPACES When there is a space in a font family name, place quotation marks around the name. This lets the browser know that space is intentional and part of the font name.

TYPE MATTERS If you think Tahoma, Verdana, and Arial are the same typeface, then font stacking probably isn't for you. Designers love their fonts and notice the subtle differences in seemingly similar typefaces.

FIGURE 3.22 *A basic font stack.*

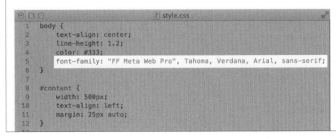

FIGURE 3.23 *An advanced font stack provides more options.*

"REAL FONTS" IN WEB PAGES

We're not limited to using the typefaces that come installed. CSS allows for *embedding* fonts into web pages. This embedding process allows web designers to bring in fonts that are not installed on a site visitor's computer and have them render properly on the screen.

FONT STACK GALLERIES

Open up your site to better web typography. Review blog posts at http://www.awayback.com/revised-font-stack/ and http://www.inspirationbit.com/striking-web-sites-with-font-stacks-that-inspire/ for inspiration for font stacks (**FIGURE 3.24**):

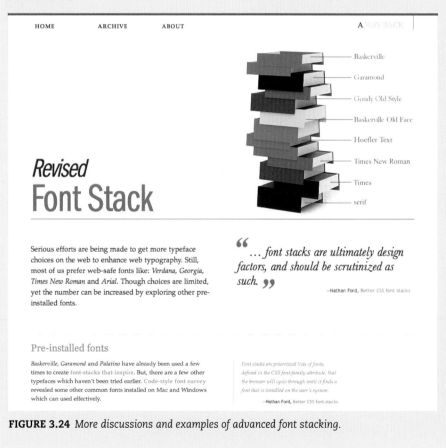

FIGURE 3.24 *More discussions and examples of advanced font stacking.*

The @font-face Property

To bring in an external font file, first use the **@font-face** property and set the value to the font name of the typeface:

```
@font-face {
  font-family: 'League Gothic Regular';
}
```

Then set the font weight and style values:

```
@font-face {
  font-family: 'League Gothic Regular';
  font-weight: normal;
  font-style: normal;
}
```

Then reference the font file:

```
@font-face {
  font-family: 'League Gothic Regular';
  src: url('/fonts/League_Gothic-webfont.eot?#iefix')
format('embedded-opentype'),
  font-weight: normal;
  font-style: normal;
}
```

Only IE browsers understand Embedded OpenType (EOT) files, which they have been doing since IE4. To deliver embedded font files for other browsers, we need to give each browser a font file it can recognize. So, the **font-face** rule should reference different file types for the same font:

```
@font-face {
  font-family: 'League Gothic Regular';
  src: url('/fonts/League_Gothic-webfont.eot?#iefix')
format('embedded-opentype'),
  url('/fonts/League_Gothic-webfont.woff') format('woff'),
  url('/fonts/League_Gothic-webfont.ttf') format('truetype'),
  url('/fonts/League_Gothic-webfont.svg#LeagueGothicRegular')
format('svg');
  font-weight: normal;
  font-style: normal;
}
```

> **! DIFFERENT STYLES NEED DIFFERENT FONT FILES**
>
> If you're using a normal and a bold font from the same family, both font faces need to be referenced through two **@font-face** declarations. Without embedding the actual bold font, the browser will badly recreate what it thinks is the bold version of the original font.

Walden
by Henry David Thoreau

FIGURE 3.25 *Before the font is embedded.*

Walden
by Henry David Thoreau

FIGURE 3.26 *After the font is embedded.*

Then set the family name within the font stack in the CSS to tell the browser where to apply the font (**FIGURES 3.25** and **3.26**):

```
header h2 {
    font-family: "League Gothic", "League Gothic Regular", serif;
}
```

In the example, we set League Gothic in the hope that the user has the font already installed on his computer, thereby eliminating the need to download another asset. If the user doesn't have it installed, that's okay, as the browser will pick a font file it can handle and render the font in the browser.

You can find typefaces that are free for commercial use to embed into your web pages at Font Squirrel (http://fontsquirrel.com/). Select a font that you'd like to use and download all the files and CSS rules you need to embed the font along with sample web pages.

Generating Files for Embedding

If you have a font file already and want to use it for a web page, Font Squirrel provides an online, free generator that lets you convert the font file to the other formats for cross-browser support (**FIGURE 3.27**):

FIGURE 3.27 *The font generator at Font Squirrel.*

TO GENERATE A SET OF FONT FILES TO EMBED INTO A WEB PAGE, FOLLOW THESE ③ STEPS:

① Click the Add Fonts button. If you're new to @font-face generator, select Optimal.

② Check the agreement that you're legally allowed to use the font for embedding.

③ Click "Download Your Kit" to download all the generating font files.

Companies that sell font files have licenses that forbid or restrict using their wares for embedding. Make sure to check the license agreement for each font you own before you upload it to the web.

Free Real Fonts

At the time of this writing, Google's free web font service (www.google.com/webfonts) has more than 550 fonts that can be embedded into web pages and the number continues to grow. With Google's focus on speed, utilizing their quick servers won't drag down your web pages much (**FIGURE 3.28**).

> ❗ **FONT FILE SIZES**
>
> While custom fonts allow more design flexibility, they come with a price. A good typeface's file size is rather large. Adding multiple fonts reduces a web page's load speed. Slow web pages create poor user experiences and decrease online sale conversions. So, be judicious with your font selections.

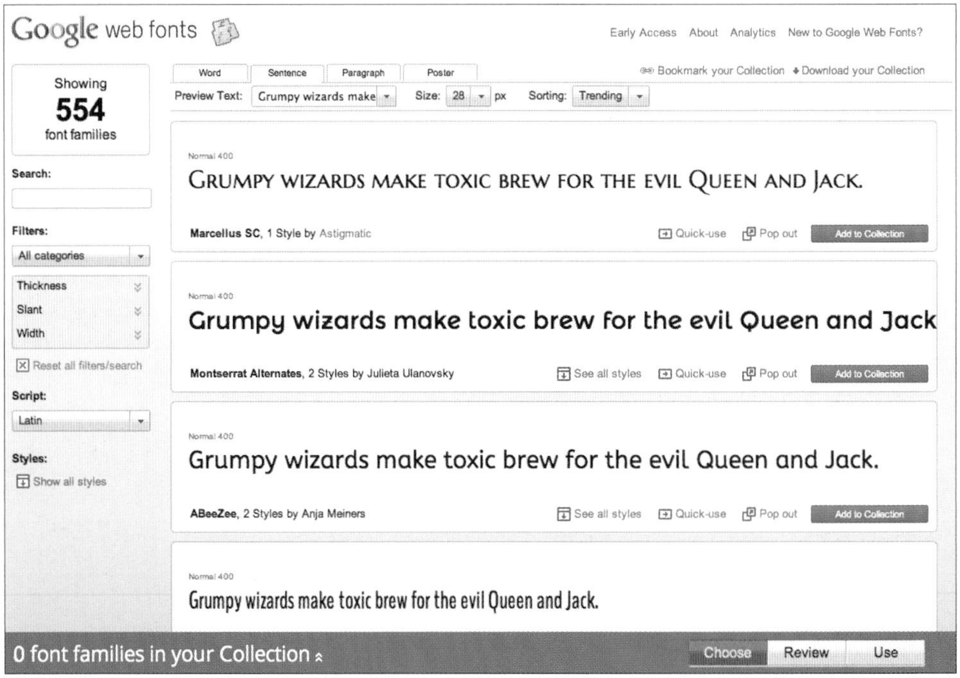

FIGURE 3.28 *Google's Web Font home page.*

TO USE GOOGLE'S WEB FONTS, FOLLOW THESE ④ STEPS:

① Find a font in Google's directory and select Quick Use below the font example.

② Copy the link element from Google's code box.

③ Insert the link element into the HTML document.

```
<head>
  <link rel="stylesheet" type="text/css" href="http://fonts.googleapis.com/
css?family=Didact+Gothic">
</head>
```

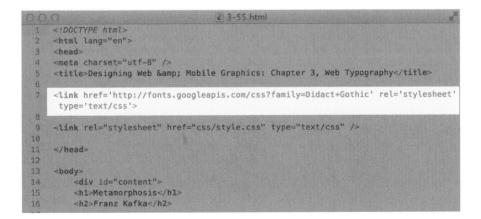

④ In a separate CSS file, such as style.css, list the family name in the font stack:

```
h1 {
  font-family:"Didact Gothic", serif;
  font-size: 2em;
}
```

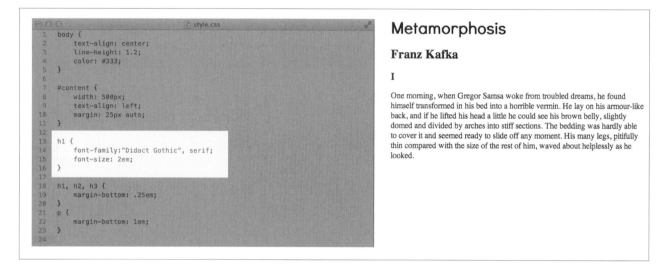

REDUCE THE NUMBER OF LINK ELEMENTS

If we use multiple links embedded in the HTML for each additional font, we then need to update those HTML files every time a design change comes up. To bring back design control to a CSS file, look to the @import rule also provided by Google (**FIGURE 3.29**).

```
@import url(http://fonts.googleapis.com/css?family=Didact+Gothic);
```

Then place the @import rule at the top of the CSS file.

FIGURE 3.29 *The @import rule for a Google web font for copy and pasting into your web page.*

ANOTHER FREE FONT SERVICE In partnership with Google Fonts, Adobe has released its own web font service called Adobe Edge Web Fonts (http://html.adobe.com/edge/webfonts/), as shown in **FIGURE 3.30**. Picking fonts is as simple as picking a font name from the drop-down menu and copying and pasting the script and CSS rules.

Huge selection. Fast. Free!

Edge Web Fonts gives you access to a vast web font library made possible by contributions from Adobe, Google, and designers around the world. The fonts are served by Typekit, so you can be sure of high performance and stability. Plus, it's free! Learn more.

Integrated with Edge Tools & Services

Edge Web Fonts is conveniently built into Edge Code today and will be available in Edge Reflow and other Edge Tools & Services soon.

FIGURE 3.30 *Adobe Edge Web Fonts.*

Commercial Font Services

Adobe's Typekit (https://typekit.com/) is a commercial font service that offers sub-scriptions to online embedding of typography. Typekit isn't a type foundry itself, but rather a clearinghouse for many other font shops' typefaces.

TO ADD A TYPEFACE FROM TYPEKIT TO A WEB PAGE, FOLLOW THESE ⑨ STEPS:

① Sign in to Typekit.

② Enter the name and domain name of the site. The web fonts will be displayed.

③ Place the JavaScript lines of code in the **head** element of the web page.

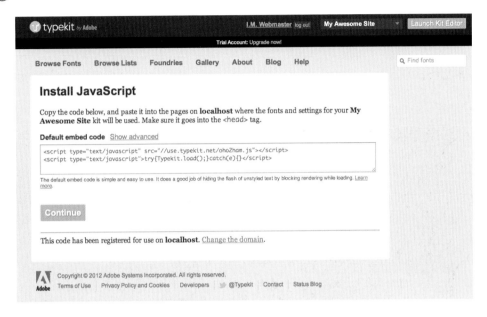

④ Search and find a typeface for embedding.

⑤ Once you've found a typeface, select "+ Add to Kit."

JAVASCRIPT IS POPULAR JavaScript is very popular. Currently 1 percent or less of web surfers turn off JavaScript in their browser.

⑥ A browser window pops open. Adjust which weights of the font you want to include.

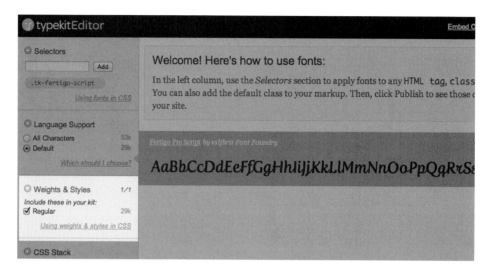

⑦ List any CSS selectors that should receive the web font. In this example, the font is for paragraphs.

> ! **CLASS SELECTORS IN TYPEKIT**
>
> Note that the class selector is premade. In the event that you want to apply the web font elsewhere in the page, you don't have to go back to Typekit and make adjustments. Rather, you can set a class attribute in the HTML element(s) that should get the web fonts.

(8) When finished, select Publish.

Kit Size: 29K 1 font, 2 selectors for My Awesome Site   Publish

(9) After a few minutes, the web fonts are brought in through JavaScript and applied to the paragraphs.

Designing Web & Mobile Graphics: Chapter 3, Web Typography

Think left and think right and think low and think high. Oh, the thinks you can think up if only you try!
~ Dr. Seuss

Fonts from

COMMERCIAL TYPE SERVICES

Typekit is not the only commercial web font service. Others include Fontdeck (http://fontdeck.com), fonts.com, and WebINK (http://www.webink.com/).

IN CONCLUSION

As we saw in the opening example, typography can enrich web design. Judicious balance of web-safe fonts and embedded fonts, as demonstrated in this chapter, can deliver a better experience to just about any site visitor.

In the next chapter, we'll look at more challenges associated with delivering the best experience possible to our site visitors.

The Challenges of

Web & Mobile

"I like the challenge of trying different things
and wondering whether it's going to work
or whether I'm going to fall flat on my face."

—*Johnny Depp*

Chapter **4**

CHALLENGES IN WEB DESIGN

Developing a new version of a browser once took a year; now,
browser companies update their products every couple of months.
The World Wide Web Consortium (W3C), the web standards body,
frequently updates its recommendations on how browsers should
work. Users are no longer chained to the desktop; they can access
the Web on their smartphones, game consoles, kiosks, and so on.
The websites we build need to adapt to meet the challenges of these
different browsers and environments.

THE WEB ENVIRONMENT

Browsers have come a long way to produce a great base experience for visitors, but you might be inadvertently creating a situation where visitors see a different presentation than the one you think you're giving them.

Revealing Browser Issues

The following screenshots show how one page compares in different browsers: Internet Explorer 9 (**FIGURE 4.1**), Safari (**FIGURE 4.2**), Chrome (**FIGURE 4.3**), Firefox (**FIGURE 4.4**), Nexus 7 Chrome (**FIGURE 4.5**), Opera (**FIGURE 4.6**), and Mobile Safari iOS on an iPad (**FIGURE 4.7**).

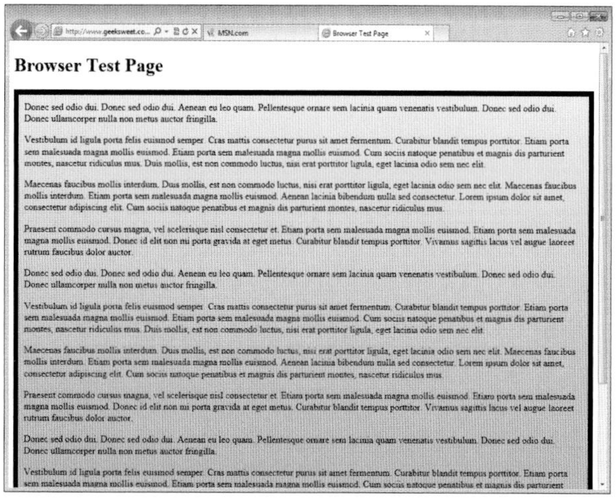

FIGURE 4.1 *A test page in Internet Explorer 9.*

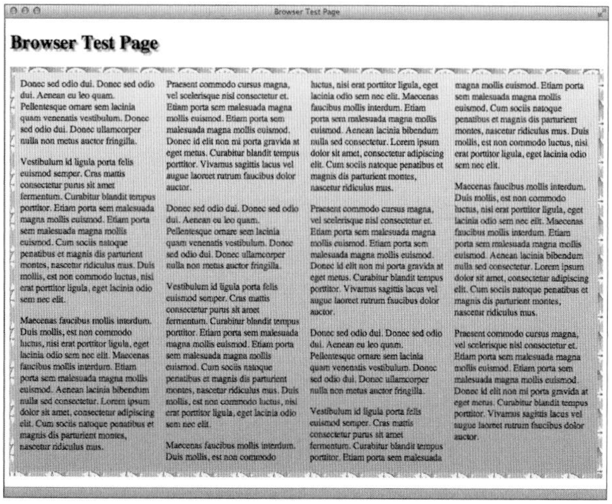

FIGURE 4.3 *A test page in Chrome.*

FIGURE 4.2 *A test page in Safari 6.*

FIGURE 4.4 *A test page in Firefox.*

FIGURE 4.5 *A test page in Nexus 7 Chrome.*

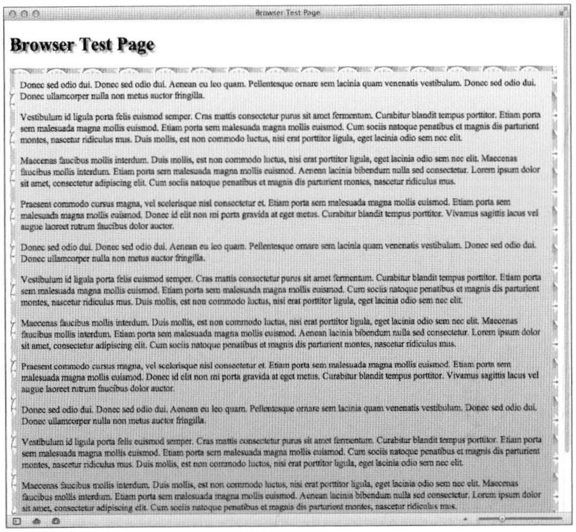

FIGURE 4.6 *A test page in Opera.*

FIGURE 4.7 *A test page in Mobile Safari on an iPad.*

TABLE 4.1 showcases which Cascading Style Sheets (CSS) features are supported by various browsers. A "Y" means the browser supports the CSS feature natively. An "N" means the browser does not support it. A "P" means the browser does support the feature, but it needs a custom CSS prefix in order for the feature to display. The custom prefixes will be explained in more detail in Vendor Prefixes later in this chapter.

TABLE 4.1 *CSS Feature Support by Browser*

Browser	Columns	Border Image	Gradients	Text Shadows
Internet Explorer 9	N	N	N	Y
Safari 6	P	Y	P	Y
Chrome	P	Y	P	Y
Firefox	P	Y	P	Y
Nexus 7 Chrome	P	P	P	Y
Opera	Y	P	P	Y
Mobile Safari iOS on iPad	P	P	P	Y

Using a Test Page

Now let's break down the test page to show which features are in it and how they are implemented. The test page covers some basic and advanced CSS functionality:

- **CSS3 multi-column** lets you set text in columns. In web design, you don't see multiple text columns unless the designer manually adjusts the number of words for each column or uses a JavaScript patch.

```
div {
  column-count: 4;
}
```

- **CSS3 border-image** lets you wrap an image around an HTML element. As the HTML stretches as text is added or removed, for example, the image stretches and adapts.

```
div {
  column-count: 4;
  border-image: url(border-img.png) 10px;
}
```

- **CSS3 gradients** sets color transitions in the background of elements.

```
div {
background: linear-gradient(to bottom,
rgba(30,87,153,1) 0%,
rgba(41,137,216,1) 50%,
rgba(32,124,202,1) 51%,
rgba(125,185,232,1) 100%);
}
```

- **CSS3 text-shadows** lets you put one or more shadows on text.

```
div h1 {
text-shadow: 0 1px 1px #bbb,
   0 2px 0 #999,
   0 3px 0 #888,
   0 4px 0 #777,
   0 5px 0 #666,
   0 6px 0 #555,
   0 7px 0 #444,
   0 8px 0 #333,
   0 9px 7px #302314;
}
```

Color

We perceive the color around us thanks to our eyes, which are electromagnetic spectrum detectors. Colors make up only a small portion of this spectrum, which encompasses x-rays, gamma rays, microwaves, radio waves, all the colors we see, and much more.

A computer screen is made of tiny dots, or pixels, arranged in a grid. These pixels change color depending on what the computer instructs the monitor to display (**FIGURE 4.8**).

FIGURE 4.8 *Zooming in closely on a raster image shows the blocks of color arranged in a grid like the grid of pixels that makes up the screen.*

When you see an option for CYMK in a digital imaging tool like InDesign or Photoshop, it's only there to help give a representation of what the colors look like when *printed*—not how they should appear on screen. Be sure to stick with RGB color mode when creating images or mocking up layouts.

The screens in our desktop PCs and mobile devices don't show colors the same way. No universal calibration system for on-screen color currently exists. Color on computer monitors can vary due to the display brand, the video card brand, the screen's age, the operating system, the amount of ambient light, colors appearing next to each other, and the age and condition of the viewer's eyes. A further translation happens in printing: some colors that are visible on a screen, where they're made with light, can't be printed with any kind of ink or toner (bright, pure blue is the classic example).

No matter how carefully you choose the colors on your screen, they'll never be absolutely accurate since there is no single standard for displaying them.

Screens and Pixels

Units of measurement are expected to be a constant. The problem with constants is that they change.

Take the humble meter, for example. How we determine the starting and ending point of the meter has altered over human history. In the 17th century, a meter was proposed to be part of the distance of the equator to the North Pole. One ten-millionth of the distance to be exact.

In 1875, a meter was then defined as the length of a platinum-iridium bar created by the International Bureau of Weights and Measures near Paris (see http://museum.nist.gov/object.asp?ObjID=37). Numerous bars of the same length were made and distributed around the world.

Some two hundred years later, the meter transformed again and is no longer tied to a physical object. A meter is now the distance *light* travels in a vacuum over 1/299,792,458th of a second. What will it be in the future? And don't ask me what happens to the length of a meter if you happen to be near a black hole, where light can't escape.

Defining a Pixel

The pixel has similar identity issues. What defines a pixel is a matter of when you ask the question. If you are a web designer working in the 1990s, the pixel would be about 1/96th of an inch and it would be fairly constant across operating systems and monitors. *Now* when you ask about the size of a pixel, the answer will depend on which kind of pixel you mean.

These days, people aren't "surfing the World Wide Web" with just the desktop anymore. The web can be accessed on screens that are 3.5 inches diagonal held close to the face, and on 60-inch TVs from across the room. To provide roughly the same experience on this wide range of devices, on-screen elements need to end up looking about the same whether they're being seen from 10 inches or 10 feet.

Let's say we set a head's font size to 24px. If we then look at that head on a retina display and a regular laptop, there should be no difference in size (**FIGURE 4.9**).

The W3C has recommended a standard visual angle pixel size that hardware and software manufacturers can refer to while developing their products. What this means is that web developers can use the CSS pixel as their unit of measurement, and let the browser and OS take care of mapping it to the device pixel, whatever its physical size may be. (There's just one hitch: so far, a perfect solution for scaling up photographic images hasn't been found, as we'll see in Chapter 13, "Images for Responsive Web Design.") The CSS pixel is an absolute length unit that is anchored to the reference pixel, which is an angular measurement (**TABLE 4.2**).

FIGURE 4.9 *The same headline seen in Chrome on an iPhone 5 with a 4-inch, 1136 × 640-pixel screen and in Safari on a MacBook Pro with a 13-inch, 1280 × 800-pixel screen.*

Accessibility

While monitors continue to improve in terms of color clarity, generating millions of colors as faithfully as possible, there are segments of the population who won't be able to see them. Seven percent of men cannot distinguish between red and green colors. Can you see the colors in **FIGURE 4.10**?

These deutan color vision deficiencies, along with others, must be taken into consideration when designing with color.

EYESIGHT STATISTICS   According to the World Health Organization, 285 million people worldwide are visually impaired. That includes 39 million blind and 246 million low-vision people.

TABLE 4.2 *The CSS Pixel and the Reference Pixel*

	Type	Derived from	Used by
reference pixel	visual angle	physics of light	hardware+OS makers
CSS pixel	fixed+anchored	reference pixel	designers/developers

FIGURE 4.10 *A "normal" image compared to an image seen as a red-green color blind person sees it.*

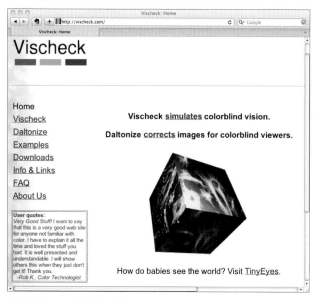

FIGURE 4.11 *The Vischeck page.*

Testing for Color Blindness

To check your design for color blindness issues, there are a couple of online tools.

- **Vischeck** (http://vischeck.com/) provides examples of color blindness and converts existing websites to showcase how they appear to people with different types of color blindness (**FIGURE 4.11**).

- **Contrast Analyser** (http://www.paciellogroup.com/resources/contrastAnalyser) uses the W3C's contrast ratio algorithm to determine whether colors have enough visibility or contrast and shows how colors look to people with different types of color blindness (**FIGURE 4.12**).

Color Vision Is Only One Part of Accessibility

Color blindness is just one accessibility issue. Designing for accessibility in general is another of the challenges of web design:

- People with mobility issues, such as those with carpal tunnel syndrome, may prefer to navigate via keyboard (http://webaim.org/techniques/keyboard/).

- People with reduced dexterity appreciate clickable areas that aren't too tiny, and forms that don't time out before they can finish filling them in (http://otal.umd.edu/UUPractice/mobility/).

- People with hearing impairments rely on captions or transcripts (http://webaim.org/articles/auditory/).

- People who are susceptible to photosensitive epileptic seizures want to avoid blinking elements (http://www.w3.org/TR/understanding-WCAG20/seizure-does-not-violate.html).

- People with learning disabilities that affect reading, such as dyslexia, can be helped by good typography, user-selectable type and background colors, and having content available in audio format (http://www.bdadyslexia.org.uk/about-dyslexia/further-information/dyslexia-style-guide.html); audio content also helps people with low vision.

FIGURE 4.12 *The Contrast Analyser.*

- People with cognitive disabilities affecting memory and attention do better with simple navigation and no distracting animation (http://www.ncdae.org/resources/articles/cognitive/).

- Best practices include the use of **alt** attributes, unambiguous copy, **title** attributes for links, proper HTML structure, and graceful degradation (http://webaim.org/techniques/alttext/).

DETERMINING *YOUR* CROSS-BROWSER GOALS

To determine how to handle different browser issues, you need to understand your visitors. To do that, you need to look at your site statistics.

Analyzing Your Site Traffic

One of the most popular methods for tracking site statistics is Google Analytics (GA), which collects information about site visitors' behavior.

Setting Up Google Analytics

If you already have a Google account (like one for Gmail), use it to set up a Google Analytics account.

TO SET UP GOOGLE ANALYTICS, FOLLOW THESE ⑥ STEPS:

① If you already have a Google account, go to Google Analytics at http://www.google.com/analytics/ and click the Create an account button, and then enter your Email and Password and click the Sign In button.

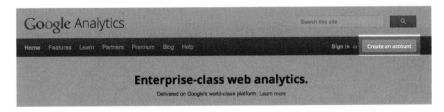

GOOGLE ANALYTICS IS FREE

While there are two available versions, free and premium, most of the time the free version is all you need.

SIGNING UP FOR A GOOGLE ACCOUNT

Don't have a Google account? It's free and opens up a lot of other free resources, like email, web alerts, online word processing and spreadsheets, and more. Sign up at https://accounts.google.com/NewAccount.

② Fill out the new account creation form with details about your account name, site URL, industry category, and time zone. Also, review the Terms of Service for the account.

③ At this main page of Google Analytics, you see a listing of the site you've entered. Click Tracking Code from the navigation menu.

④ Select the domain name you're using. If you're hosting your own domain name, select "A single domain."

(5) Copy and paste the code from Google's form field in every page of your site above the closing **body** tag.

! SERVING USERS, NOT OURSELVES

By placing the JavaScript code at the bottom of the document, the browser gets to it later on and focuses on the other elements of the page instead.

While instructions from Google Analytics state to place the code in the head element, this slows the rendering of a web page ever so slightly. Ensuring that your pages render as quickly as possible is more important than finding out how visitors are using the site. If pages render quickly, then visitors are more inclined to surf more of your site.

(6) Upload the new pages to the server.

Once the code has been added to your site, the next step is to wait. It takes anywhere from four hours to a couple of days for Google to start publishing data to review.

Finding Browser Statistics

Finding browser statistics about your site's visitors is pretty straightforward. You can find information such as the types of browser your visitors use, and how often they use each browser both in number and percentage. You can even find out these details for specific browser versions.

TO FIND BROWSER INFORMATION ON YOUR SITE'S VISITORS, JUST FOLLOW THESE ⑤ STEPS:

① After logging into Google Analytics, you see the Visitors Overview page.

② Click on the large date text in the upper right corner to select the date range you want to review.

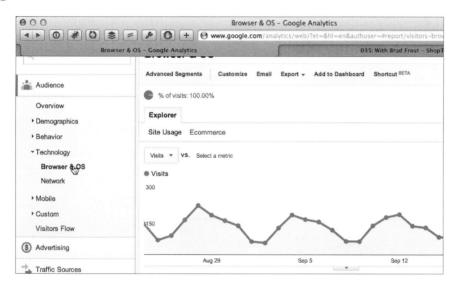

③ In the left column, select Technology > Browser & OS.

(4) The different browsers are listed on the page and color-coded to a pie chart.

(5) For a breakdown on the different versions of a browser visiting a site, click on the browser name. The example shown here is the breakdown of the versions of Firefox visiting the site.

Updating Google Analytics Settings

Going back to your profile to keep your site information and goals updated ensures that Google Analytics is gathering the right data to give you an accurate picture of your site usage.

TO UPDATE SITE INFORMATION AS IT CHANGES, FOLLOW THESE ④ STEPS:

① Click on the Profile name.

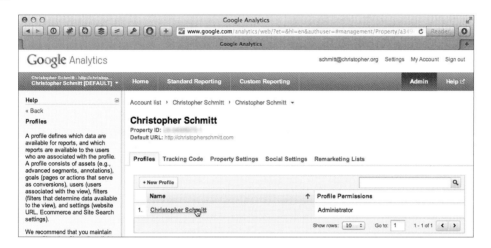

② Select Profile Settings from the navigation submenu.

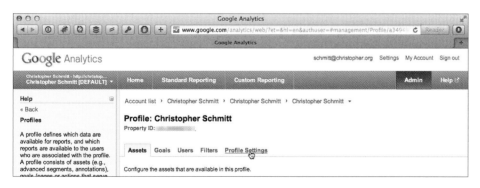

(3) Make updates to the information.

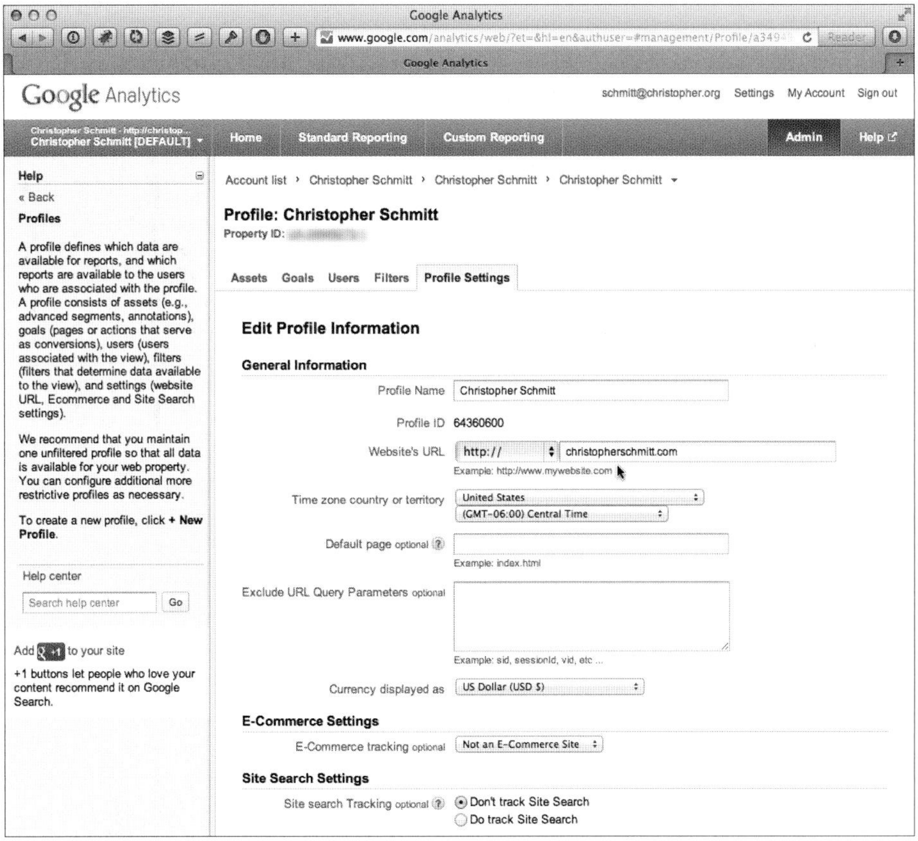

(4) Select Apply.

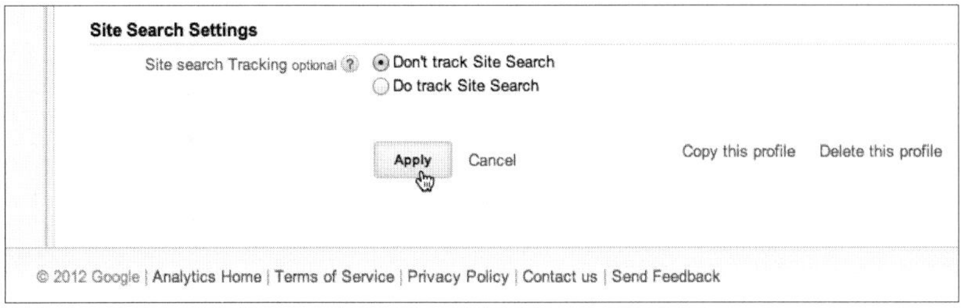

DEVELOPING YOUR SITE FOR DIFFERENT DEVICES

As we have found out already, browsers have varied support for CSS features. Another difference in browsers is in how they display HTML text and white space that doesn't have any CSS customization. The underlying browser styles can influence the CSS presentation layer, so we try to take the browser styles back to a basic and common foundation.

Resetting and Normalizing Browser Styles

Browsers have their own internal style sheets, which designers use to render basic default styles for everything from the distance between lines of text to link colors (**FIGURE 4.13**).

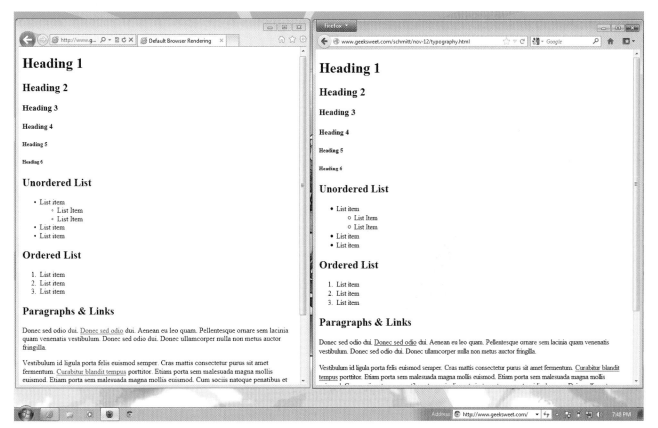

FIGURE 4.13 *Differences in Internet Explorer 9 vs. Firefox browser rendering on Windows.*

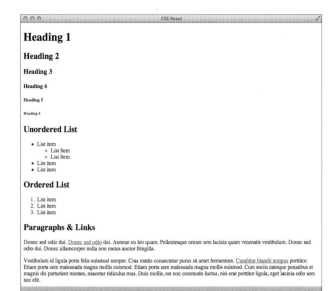

FIGURE 4.14 *Before the CSS Reset.*

Resetting Styles

One way to address browser inconsistencies is to remove or set all CSS properties to zero. This is done through a CSS style sheet known as CSS Reset, like the one premade from Yahoo! through its YUI Library. To set up a reset for a web page (**FIGURE 4.14**), place a link element at the top of any other reference to the style sheet (**FIGURE 4.15**):

```
<link rel="stylesheet" type="text/css"
href="http://yui.yahooapis.com/3.7.1/build/
cssreset/cssreset-min.css">
<link rel="stylesheet" type="text/css"
href="style.css">
```

Normalizing Styles

Using the CSS Reset approach means that all default settings are dialed back. What's left is an empty canvas with no hint of design or standards. That's where **normalize.css** steps in. Rather than removing everything, Normalize.css (http://necolas.github.com/normalize.css/) creates a cohesive standard for the default rendering of HTML elements (**FIGURE 4.16**).

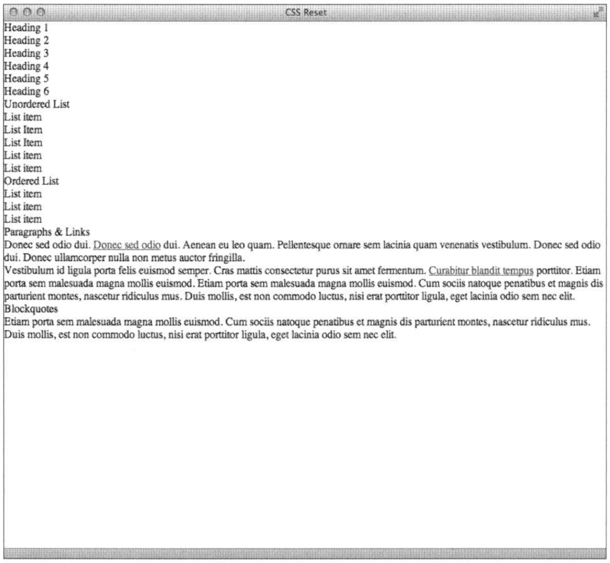

FIGURE 4.15 *After the CSS Reset.*

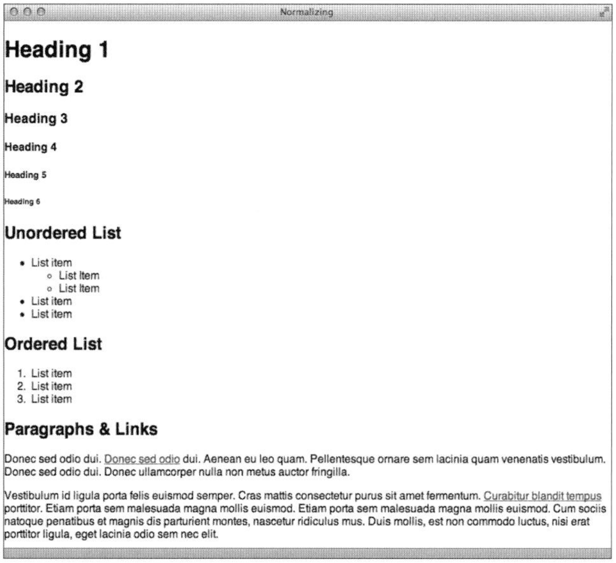

FIGURE 4.16 *After **normalize.css**.*

Normalizing style sheets gives you a solid base to build web pages without having to worry about little discrepancies in browser renderings.

Vendor Prefixes

Sometimes a new CSS feature brought into a browser is still in its beginning stages and needs more work. When this happens, the browser vendor usually provides what's called a **prefix CSS property**.

The Simple CSS Workaround

For example, a simple CSS gradient like the following code will be ignored in Safari 6:

```
div {
  background-image: linear-gradient(#fff, #000);
}
```

To get Safari to work, we have to add a line of code that only Safari will recognize:

```
div {
  background-image: -webkit-linear-gradient(#fff, #000);
  background-image: linear-gradient(#fff, #000);
}
```

The software that powers the rendering or display of a page in Safari is known as WebKit. Therefore, to specify a special feature like a gradient, we need to add "webkit" surrounded by hyphens. To support other browsers that have the same approach to new CSS features, we need to add the special vendor prefix for each of them (**TABLE 4.3**):

```
div {
  background-image: -webkit-linear-gradient(#fff, #000);
  background-image: -moz-linear-gradient(#fff, #000);
  background-image: -ms-linear-gradient(#fff, #000);
  background-image: -o-linear-gradient(#fff, #000);
  background-image: linear-gradient(#fff, #000);
}
```

TABLE 4.3 *WebKit Vendor Prefixes*

Browser	Vendor Prefix
Safari	-webkit-
Firefox	-moz-
Internet Explorer	-ms-
Opera	-o-

WHY DO BROWSERS HAVE UNTESTED FEATURES?

Sometimes browser vendors want to gain an advantage over their competitors, so they put out a new feature that the others don't yet have. This scenario played out over and over again in what's been called the Browser Wars. Other times, browser vendors want to see if a new feature will be adopted by web developers, or they might feel that a feature is worthwhile to implement without consulting other interested parties.

The group that writes the CSS standards will not approve a CSS property that begins with a hyphen. This enables browser vendors to create vendor-prefixes that start with hyphens for the testing of features. For the specification, check out http://www.w3.org/TR/CSS21/syndata.html#vendor-keywords.

Automatic Vendor Prefixing

For one CSS feature in our text shadow example, five additional lines of code were needed to support browsers. If we need to add additional lines of code for each browser for each new CSS feature, the lines of code we generate would quickly get out of control. Web developer Lea Verou realized the vendor prefixes situation and developed a piece of JavaScript called -prefix-free (http://leaverou.github.com/prefixfree/), shown in **FIGURE 4.17**:

FIGURE 4.17 *The -prefix-free homepage.*

By downloading the file and placing the -prefix-free JavaScript file in the head element of your web page, the vendor-prefixes are automatically applied to the user's browsers *if* they need them:

```
<head>
<meta charset="utf-8">
<title>My Web Page</title>
<link rel="stylesheet" href="style.css" />
<script src="prefixfree.js"></script>
</head>
```

That means you can focus on writing clean code and not worry about double-checking browser support features in the CSS.

Validation

Once you're satisfied with your design, you'll want to validate your HTML and CSS code to make sure it complies with all the requirements and rules that we've established thus far. A **validator** is a tool that checks the code for proper HTML and CSS syntax by making sure that all tags are closed and properly nested. If there are no syntax errors, then the page is said to *validate*.

FIGURE 4.18 *Validator reporting errors.*

W3C°	Unicorn - W3C's Unified Validator
	Improve the quality of the Web

▼ This document has not passed the test: *W3C HTML Validator* 🗗   ⓘ 2 ⊗ 24 ⚠ 1 🗗

– Info (2)

URI: http://www.google.com/

Using experimental feature: HTML5 Conformance Checker
The validator checked your document with an experimental feature: *HTML5 Conformance Checker*. This feature has been made available for your convenience, but be aware that it may be unreliable, or not perfectly up to date with the latest development of some cutting-edge technologies. If you find any issues with this feature, please report them. Thank you.

No Character encoding declared at document level
No character encoding information was found within the document, either in an HTML meta element or an XML declaration. It is often recommended to declare the character encoding in the document itself, especially if there is a chance that the document will be read from or saved to disk, CD, etc. See this tutorial on character encoding for techniques and explanations.

– Errors (24)

URI: http://www.google.com/

8	2076	... </head><body dir="ltr" bgcolor="#fff" > <script>(function(){var src=//images/sr...	The bgcolor attribute on the body element is obsolete. Use CSS instead.
11	99	...area><div id="mngb"><div id=gbar><nobr> <b class=gb1>Search</b> <a class=gb1 hr...	Element nobr not allowed as child of element div in this context. (Suppressing further errors from this subtree.)
11	176	...ref="http://www.google.com/imghp?hl=en & tab=wi">Images</a> <a class=gb1 href="h...	& did not start a character reference. (& probably should have been escaped as &.)
11	245	...1 href="http://video.google.com/?hl=en & tab=wv">Videos</a> <a class=gb1 href="h...	& did not start a character reference. (& probably should have been escaped as &.)
11	317	...ref="http://maps.google.com/maps?hl=en & tab=wl">Maps</a> <a class=gb1 href="htt...	& did not start a character reference. (& probably should have been escaped as &.)
11	388	...ef="http://news.google.com/nwshp?hl=en & tab=wn">News</a> <a class=gb1 href="htt...	& did not start a character reference. (& probably should have been escaped as &.)

More than likely your pages won't validate the first time you code them—it's surprisingly easy to forget a tag or a quote. Luckily the validators are specific as to what the error is and where it's located (**FIGURE 4.18**):

At first, validating your code may seem impossible, but it becomes easier as you get used to what clean, syntactical code looks like. The W3C has a markup validation service at http://validator.w3.org/unicorn/. Simply upload your document or provide its address, and the validator quickly gives you a report on both HTML and CSS errors. Working through the validator can be a little puzzling at times because of the error messages, but once you clean up any errors you get a clean bill of health (**FIGURE 4.19**).

Another valuable tool is HTML Tidy (http://infohound.net/tidy/). This tool actually fixes badly formed markup: it adds closing tags, changes mismatched tags, adds quotes to attribute values, and properly nests tags that are not nested (**FIGURE 4.20**). Stand-alone tidy applications are available for various platforms, and there are online versions as well. HTML Tidy also comes with many HTML and text editors.

> **BUILT-IN VALIDATORS** WYSIWYG editors like Dreamweaver come with their own built-in validators.

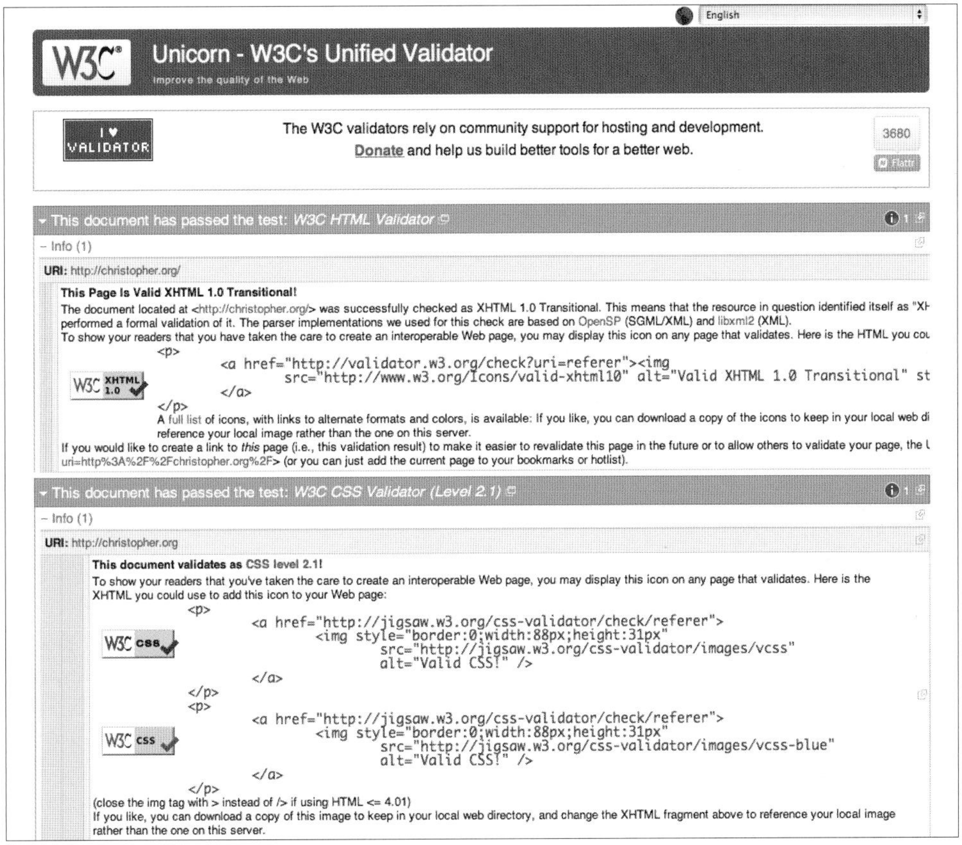

FIGURE 4.19 *Gaining the coveted seal of approval from a validator.*

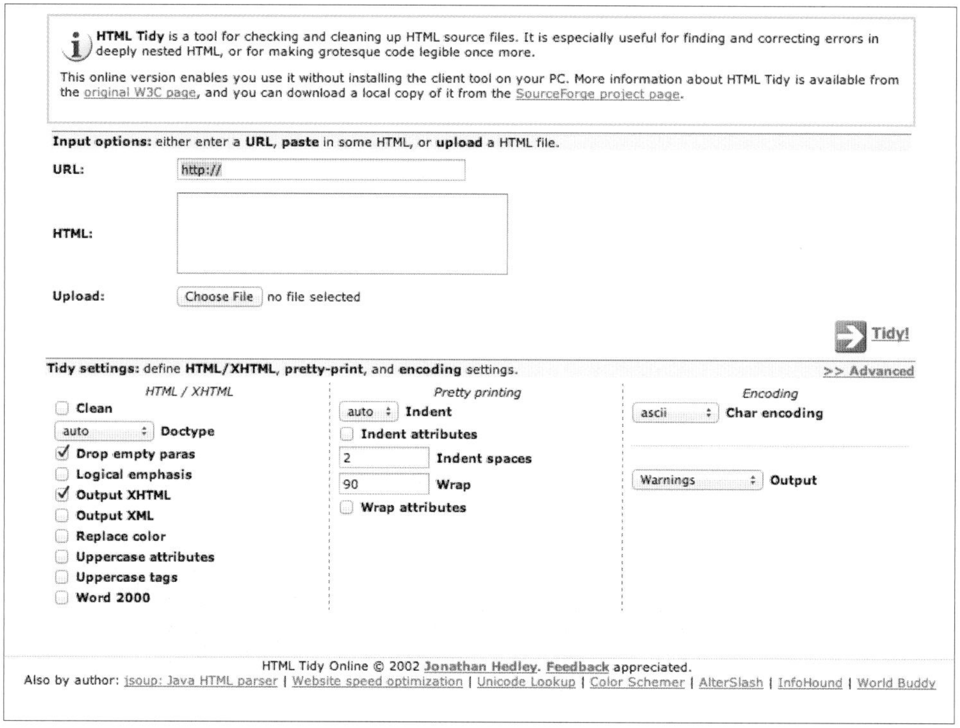

FIGURE 4.20 *HTML Tidy makes your code cleanly spaced and balanced.*

Testing

When designing for the web, it's important to test against as many browsers and devices as possible. It can be difficult to maintain a number of desktop browser installations—both new and older—and get your hands on a wide range of devices to create a full mobile testing suite. Here are some suggestions to make cross-device development a little less complex.

Software

Use services like BrowserStack (http://www.browserstack.com/) to quickly test different platforms, browsers, resolutions, and connection speeds (**FIGURE 4.21**).

If you own a Mac, buy a software package like Parallels (http://www.parallels.com/products/desktop/) or VMware Fusion (http://www.vmware.com/products/fusion/overview.html). You can download Oracle VirtualBox (https://www.virtualbox.org/) for free (**FIGURE 4.22**). These software packages allow for **virtualization**—running Windows and Windows-based browsers on a Mac. You'll still need to purchase a Windows OS license, but you won't have to buy a separate machine.

FIGURE 4.21 *Using the Browser-Stack interface to check out a page design.*

FIGURE 4.22 *Oracle VirtualBox.*

Hardware

After creating a test page, upload it to the web and then take a breather. Go to your local computer store and check out your web page design in the store's display models. Check in on cell phone stores, too, to see how your page looks in their mobile devices.

If you can, buy a smartphone on eBay or ask friends and colleagues for their old phones and devices when they upgrade. You might be surprised how many people have old devices hanging around in a junk drawer. When *you* upgrade to a new device, keep your old one around for testing to create your own mini testing lab. Use services like Adobe Edge Inspect to test web pages on different devices. MobileTh.at is a new service, just being coded at the time of writing, that promises to simplify mobile testing.

IN CONCLUSION

Browsers have different levels of support for CSS features, as well as different interpretations of how to render HTML. By using tools like normalize.css and validating on multiple devices, we can address many of the challenges of web design. However, there's no substitute for knowing and learning about your audience and working to build them the best site possible. In the next chapter, we'll look at one of the most powerful parts of graphics and design: color.

> "I found I could say things with color and shapes that I couldn't say any other way—things I had no words for."
>
> —*Georgia O'Keeffe*

Chapter 5

COLOR FOR THE WEB

Color is the first item by which one can judge a site. It's the splashes of color and an eye-grabbing design that a visitor to your site sees. Better use of color means a better website. If you can carry a color scheme to every page, you'll automatically create a cohesive look and feel for your site.

A **color scheme** is a set of colors that helps define the mood, educate the user about navigation (subtly signaling what's "hot" or "clickable"), and reinforce the site's identity, or brand image. Developing simple color schemes becomes second nature the more you work with color.

CODING WEB COLOR

Unless you specify otherwise, HTML applies default colors to your content as shown in **FIGURE 5.1**:

FIGURE 5.1 *Default colors in HTML are a white background, black text, blue links, and purple visited links.*

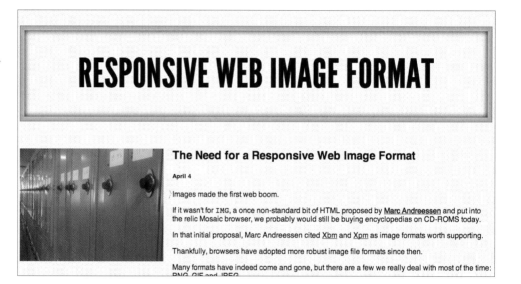

Hexadecimal Color Notation

You're probably used to seeing the six alphanumeric characters that generally define color in HTML and CSS. You probably know that the hex notation #fffff is white and #00000 is black. But did you know that these are simply RGB values converted to base 16? There are actually just three values, not six, for each color. This was a clever way of saving characters in the early days; instead of three digits for each RGB value (from 0 to 255), hexadecimal takes two digits to express the same number (from 00 to ff).

Since CSS3, however, we can also directly give the RGB values of a color this way: RGB (60, 100, 100).

HEXADECIMAL SHORTHAND

If a color notation has repeating characters, you can shorten it by leaving off one of the repeated characters. For example, the hex code of a fuchsia color is **#ff00ff** but with shorthand notation, the very same color can be written with three characters: **#f0f**. A dark yellow (**#ffcc00**) can be shortened to **#fc0**.

Overriding HTML's Default Colors

In the following HTML example, notice how CSS is tied to an **h1** element to set its color:

```
<!DOCTYPE html>
<html>
 <head>
  <title>The Need for a Responsive Web Image Format</title>
  <style type="text/css">
   h1 {color: #660033;}
  </style>
 </head>
 <body>
   <h1>The Need for a Responsive Web Image Format</h1>
 </body>
</html>
```

The **style** element contains one rule applied to the **h1** element. The selector is **h1**, the property is color, and the value is #660033 (**FIGURE 5.2**).

CSS can change the background color of the **body** element with the **background-color** property.

```
body {
   background-color: #fec3c0;
}
```

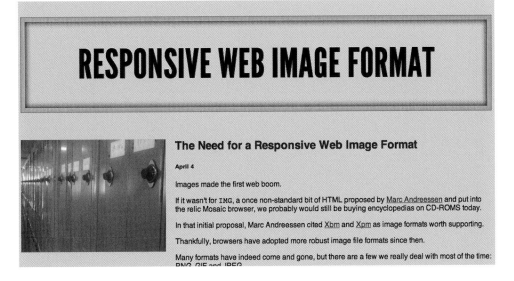

FIGURE 5.2 *A CSS rule applied to the **h1** element changes its color property. The background color of a web page comes from the **body** element, which can be changed with the* CSS **background-color** *property.*

It's not only backgrounds that can be colored with CSS. The CSS **color** property sets the foreground color of any element. In the body element, the text is equivalent to the foreground. Set the text color of the **body** element with the **color** property, in this case a red-violet (**FIGURE 5.3**).

```
body {
  color: #660033;
  background-color: #fec3c0;
}
```

Another part of an element that can be colored with CSS is the border. If an element has a border specified, but that border has no color assigned to it, then the border takes the color of the foreground of the element. The **border-color** property overrides that default. Link elements, whether text or image links, are often the subject of a CSS color makeover.

FIGURE 5.3 *The basic text color of a web page is determined by the* **body** *element.*

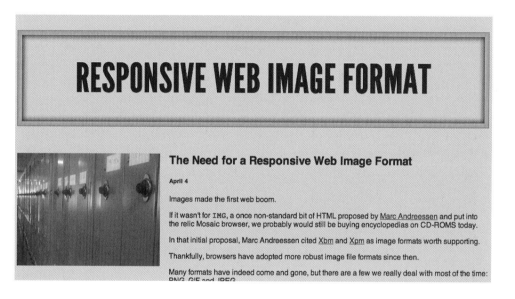

Setting the link colors requires a few more steps (**FIGURE 5.4**):

```
/* set color for visited links */
a:visited {
 color: #003333;
}
/* set link colors for rollover on text links */
a:link:hover, a:visited:hover {
 color: #ff0066;
}
/* set link colors when clicking link */
a:link:active, a:visited:active{
 color: purple;
 /* what's the hexadecimal equlavent of purple? */
}
```

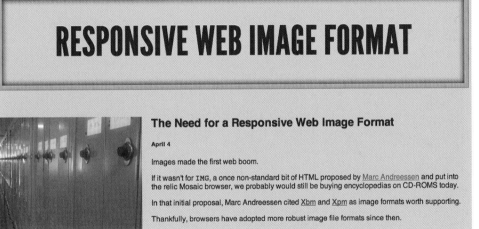

FIGURE 5.4 *Rollovers on text links set to bright pink.*

Image Borders

The **border** attribute on the **img** element sets the width of the border. In this case, we're adding a color border only to images that are links (**FIGURE 5.5**):

```
<html>
 <head>
  <title>CSS Example</title>
   <style type="text/css">
a img {
 border: 2px red solid;
 padding: 2px;
}
</style>
 </head>
 <body>
   <h1>The Need for a Responsive Web Image Format</h1>
   <img src="filename.gif" alt="" />
 </body>
</html>
```

FIGURE 5.5 *Setting a color border around an image with a link, including a bit of padding.*

Transparency with CSS Color

CSS lets you include many other vibrant color features and subtleties in your web pages. One such feature is **RGBa color**. The "a" stands for "alpha," a value that allows designers to adjust the opacity of the RGB color it modifies.

The fourth value in RGBa sets the opacity of the color from 0 to 1. If the value is set to 1, the color is 100% visible. If it's set to .5, it's 50% transparent. If it's set to 0, it's completely transparent. As shown in **FIGURE 5.6**, the body text is set to 50% opacity allowing the background image to shine through. For more on transparency, see Chapter 8, Transparency and Shadow.

```
/* set font color, with 50% opacity */
p {
color: rgba(102,0,51,.5);
}
```

! ONLY TWO COLOR SYSTEMS CREATE TRANSPARENCY IN CSS

RGBa and HSLa are the only two color systems with a transparency channel. So, if you want an element whose color can be set by CSS to be transparent, you need to specify its color values in one of those two color notation systems.

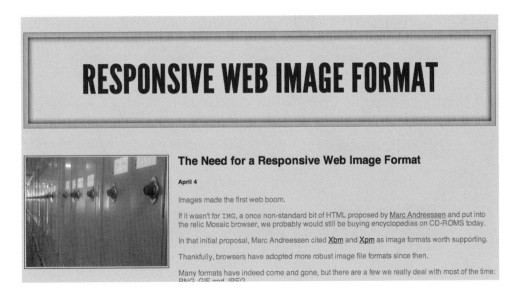

FIGURE 5.6 *Body text color transparency set through CSS.*

COLOR PROPERTIES

FIGURE 5.7 *Color spectrum represented as a band.*

The most basic attribute of a color is also known as **hue**. Each *hue* is a specific spot on the color spectrum. A spectrum can be as simple as a band (**FIGURE 5.7**) or a wheel (**FIGURE 5.8**). Additional color attributes you should know about are *value*, *contrast*, *brightness*, and *saturation*.

The range from black to white is called *value* (**FIGURE 5.9**). It's good to be aware of situations where colors have different hue but are close in value; in some cases, they can be hard to distinguish. **Brightness** adds white to an image; reducing brightness tones down the image (**FIGURE 5.10**). **Contrast** is the degree of separation between values (**FIGURE 5.11**). **Saturation** is the measurement of color intensity (**FIGURE 5.12**). The lack of saturation looks like a black-and-white television picture.

FIGURE 5.8 *Color spectrum represented as a color wheel; each position on the circle represents a hue.*

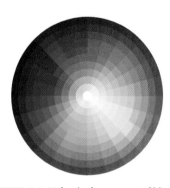

FIGURE 5.9 *Value is the amount of black or white within a color.*

FIGURE 5.10 *Brightness levels from low (left) to normal to high (right).*

FIGURE 5.11 *Contrast levels from low (left) to normal to high (right).*

FIGURE 5.12 *Full saturation (top), half saturation (center), and no saturation (bottom).*

PRIMARY COLOR SYSTEMS

The three **additive primary colors**—● red, ● green, ● blue—were deter-mined in 1861 by Scottish physicist Sir James Clerk Maxwell (**FIGURE 5.13**).

When the colors come together in various combinations and levels, they produce other colors in the spectrum. When all three are combined at full intensity they produce white light (**FIGURE 5.14**). This, in a roundabout way, is how color is achieved on your computer monitor right now.

The **subtractive primaries** found by Louis Ducos du Hauron (**FIGURE 5.15**) are ● cyan, ● magenta, and ○ yellow; mixing these colors, you get a color that closely resembles black. Take away these colors, and you're left with your original background, usually white (**FIGURE 5.16**).

The subtractive primary system is used in printing, and is commonly referred to as **CYMK** (with the "K" representing black ink, the *key*). The fourth ink is needed to produce a "true" dark black unlike the muddy black that cyan, yellow, and magenta together produce. **Note that the web can-not display CMYK colors.**

FIGURE 5.13 *Sir James Clerk Maxwell looks to his right, finds color.*

FIGURE 5.15 *Louis Ducos du Hauron found the subtractive primaries.*

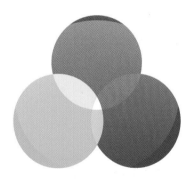

FIGURE 5.14 *An approximation of red, green, and blue light, the additive colors.*

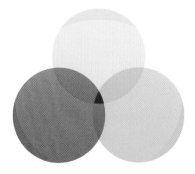

FIGURE 5.16 *Cyan, magenta, and yellow are the subtractive colors.*

COLOR COMBINATIONS

There are no definites with color. Sure, you have your red, your green, and so on—but even that is relative. Try to describe a type of red to a friend, for example: is it brick red or a more pink red?

When a color is placed near other colors, it takes on a different hue because of the way we perceive colors in relation to one another (**FIGURE 5.17**).

In **FIGURE 5.18**, the solid gray bars are the same, but in the bottom example it appears to contain a gradient because of the background around it.

FIGURE 5.17 *Although both circles are the same red color, the circle on the left looks lighter than the circle on the right.*

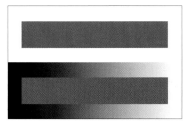

FIGURE 5.18 *Though both bars are solid gray, the bottom bar seems to contain a gradient of light gray (left) to dark gray (right).*

THE HSL SYSTEM

HSL color model is another digital color system based on *hue, saturation,* and *lightness* (**FIGURE 5.19**). HSL manipulates the hue based on degrees (the full circle from 0 to 360) and percentages of saturation and lightness (0% to 100%). For example, the following code signifies red:

```
.alert {
  color: hsl(0, 100%, 50%)
}
```

And a light green color is written out like:

```
.good {
  color: hsl(120, 100%, 75%)
}
```

Alpha transparency support has been brought in through HSLa. Much like RGBa, it supports transparency in the same manner. The following code snippet is for transparent yellow:

```
.warning {
  color: hsla(60, 85%, 55%, 0.8);
}
```

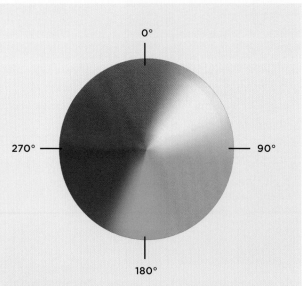

FIGURE 5.19 *A representation of the HSL color system commonly used in color pickers.*

On a color wheel, similar or **analogous colors** are found next to each other. To pick analogous colors, simply pick one color on the color wheel and its nearest neighbor to the left and right (**FIGURE 5.20**).

Monochromatic color schemes essentially use variations in value of a single hue, using more or less black. For this example (**FIGURE 5.21**), colors are picked from the red "pie slice."

Gradated color schemes, related to monochromatic color schemes, incorporate a series of small changes in hue that seem to blend smoothly from one endpoint to the other (**FIGURE 5.22**).

Complementary color schemes are color choices that are opposites in terms of hue. These are literally on the opposite sides of the wheel, but usually the same distance from the center, of similar value (**FIGURE 5.23**).

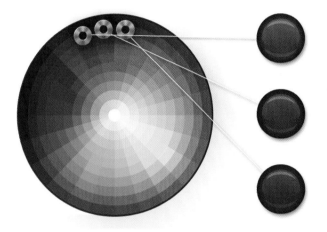

FIGURE 5.20 *An analogous color scheme.*

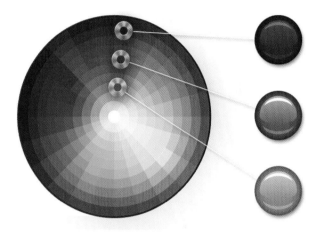

FIGURE 5.22 *A gradated color scheme.*

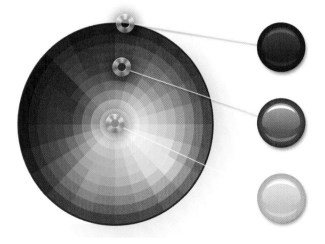

FIGURE 5.21 *A monochromatic color scheme.*

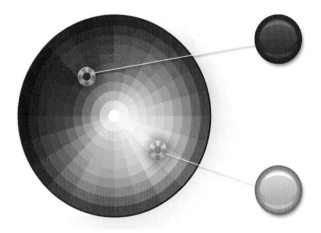

FIGURE 5.23 *A complementary color scheme.*

BUILDING A COLOR SCHEME

Here are a few techniques you can use to help find the right color scheme for a design project.

Finding the Base Color

The first step is to pick the base or central color. When making this selection, consider your audience, the subject matter of the project, and the client's ideas. For example, if you're building a website for a financial institution, you may want to go with a conservative color. Blue is associated with legitimacy and expertise. If the site is about an action movie or a sports star, you might want to pick red. Red is a good choice when you want to convey force and spontaneity.

Once you know which emotions you want to elicit in your site's visitors, you can pick a central color to build your color scheme around. **TABLE 5.1** shows colors and the positive and negative traits associated with them from a North American perspective.

TABLE 5.1 *Color meanings*

Color		Positive Traits	Negative Traits
	White	Purity, Space, Salvation, Innocence	Surrender, Unwantedness, Concealment
	Red	Power, Hunger, Impulsiveness	Anger, Forcefulness, Impatience, Intimidation, Conquest, Violence
	Orange	Steadfastness, Courage, Confidence, Friendliness, Cheerfulness, Safety	Ignorance, Inferiority, Sluggishness, Superiority
	Yellow	Intelligence, Joy, Organization	Cowardice, Laziness, Cynicism
	Green	Hope, Growth, Good Health, Freshness, Soothing, Sharing	Greed, Inexperience, Guilt, Jealousy, Disorder
	Blue	Wisdom, Love, Acceptance, Patience, Knowledge, Understanding	Fear, Coldness, Passivity, Depression
	Purple	Royalty, Reincarnation	Mourning
	Pink	Feminine, Relaxation, Acceptance	Weakness, Shallowness, Immaturity
	Black	Opulence, Power, Strength	Death, Evil, Rebellion
	Brown	Health, Earth, Nature	Poverty

This site design utilizes a white color scheme.

This site design utilizes an orange color scheme.

This site design utilizes a red color scheme.

This site design utilizes a yellow color scheme.

This site design utilizes a green color scheme.

This site design utilizes a blue color scheme.

This site design utilizes a purple color scheme.

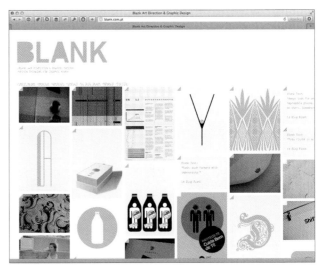

This site design utilizes a pink color scheme.

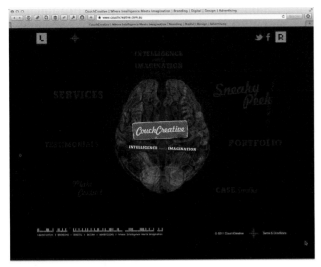

This site design utilizes a black color scheme.

This site design utilizes a brown color scheme.

Cultures and Color

Although the Internet is an international medium, you might have a project where you're localizing a website. **Localization** refers to the process of translating or adapting a site to different places or cultures. Different cultures associate different meanings with colors. Designers must work with the psychology of color and the cultural meanings of color. Be sure to do your research and consult your client about color choices. **TABLE 5.2** showcases a few meanings of colors around the world.

TABLE 5.2 *Sample of Meanings Associated with Color in Various Cultures*

Color	Culture or Country	Meaning
White	Eastern and Western	Mourning
Red	China	Luck, Celebration
Orange	India	Religious, Sacred
Yellow	Asian	Sacred, Imperial
Green	Japan	Advanced technology
Blue	Iran	Mourning
Purple	Egypt	Virtue
Pink	South Africa	Trust
Black	China	Traditional clothing for boys
Brown	Nicaragua	Disapproval

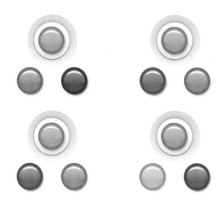

FIGURE 5.24 *Supporting colors.*

Browsing for Color Inspiration

Once you know the main color you want to build your design around, you have a direction to look for supporting colors (**FIGURE 5.24**). Let's look at a couple possible ways to find them.

Collect photos, magazine layouts, and mood boards in an Evernote folder (http://evernote.com) that's dedicated to inspiration (**FIGURE 5.25**). Evernote has a website along with mobile and tablet apps for both iOS and Android OS, so you'll always be near your design folder, ready to review or add photos, sketches, or ideas whenever inspiration hits.

MATH COLOR HARMONIES   If you're mathematically inclined, read the "Color Harmonization" paper by Daniel Cohen-Or and his colleagues (http://www.igl.ethz.ch/projects/color-harmonization/harmonization.pdf). Cohen-Or runs through traditional color harmonies while proposing mathematical formulas for automatically harmonizing images without the need for the artist's eye or intuition.

FIGURE 5.25 *Accessing an Evernote design inspiration folder through the web browser.*

DESIGN INSPIRATION IN THE CLOUD

I've gone through the process of keeping physical design inspiration folders many times since design school. I always lose them. Evernote stores the folder in the cloud, so you can pull up the folder via a mobile app, desktop app, or through a web browser, and they're never lost.

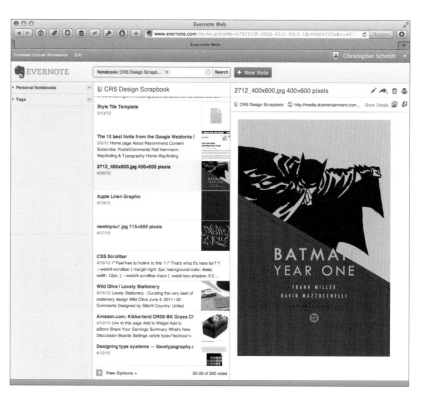

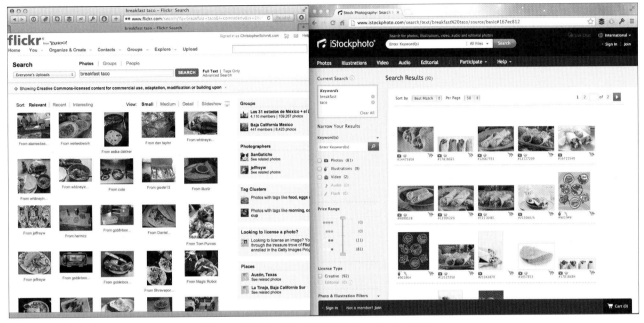

FIGURE 5.26 *Advanced photo search in Flickr, and looking through iStockphoto for inspiration.*

Another option is to use Google's image search. Type in a base color and emotion that you want to include in the design project. Continue this search in photo sharing and stock photography sites like Flickr (http://flickr.com) and iStockphoto (http://istockphoto.com/), as shown in **FIGURE 5.26.**

Some sites focus solely on color schemes, for example, ColorCombos.com (**FIGURE 5.27**), COLOURlovers.com (**FIGURE 5.28**), and Adobe Kuler (kuler. adobe.com) (**FIGURE 5.29**). Look through for inspiration or, if there's one that seems to work, use the color combinations for your project.

! ADVANCED FLICKR SEARCH

Not only is Flickr a great place for color inspiration, but you can find photography that you can actually use. Be sure to go to the Advanced Search (http://www.flickr.com/search/advanced/) and pick Creative Commons–licensed content that you can modify and use commercially. While you will need to cite the source of the files in your work, Creative Commons–licensed material lets you use other people's work without having to directly ask them for permission. For more information on Creative Commons, see http://creativecommons.org.

FIGURE 5.27 *ColorCombos.*

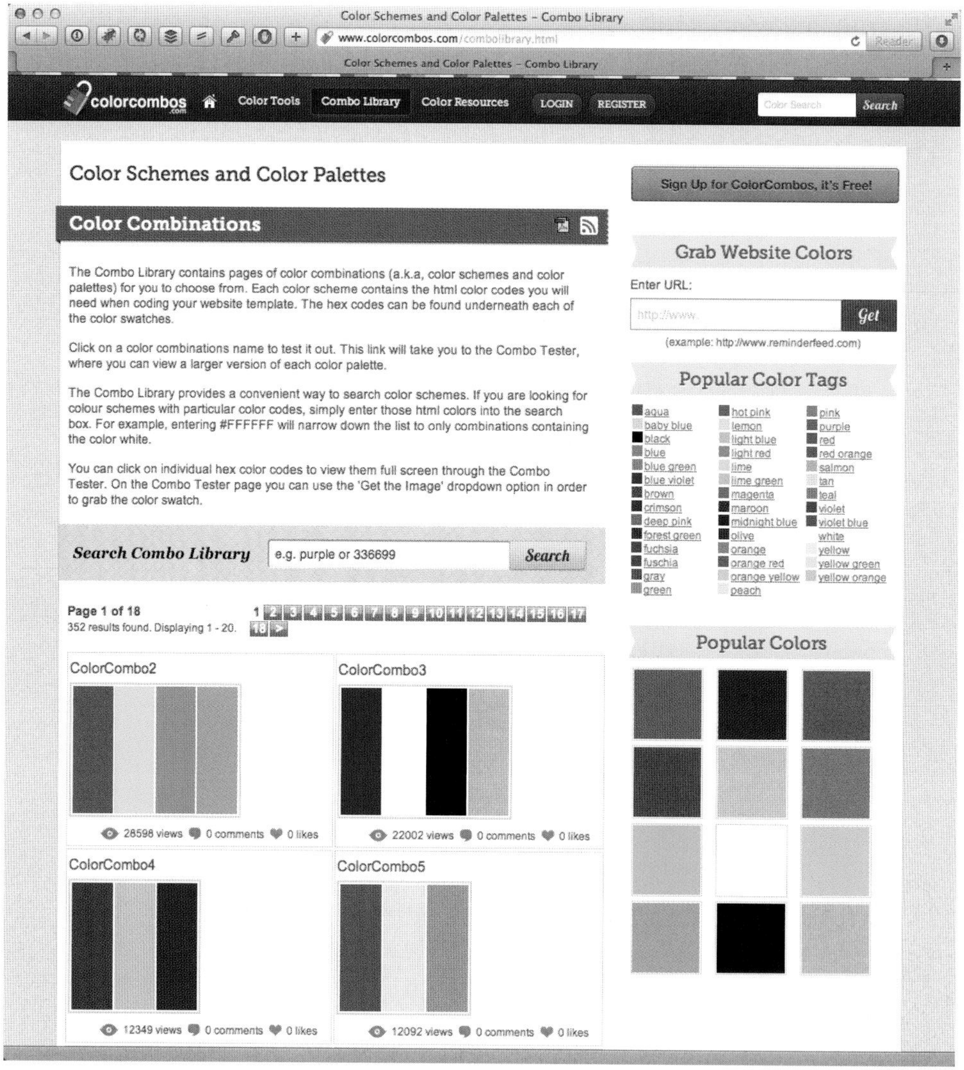

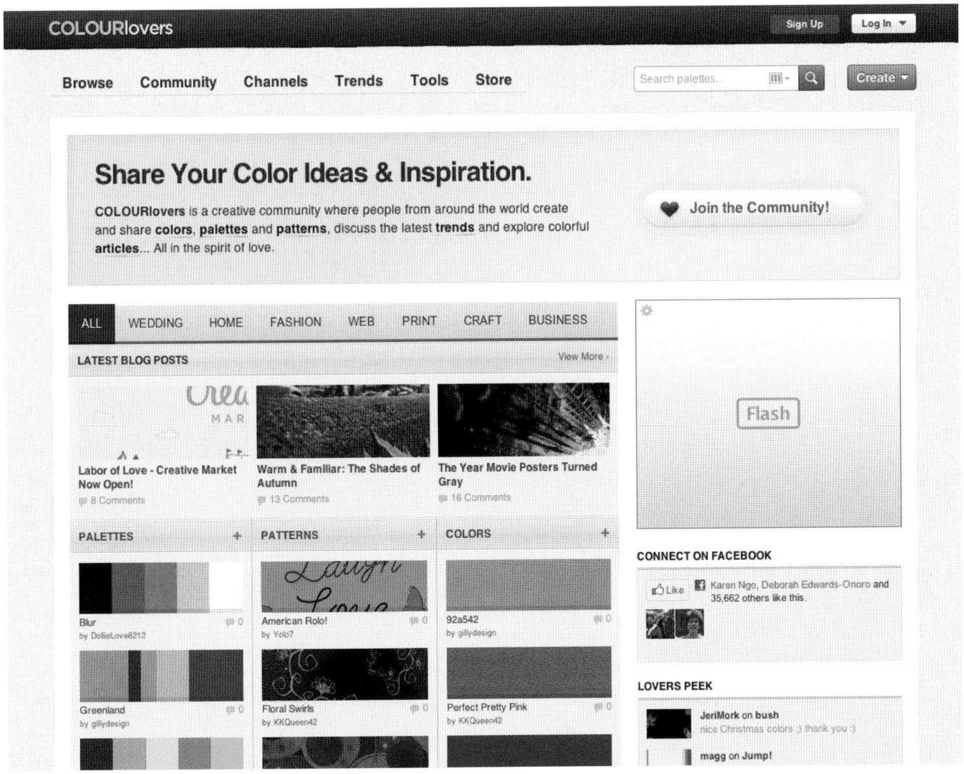

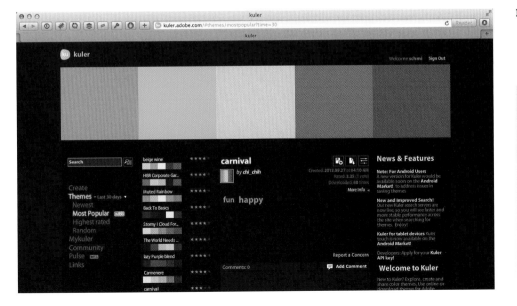

FIGURE 5.28
COLOURlovers.

FIGURE 5.29 *Adobe Kuler.*

UTILIZING ADOBE'S ECOSYSTEM

Adobe Kuler is a great site if you use Adobe's suite of imaging and publishing tools. You can download a color palette and load it into your Adobe application.

Picturing a Color Scheme

Another way to cheat your way to a color scheme is to find a photo or piece of artwork you like and use the colors in it to create the color scheme. If the colors in the photograph or artwork are pleasing to your eye, then they stand a very good chance of working in another design project.

USE THESE ④ STEPS TO PICK COLORS OUT OF A DIGITAL IMAGE.

① Bring a photograph or artwork with colors that work well together into an image editor.

② Select Blur > Gaussian Blur until only the abstract colors remain.

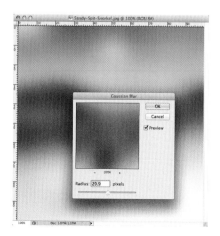

③ Use the Color Picker Tool to select each color.

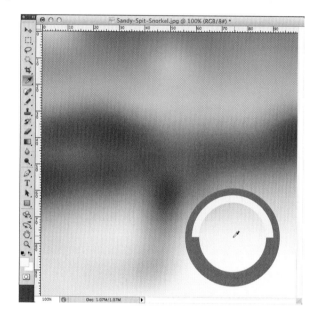

④ Add the color to your Swatch palette for future reference.

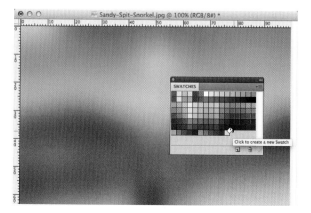

CONSISTENT COLORS

Color is relative. How we perceive a color depends on the context in which it's presented. As designers, it's our job to select and arrange colors in color schemes and compositions, which is hard enough. But there's another challenge when it comes to color on computers: our digital workspace can work against us.

How long have you owned your computer? Did you know that as computer monitors age, they tend to display darker?

Calibrating Colors

To help stabilize color shifting, calibrate or tune the monitor's colors on a regular basis. Ideally, this is something you want to do weekly.

For Windows OS calibration steps, see http://windows.microsoft.com/is-IS/windows7/Calibrate-your-display. For Macintosh OS calibration procedure, see http://www.maclife.com/article/howtos/how_calibrate_any_display_mac_os_x.

To help with color calibration, use a tool like ColorMunki Display (**FIGURE 5.30**) or ColorMunki Design (**FIGURE 5.31**).

Although it has a funny name, the Pantone ColorMunki Design (US $449) is serious about color. The device takes measurements of not only your computer screen, but also the light in your work area to determine the best color profile for your computer.

Picking Up Colors

The ColorMunki has another neat trick: it can pick up or extract colors from physical objects. So, colors from magazine spreads, photographs, and so on can be picked up and matched to color values for you to use in your designs.

CSS COLOR CHART

In CSS, colors can be designated in numerous ways. We've discussed using hex notation, as RGB or RGBa colors. But they can also be marked as HSL colors, or even certain *color names*.

TABLE 5.3 shows the 147 color names that HTML and CSS recognize, including 17 standard colors that are supported by all browsers: aqua, black, blue, fuchsia, gray, grey, green, lime, maroon, navy, olive, purple, red, silver, teal, white, and yellow.

FIGURE 5.30 *A Pantone ColorMunki Display calibrator.*

FIGURE 5.31 *A ColorMunki Design handheld device.*

TABLE 5.3 *CSS Color Keywords with Approximate Color Examples*

Keyword		Decimal RGB	HSL	Hex	Short
	aliceblue	rgb(240,248,255)	hsl(208,100%,97.1%)	#F0F8FF	
	antiquewhite	rgb(250,235,215)	hsl(34,77.8%,91.2%)	#FAEBD7	
	aqua	rgb(0,255,255)	hsl(180,100%,50%)	#00FFFF	#0FF
	aquamarine	rgb(127,255,212)	hsl(160,100%,74.9%)	#7FFFD4	
	azure	rgb(240,255,255)	hsl(180,100%,97.1%)	#F0FFFF	
	beige	rgb(245,245,220)	hsl(60,55.6%,91.2%)	#F5F5DC	
	bisque	rgb(255,228,196)	hsl(33,100%,88.4%)	#FFE4C4	
	black	rgb(0,0,0)	hsl(0,0%,0%)	#000000	#000
	blanchedalmond	rgb(255,235,205)	hsl(36,100%,90.2%)	#FFEBCD	
	blue	rgb(0,0,255)	hsl(240,100%,50%)	#0000FF	#00F
	blueviolet	rgb(138,43,226)	hsl(271,75.9%,52.7%)	#8A2BE2	
	brown	rgb(165,42,42)	hsl(0,59.4%,40.6%)	#A52A2A	
	burlywood	rgb(222,184,135)	hsl(34,56.9%,70%)	#DEB887	
	cadetblue	rgb(95,158,160)	hsl(182,25.5%,50%)	#5F9EA0	
	chartreuse	rgb(127,255,0)	hsl(90,100%,50%)	#7FFF00	
	chocolate	rgb(210,105,30)	hsl(25,75%,47.1%)	#D2691E	
	coral	rgb(255,127,80)	hsl(16,100%,65.7%)	#FF7F50	
	cornflowerblue	rgb(100,149,237)	hsl(219,79.2%,66.1%)	#6495ED	
	cornsilk	rgb(255,248,220)	hsl(48,100%,93.1%)	#FFF8DC	
	crimson	rgb(220,20,60)	hsl(348,83.3%,47.1%)	#DC143C	
	cyan	rgb(0,255,255)	hsl(180,100%,50%)	#00FFFF	#0FF
	darkblue	rgb(0,0,139)	hsl(240,100%,27.3%)	#00008B	
	darkcyan	rgb(0,139,139)	hsl(180,100%,27.3%)	#008B8B	

Keyword	Decimal RGB	HSL	Hex	Short
darkgoldenrod	rgb(184,134,11)	hsl(43,88.7%,38.2%)	#B8860B	
darkgray	rgb(169,169,169)	hsl(0,0%,66.3%)	#A9A9A9	
darkgreen	rgb(0,100,0)	hsl(120,100%,19.6%)	#006400	
darkgrey	rgb(169,169,169)	hsl(0,0%,66.3%)	#A9A9A9	
darkkhaki	rgb(189,183,107)	hsl(56,38.3%,58%)	#BDB76B	
darkmagenta	rgb(139,0,139)	hsl(300,100%,27.3%)	#8B008B	
darkolivegreen	rgb(85,107,47)	hsl(82,39%,30.2%)	#556B2F	
darkorange	rgb(255,140,0)	hsl(33,100%,50%)	#FF8C00	
darkorchid	rgb(153,50,204)	hsl(280,60.6%,49.8%)	#9932CC	
darkred	rgb(139,0,0)	hsl(0,100%,27.3%)	#8B0000	
darksalmon	rgb(233,150,122)	hsl(15,71.6%,69.6%)	#E9967A	
darkseagreen	rgb(143,188,143)	hsl(120,25.1%,64.9%)	#8FBC8F	
darkslateblue	rgb(72,61,139)	hsl(248,39%,39.2%)	#483D8B	
darkslategray	rgb(47,79,79)	hsl(180,25.4%,24.7%)	#2F4F4F	
darkslategrey	rgb(47,79,79)	hsl(180,25.4%,24.7%)	#2F4F4F	
darkturquoise	rgb(0,206,209)	hsl(181,100%,41%)	#00CED1	
darkviolet	rgb(148,0,211)	hsl(282,100%,41.4%)	#9400D3	
deeppink	rgb(255,20,147)	hsl(328,100%,53.9%)	#FF1493	
deepskyblue	rgb(0,191,255)	hsl(195,100%,50%)	#00BFFF	
dimgrey	rgb(105,105,105)	hsl(0,0%,41.2%)	#696969	
dimgrey	rgb(105,105,105)	hsl(0,0%,41.2%)	#696969	
dodgerblue	rgb(30,144,255)	hsl(210,100%,55.9%)	#1E90FF	
firebrick	rgb(178,34,34)	hsl(0,67.9%,41.6%)	#B22222	

continues

TABLE 5.3 *CSS Color Keywords with Approximate Color Examples (continued)*

Keyword	Decimal RGB	HSL	Hex	Short
floralwhite	rgb(255,250,240)	hsl(40,100%,97.1%)	#FFFAF0	
forestgreen	rgb(34,139,34)	hsl(120,60.7%,33.9%)	#228B22	
fuchsia	rgb(255,0,255)	hsl(300,100%,50%)	#FF00FF	#F0F
gainsboro	rgb(220,220,220)	hsl(0,0%,86.3%)	#DCDCDC	
ghostwhite	rgb(248,248,255)	hsl(240,100%,98.6%)	#F8F8FF	
gold	rgb(255,215,0)	hsl(51,100%,50%)	#FFD700	
goldenrod	rgb(218,165,32)	hsl(43,74.4%,49%)	#DAA520	
gray	rgb(128,128,128)	hsl(0,0%,50.2%)	#808080	
green	rgb(0,128,0)	hsl(120,100%,25.1%)	#008000	
greenyellow	rgb(173,255,47)	hsl(84,100%,59.2%)	#ADFF2F	
grey	rgb(128,128,128)	hsl(0,0%,50.2%)	#808080	
honeydew	rgb(240,255,240)	hsl(120,100%,97.1%)	#F0FFF0	
hotpink	rgb(255,105,180)	hsl(330,100%,70.6%)	#FF69B4	
indianred	rgb(205,92,92)	hsl(0,53.1%,58.2%)	#CD5C5C	
indigo	rgb(75,0,130)	hsl(275,100%,25.5%)	#4B0082	
ivory	rgb(255,255,240)	hsl(60,100%,97.1%)	#FFFFF0	
khaki	rgb(240,230,140)	hsl(54,76.9%,74.5%)	#F0E68C	
lavender	rgb(230,230,250)	hsl(240,66.7%,94.1%)	#E6E6FA	
lavenderblush	rgb(255,240,245)	hsl(340,100%,97.1%)	#FFF0F5	
lawngreen	rgb(124,252,0)	hsl(90,100%,49.4%)	#7CFC00	
lemonchiffon	rgb(255,250,205)	hsl(54,100%,90.2%)	#FFFACD	
lightblue	rgb(173,216,230)	hsl(195,53.3%,79%)	#ADD8E6	
lightcoral	rgb(240,128,128)	hsl(0,78.9%,72.2%)	#F08080	

Keyword		Decimal RGB	HSL	Hex	Short
	lightcyan	rgb(224,255,255)	hsl(180,100%,93.9%)	#E0FFFF	
	lightgoldenrodyellow	rgb(250,250,210)	hsl(60,80%,90.2%)	#FAFAD2	
	lightgray	rgb(211,211,211)	hsl(0,0%,82.7%)	#D3D3D3	
	lightgreen	rgb(144,238,144)	hsl(120,73.4%,74.9%)	#90EE90	
	lightgrey	rgb(211,211,211)	hsl(0,0%,82.7%)	#D3D3D3	
	lightpink	rgb(255,182,193)	hsl(351,100%,85.7%)	#FFB6C1	
	lightsalmon	rgb(255,160,122)	hsl(17,100%,73.9%)	#FFA07A	
	lightseagreen	rgb(32,178,170)	hsl(177,69.5%,41.2%)	#20B2AA	
	lightskyblue	rgb(135,206,250)	hsl(203,92%,75.5%)	#87CEFA	
	lightslategray	rgb(119,136,153)	hsl(210,14.3%,53.3%)	#778899	#789
	lightslategrey	rgb(119,136,153)	hsl(210,14.3%,53.3%)	#778899	#789
	lightsteelblue	rgb(176,196,222)	hsl(214,41.1%,78%)	#B0C4DE	
	lightyellow	rgb(255,255,224)	hsl(60,100%,93.9%)	#FFFFE0	
	lime	rgb(0,255,0)	hsl(120,100%,50%)	#00FF00	#0F0
	limegreen	rgb(50,205,50)	hsl(120,60.8%,50%)	#32CD32	
	linen	rgb(250,240,230)	hsl(30,66.7%,94.1%)	#FAF0E6	
	magenta	rgb(255,0,255)	hsl(300,100%,50%)	#FF00FF	#F0F
	maroon	rgb(128,0,0)	hsl(0,100%,25.1%)	#800000	
	mediumaquamarine	rgb(102,205,170)	hsl(160,50.7%,60.2%)	#66CDAA	
	mediumblue	rgb(0,0,205)	hsl(240,100%,40.2%)	#0000CD	
	mediumorchid	rgb(186,85,211)	hsl(288,58.9%,58%)	#BA55D3	
	mediumpurple	rgb(147,112,219)	hsl(260,59.8%,64.9%)	#9370DB	
	mediumseagreen	rgb(60,179,113)	hsl(147,49.8%,46.9%)	#3CB371	

continues

TABLE 5.3 *CSS Color Keywords with Approximate Color Examples (continued)*

Keyword		Decimal RGB	HSL	Hex	Short
	mediumslateblue	rgb(123,104,238)	hsl(249,79.8%,67.1%)	#7B68EE	
	mediumspringgreen	rgb(0,250,154)	hsl(157,100%,49%)	#00FA9A	
	mediumturquoise	rgb(72,209,204)	hsl(178,59.8%,55.1%)	#48D1CC	
	mediumvioletred	rgb(199,21,133)	hsl(322,80.9%,43.1%)	#C71585	
	midnightblue	rgb(25,25,112)	hsl(240,63.5%,26.9%)	#191970	
	mintcream	rgb(245,255,250)	hsl(150,100%,98%)	#F5FFFA	
	mistyrose	rgb(255,228,225)	hsl(6,100%,94.1%)	#FFE4E1	
	moccasin	rgb(255,228,181)	hsl(38,100%,85.5%)	#FFE4B5	
	navajowhite	rgb(255,222,173)	hsl(36,100%,83.9%)	#FFDEAD	
	navy	rgb(0,0,128)	hsl(240,100%,25.1%)	#000080	
	oldlace	rgb(253,245,230)	hsl(39,85.2%,94.7%)	#FDF5E6	
	olive	rgb(128,128,0)	hsl(60,100%,25.1%)	#808000	
	olivedrab	rgb(107,142,35)	hsl(80,60.5%,34.7%)	#6B8E23	
	orange	rgb(255,165,0)	hsl(39,100%,50%)	#FFA500	
	orangered	rgb(255,69,0)	hsl(16,100%,50%)	#FF4500	
	orchid	rgb(218,112,214)	hsl(302,58.9%,64.7%)	#DA70D6	
	palegoldenrod	rgb(238,232,170)	hsl(55,66.7%,80%)	#EEE8AA	
	palegreen	rgb(152,251,152)	hsl(120,92.5%,79%)	#98FB98	
	paleturquoise	rgb(175,238,238)	hsl(180,64.9%,81%)	#AFEEEE	
	palevioletred	rgb(219,112,147)	hsl(340,59.8%,64.9%)	#DB7093	
	papayawhip	rgb(255,239,213)	hsl(37,100%,91.8%)	#FFEFD5	
	peachpuff	rgb(255,218,185)	hsl(28,100%,86.3%)	#FFDAB9	
	peru	rgb(205,133,63)	hsl(30,58.7%,52.5%)	#CD853F	

Keyword	Decimal RGB	HSL	Hex	Short
pink	rgb(255,192,203)	hsl(350,100%,87.6%)	#FFC0CB	
plum	rgb(221,160,221)	hsl(300,47.3%,74.7%)	#DDA0DD	
powderblue	rgb(176,224,230)	hsl(187,51.9%,79.6%)	#B0E0E6	
purple	rgb(128,0,128)	hsl(300,100%,25.1%)	#800080	
red	rgb(255,0,0)	hsl(0,100%,50%)	#FF0000	#F00
rosybrown	rgb(188,143,143)	hsl(0,25.1%,64.9%)	#BC8F8F	
royalblue	rgb(65,105,225)	hsl(225,72.7%,56.9%)	#4169E1	
saddlebrown	rgb(139,69,19)	hsl(25,75.9%,31%)	#8B4513	
salmon	rgb(250,128,114)	hsl(6,93.2%,71.4%)	#FA8072	
sandybrown	rgb(244,164,96)	hsl(28,87.1%,66.7%)	#F4A460	
seagreen	rgb(46,139,87)	hsl(146,50.3%,36.3%)	#2E8B57	
seashell	rgb(255,245,238)	hsl(25,100%,96.7%)	#FFF5EE	
sienna	rgb(160,82,45)	hsl(19,56.1%,40.2%)	#A0522D	
silver	rgb(192,192,192)	hsl(0,0%,75.3%)	#C0C0C0	
skyblue	rgb(135,206,235)	hsl(197,71.4%,72.5%)	#87CEEB	
slateblue	rgb(106,90,205)	hsl(248,53.5%,57.8%)	#6A5ACD	
slategray	rgb(112,128,144)	hsl(210,12.6%,50.2%)	#708090	
slategrey	rgb(112,128,144)	hsl(210,12.6%,50.2%)	#708090	
snow	rgb(255,250,250)	hsl(0,100%,99%)	#FFFAFA	
springgreen	rgb(0,255,127)	hsl(150,100%,50%)	#00FF7F	
steelblue	rgb(70,130,180)	hsl(207,44%,49%)	#4682B4	
tan	rgb(210,180,140)	hsl(34,43.8%,68.6%)	#D2B48C	
teal	rgb(0,128,128)	hsl(180,100%,25.1%)	#008080	

continues

TABLE 5.3 *CSS Color Keywords with Approximate Color Examples (continued)*

Keyword	Decimal RGB	HSL	Hex	Short
thistle	rgb(216,191,216)	hsl(300,24.3%,79.8%)	#D8BFD8	
tomato	rgb(255,99,71)	hsl(9,100%,63.9%)	#FF6347	
turquoise	rgb(64,224,208)	hsl(174,72.1%,56.5%)	#40E0D0	
violet	rgb(238,130,238)	hsl(300,76.1%,72.2%)	#EE82EE	
wheat	rgb(245,222,179)	hsl(39,76.7%,83.1%)	#F5DEB3	
white	rgb(255,255,255)	hsl(0,0%,100%)	#FFFFFF	#FFF
whitesmoke	rgb(245,245,245)	hsl(0,0%,96.1%)	#F5F5F5	
yellow	rgb(255,255,0)	hsl(60,100%,50%)	#FFFF00	#FF0
yellowgreen	rgb(154,205,50)	hsl(80,60.8%,50%)	#9ACD32	

IN CONCLUSION

We covered a lot in this chapter because color is a key step in creating a visually pleasing website. From the conservative blue tones of a financial website to the warm colors of a sports site, colors relate to emotions. Color reaches every aspect of a web design, from the foreground to the background, from the text to the images. It can turn passive users into active users.

Now that you've worked through the basics of color theory and building a color scheme, you can confidently create custom color schemes for your web projects. Next, we'll start working with images for the web.

Chapter **6**

IMAGES FOR THE WEB

Images made the web boom. In its early days, the World Wide Web was about colleagues sharing scientific papers written in text so dry it would make Shakespeare weep. If it wasn't for the simple img element, a once nonstandard bit of HTML proposed by Marc Andreessen (http://1997.webhistory.org/www.lists/www-talk.1993q1/0182.html) and coded into the now-relic Mosaic browser, we'd probably still be buying encyclopedias on CD-ROMs just to figure out what all those authors of scientific papers were talking about.

In that initial proposal, Andreessen cited XBM and XPM as image formats worth supporting, since those image formats were already supported on the X Window System that the Mosaic browser was built on (**FIGURE 6.1**).

proposed new tag: IMG

Marc Andreessen (*marca@ncsa.uiuc.edu*)
Thu, 25 Feb 93 21:09:02 -0800

- **Messages sorted by:** [date][thread][subject][author]
- **Next message:** Tony Johnson: "Re: proposed new tag: IMG"
- **Previous message:** Bill Janssen: "Re: xmosaic experience"
- **Next in thread:** Tony Johnson: "Re: proposed new tag: IMG"

I'd like to propose a new, optional HTML tag:

IMG

Required argument is SRC="url".

This names a bitmap or pixmap file for the browser to attempt to pull over the network and interpret as an image, to be embedded in the text at the point of the tag's occurrence.

An example is:

<IMG SRC="file://foobar.com/foo/bar/blargh.xbm">

(There is no closing tag; this is just a standalone tag.)

This tag can be embedded in an anchor like anything else; when that happens, it becomes an icon that's sensitive to activation just like a regular text anchor.

Browsers should be afforded flexibility as to which image formats they support. Xbm and Xpm are good ones to support, for example. If a browser cannot interpret a given format, it can do whatever it wants instead (X Mosaic will pop up a default bitmap as a placeholder).

This is required functionality for X Mosaic; we have this working, and we'll at least be using it internally. I'm certainly open to suggestions as to how this should be handled within HTML; if you have a better idea than what I'm presenting now, please let me know. I know this is hazy wrt image format, but I don't see an alternative than to just say ``let the browser do what it can'' and wait for the perfect solution to come along (MIME, someday, maybe).

Let me know what you think.........

Cheers,
Marc

--
Marc Andreessen
Software Development Group
National Center for Supercomputing Applications
marca@ncsa.uiuc.edu

FIGURE 6.1 *Marc Andreessen's email proposing the* `img` *element.*

A MATTER OF BITS

To understand image formats for the web, we first need to understand bit depth. An image on the web can be an *8-bit* image. But what does it mean to say 8 bits?

Bit Depth

A *bit* refers to computer languages made up of zeroes and ones. One bit can store either a zero or a one. In a 1-bit image, you get two colors to use to display an image (**FIGURE 6.2**). For example, white is represented by a zero (0) and black is represented by a one (1).

Increasing the number of bits of information within an image format allows for more color information. The sharp contrast of a 1-bit color image can be smoothed out by going to a 2-bit image. Instead of just one digit, there are now two: 00 and 11 can represent white and black respectively, but there are new combinations: 01 and 10, which can represent light gray and dark gray (**FIGURE 6.3**).

FIGURE 6.2 *A 1-bit image has two levels of color and can be posterized (left) or dithered (right and detail).*

FIGURE 6.3 *A 2-bit image has four levels of color, for example black, dark gray, light gray, and white. It can also be posterized (left) or dithered (right and detail).*

Posterization and Dithering

When an image contains only a few colors, a choppy visual effect called *posterization* can occur: adjacent graduated shades are forced into flat areas of color.

Dithering can be applied to a more complex image, reducing a color palette to the available hues. Instead of a banding effect, the colors are spread out. Allowing a photograph or other color-rich item to display within the file's graphic limitations, dithering restructures a more complex image to blend only the 256 or fewer colors.

More Bits Means More Colors

By adding more and more information into an image file, more complex images can be stored and displayed, providing better tones (**FIGURES 6.4**, **6.5**, **6.6**, **6.7**, **6.8**, **6.9**, and **6.10**).

DITHERING VS. POSTERIZATION For photographic images, dithering often produces more visually pleasing images than posterization does.

FIGURE 6.4 *Eight levels of color in a posterized 3-bit image.*

FIGURE 6.5 *Eight levels of color in a dithered 3-bit image.*

FIGURE 6.6 *Sixteen levels of color in a posterized 4-bit image.*

FIGURE 6.7 *Sixteen levels of color in a dithered 4-bit image.*

FIGURE 6.8 *A 5-bit image with 32 levels of color.*

FIGURE 6.9 *At 64 levels of color and up, dithering and posterization become less noticable.*

FIGURE 6.10 *An 8-bit image with 256 levels of color.*

Why Is Bit-Depth Important?

As you can see from **TABLE 6.1**, the greater the bit-depth, the larger the number of colors in an image.

While this gives us more accurate photographs and rich illustrations, the increase in bit-depth also means a *larger* file size. While Internet connection speeds are increasing the world over in the last decade, it's an uneven split between desktop and mobile Internet connections (http://analytics.blogspot.com/2012/04/global-site-speed-overview-how-fast-are.html). Desktop browsing speeds are very slow in Africa, South America, and South Asia. While mobile *connection* speeds are fast, information travels more slowly over cellular networks than via desktop browsing. Always consider the balance between color data and download speed.

TABLE 6.1 *Colors possible per number of bits*

Number of bits		How many possible colors?	Examples	100 × 100px file size
1-bit	2^1	2	Atari ST	1.25kb
2-bit	2^2	4	Early Macintoshes (color)	
3-bit	2^3	8		
4-bit	2^4	16	Commodore 64	5kb
5-bit	2^5	32		
6-bit	2^6	64		
7-bit	2^7	128		
8-bit	2^8	256	Apple II, Super VGA	10kb
9-bit	2^9	512		
10-bit	2^{10}	1,024		
11-bit	2^{11}	2,048		
12-bit	2^{12}	4,096		
13-bit	2^{13}	8,192		
14-bit	2^{14}	16,384		
15-bit	2^{15}	32,768	Sega Saturn game console	
16-bit	2^{16}	65,536		20kb
24-bit	2^{24}	16,777,216		30kb
32-bit	2^{32}	4,294,967,296	HD TV	40kb
40-bit	2^{40}	1,099,511,627,776	Windows 7	
48-bit	2^{48}	281,474,976,710,656		

CHECKING YOUR SITE'S SPEED AROUND THE WORLD

How fast is your site in other locations? It's easy to check out at WebPagetest.org (**FIGURES 6.11** and **6.12**). Enter your site's URL and then select a test location from a selection of locations from Asheville, North Carolina to Wellington, New Zealand. Mobile testing can be done through Akamai's free tool, Mobitest, at http://mobitest. akamai.com/ (**FIGURE 6.13**).

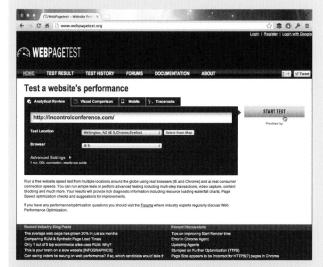

FIGURE 6.11 *Web Page Test.*

FIGURE 6.13 *An illustration of mobile speeds.*

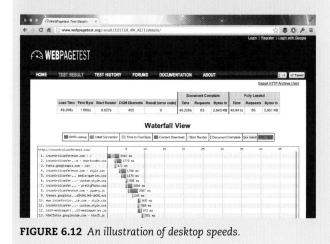

FIGURE 6.12 *An illustration of desktop speeds.*

As we look into a number of image formats for the web, we'll also look at how to squeeze the most out of each format (**FIGURE 6.14**). More importantly, by understanding how each format compresses images, we can create compelling images that are low in file size (**FIGURE 6.15**).

FIGURE 6.14 *A compressed JPEG image with a file size of 340k.*

FIGURE 6.15 *A compressed GIF image with a file size of 94k.*

RETRO GAMES AND BIT DEPTH

The designers of The Legend of Zelda, released in 1986 for the Nintendo Entertainment System, created all the graphics—from the numbers to the character animation—with 8-bit graphics (**FIGURE 6.16**).

That's not a lot of information when compared to the sequel, The Legend of Zelda: A Link to the Past, released in 1991 with 16-bit graphics. The images, while still blocky, showcase more visual information made possible by having access to more shades of colors (**FIGURE 6.17**).

FIGURE 6.16 *In 1986, The Legend of Zelda used 8-bit graphics.*

FIGURE 6.17 *Five years later, in 1991, the sequel The Legend of Zelda: A Link to the Past used 16-bit graphics.*

RASTER IMAGE FORMATS

The basic raster image format has been a part of the desktop experience for several decades and, thankfully, browsers have adopted more robust image file formats over time. Many formats have come and gone, but there are a few we deal with most of the time: GIF, PNG, and JPEG. All three of these image formats deserve closer inspection.

GIF Image Format

The Graphics Image Format, or GIF, was developed by CompuServe in 1987. It is an indexed bitmap format, meaning that it uses a fixed list of colors. The GIF employs a variable 8-bit format, which uses 8 bits per pixel and 256 *or fewer* colors in the image. This type of file is well suited for an image with a limited color palette. On the other hand, it's not a good choice for displaying a more complex image, like a photograph.

Compression Scheme

A GIF file uses *lossless* compression, which means the image does not lose quality when it is compressed. Because smaller file sizes can help a web page load faster, this provides a significant advantage for simple images. However, there is a trick to know about GIF compression. Compare two GIF images: one with a horizontal line pattern (**FIGURE 6.18**) and another image with a vertical line pattern (**FIGURE 6.19**).

The image with the horizontal stripes has a smaller file size (1.4kb) than the one with the vertical stripes (10kb).

While a GIF does provide lossless compression, the real file size savings in using a GIF is for flat areas where there aren't many horizontal changes in color.

HOW DO YOU PRONOUNCE GIF? Steve Wilhite, the creator of the GIF at CompuServe, says the name with a soft "g" as in "giraffe." You can find more on the image format's history and pronunciation at http://www.olsenhome.com/gif/.

MORE THAN THREE NATIVE IMAGE FORMATS

While Internet Explorer and Firefox dropped their support, Safari still supports XMB and XPM formats. The image formats aren't popular and don't compress as well as GIF or JPEG, so we probably won't use them. If you're the type of person who wants to dive deep into past image formats, visit www.xfree86.org/current/xpm.pdf for more on XPM, or http://en.wikipedia.org/wiki/X_BitMap for more on XMB.

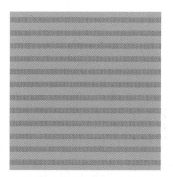

FIGURE 6.18 *Horizontal pattern.*

FIGURE 6.19 *Vertical pattern.*

FIGURE 6.20 *A JPEG example.*

FIGURE 6.21 *The more blur or gradation in an image, the better the file savings.*

JPEG Image Format

The JPEG gets its name from the Joint Photographic Experts Group, which defines standards for the file type and for other still picture coding. JPEGs allow photographs and other color-rich images to display well. The image shown in **FIGURE 6.20** weighs in at 297kb.

The JPEG has a complementary usage to GIF files: it works well for storing photographs and other color-rich images, but a simple image like a logo would be a much less efficient use of this image file type.

Compression Scheme

A JPEG is highly compressed, which means that a photograph saved as a JPEG will have a relatively small file size. However, it is a *lossy* format; whenever a JPEG image is compressed or modified, it loses some of its quality.

Compressing the image to a certain point will still allow it to display well on the web, so site designers often experiment to find the right balance between image quality and file size (**FIGURE 6.21**). The image shown in Figure 6.21 with blur applied to the background is 221kb, a savings of 76kb over the original JPEG photo.

> **BLUR THE BACKGROUND** If you are looking for ways to reduce image file size for JPEGs, blur the background of the image. This technique leverages JPEG's compression algorithms while making the focal part of your image still sharp.

Artifacts at Low Compression

When a JPEG is compressed too far, it can result in fuzzy edges and other image distortions, which are called artifacts. While compression artifacts may be applied intentionally for artistic effect, they are more often a consequence of over-compression. In **FIGURE 6.22**, compression was set to maximum and resulted in a file size of 18.3kb. Substantial savings, but the image looks pretty bad.

By testing different levels of compression for a JPEG image, you can achieve the clarity you need within the acceptable file size.

COMPRESSION MATTERS I've found a compression rate of 20–30% to be sufficient for most photographs. Ratcheting up the compression more tends to bring too many compression artifacts with marginal file size savings.

PNG Image Format

A PNG (short for Portable Network Graphics) provides either an indexed format, which works like a GIF except with more colors, or a full-color RGB format similar to a JPEG (**FIGURE 6.23**).

An indexed PNG has a much more extensive color palette than a GIF, so it can provide more image clarity. And because it's lossless, file compression doesn't cause artifacts like in a JPEG. On the other hand, the file sizes are larger, particularly for the full-color files, and PNG images display properly only on newer web browsers.

Compression Scheme

Like a GIF, a PNG is a lossless format, which means that file compression retains image quality. However, it takes more processing power to read and write PNG files than either GIF or JPEG files, and the file size is substantially larger for a PNG. Typically, a PNG file saved at 8-bit depth (PNG-8) is better than GIF.

Can you tell the difference between the two images in **FIGURE 6.24**?

FIGURE 6.24 *Comparing file sizes between PNG (left) and GIF (right). The PNG image weighs 140kb and the GIF image weighs 158kb.*

FIGURE 6.22 *Very bad compression.*

FIGURE 6.23 *A PNG-24 image contains more colors than a GIF image can.*

IMAGE COMPRESSION CHART

Banded color

JPEG maximum quality

JPEG very high quality

JPEG high quality

JPEG medium quality

JPEG low quality

JPEG zero quality

8-bit GIF

7-bit GIF

6-bit GIF

5-bit GIF

4-bit GIF

3-bit GIF

2-bit GIF

8-bit GIF, dithered

7-bit GIF, dithered

6-bit GIF, dithered

5-bit GIF, dithered

4-bit GIF, dithered

3-bit GIF, dithered

2-bit GIF, dithered

8-bit PNG

7-bit PNG

6-bit PNG

5-bit PNG

4-bit PNG

3-bit PNG

2-bit PNG

8-bit PNG, dithered

7-bit PNG, dithered

6-bit PNG, dithered

5-bit PNG, dithered

4-bit PNG, dithered

3-bit PNG, dithered

2-bit PNG, dithered

IMAGE COMPRESSION CHART

Photograph

JPEG maximum quality

JPEG very high quality

JPEG high quality

JPEG medium quality

JPEG low quality

JPEG zero quality

8-bit GIF

7-bit GIF

6-bit GIF

5-bit GIF

4-bit GIF

3-bit GIF

2-bit GIF

8-bit GIF, dithered

7-bit GIF, dithered

6-bit GIF, dithered

5-bit GIF, dithered

4-bit GIF, dithered

3-bit GIF, dithered

2-bit GIF, dithered

8-bit PNG, dithered

7-bit PNG, dithered

6-bit PNG, dithered

5-bit PNG, dithered

4-bit PNG, dithered

3-bit PNG, dithered

2-bit PNG, dithered

IMAGE COMPRESSION CHART

Pattern

JPEG maximum quality

JPEG very high quality

JPEG high quality

JPEG medium quality

JPEG low quality

JPEG zero quality

8-bit GIF

7-bit GIF

6-bit GIF

5-bit GIF

4-bit GIF

3-bit GIF

2-bit GIF

8-bit GIF, dithered

7-bit GIF, dithered

6-bit GIF, dithered

5-bit GIF, dithered

4-bit GIF, dithered

3-bit GIF, dithered

2-bit GIF, dithered

8-bit PNG

7-bit PNG

6-bit PNG

5-bit PNG

4-bit PNG

3-bit PNG

2-bit PNG

8-bit PNG, dithered

7-bit PNG, dithered

6-bit PNG, dithered

5-bit PNG, dithered

4-bit PNG, dithered

3-bit PNG, dithered

2-bit PNG, dithered

IMAGE COMPRESSION CHART

Illustration

JPEG maximum quality

JPEG very high quality

JPEG high quality

JPEG medium quality

JPEG low quality

JPEG zero quality

8-bit GIF

7-bit GIF

6-bit GIF

5-bit GIF

4-bit GIF

3-bit GIF

2-bit GIF

8-bit GIF, dithered

7-bit GIF, dithered

6-bit GIF, dithered

5-bit GIF, dithered

4-bit GIF, dithered

3-bit GIF, dithered

2-bit GIF, dithered

8-bit PNG, dithered

7-bit PNG, dithered

6-bit PNG, dithered

5-bit PNG, dithered

4-bit PNG, dithered

3-bit PNG, dithered

2-bit PNG, dithered

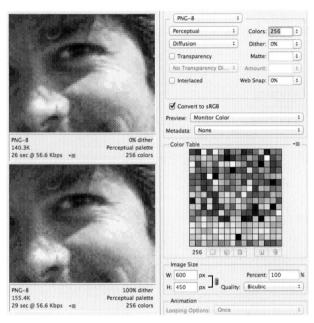

FIGURE 6.25 *The bottom image is dithered 100% to better blend colors.*

SVGZ FILES

SVGZ means that the file is an SVG file format, but it has been gzipped for smaller file sizes. If you're already using HTTP compression on text and image files (see Chapter 7, "Creating Images for the Web"), you don't need to worry about compressing SVG images further. The server compresses the files before they get sent to the browser.

Dithering

As with a GIF, an indexed PNG (PNG-8) uses dithering to translate a full-color image into the format. Because full-color PNG files are so large, this can provide a reasonable compromise between image clarity and file size. A dithered, indexed PNG retains a pixilated look that its full-color counterpart avoids (**FIGURE 6.25**).

SVG: VECTOR FILES FOR THE WEB

SVG (Scalable Vector Graphics) is a unique image file format that has been around for a while, but has recently been widely adopted by browser vendors. As the appearance and behavior of SVG images are defined by text files, they can be edited with a text editor or drawing program (**FIGURE 6.26**).

Compression Scheme

Because SVG images are composed of repeated fragments of XML text, they have lossless compression. The industry standard for compression is to use a zip algorithm, resulting in a filename ending in ".svgz."

Benefits

The greatest benefits to an SVG file are quality and searchability. Unlike most other image file types, an SVG is not pixel-based, so it can be expanded or reduced without affecting how the picture appears (**FIGURE 6.27**). In addition, because XML text defines the picture, text searches easily find the images online.

Because SVG files do not rely on pixels to define the image, expanding the file does not result in a "dotted" or jagged appearance like it does in raster images. Expanding the image size is a matter of building the XML text to define the parameters.

FIGURE 6.26 *SVG example showing editable text files associated with image.*

FIGURE 6.27 *Up close, an SVG image (right) has smoother edges than the same image exported as GIF (left).*

IN CONCLUSION

Images enhance the web, making it a richer, more visually appealing place than it was originally. As web developers we need to know how common and varied image formats work. Doing so allows us to create complex presentations without inflated image file sizes that can hinder users on slow computers or internet connections. Up next, we'll dive deeper into how to use image creation tools.

Chapter 7

CREATING IMAGES FOR THE WEB

In this chapter, we first cover tips and techniques to prepare images for web delivery while still in imaging software like Adobe Illustrator or Photoshop. Then, we go over steps to export images into various file formats. Finally, we look at ways of optimizing and compressing images for snappy web browsing.

WORKING IN ILLUSTRATOR

Adobe Illustrator is software designed for editing vector images. While most image formats for the web have been raster based, the rise in browser support for SVG makes Illustrator a contender for the web designer's main imaging application.

FIGURE 7.1 *Opening the Web workspace palette in Illustrator.*

FIGURE 7.2 *The Transform palette.*

Setting Up Workspace for Web

When you open Adobe Illustrator, you see a set of tabs and palettes. Among these is a premade palette geared toward web work. To access the Web workspace in Illustrator, go to Window > Workspace > Web (**FIGURE 7.1**).

Some of the palettes that appear in the Web workspace include:

- **Transform** for fine-tuned measurements and size or position changes (**FIGURE 7.2**).

- **Swatches** for collecting and storing color samples. Also, check out the Kuler extension by selecting Window > Extensions > Kuler, which pulls in community-driven color schemes from Adobe's social media site (**FIGURE 7.3**).

- **Symbols** collection of reusable graphic elements. If you make a change to the symbol after it's been placed in the document, the changes are automatically updated throughout (**FIGURE 7.4**).

- **Appearance** for making changes to opacity and blending. Click on the Illustrator object to change an object's stroke, fill, opacity, and more (**FIGURE 7.5**).

- **Artboards** for changing sizes and names of work areas in a document, and **Layers** for keeping the shapes within one work area sorted and named for easy navigation and selection (**FIGURE 7.6**).

FIGURE 7.3 *The Swatches palette.*

FIGURE 7.4 *The Symbols palette.*

FIGURE 7.5 *The Appearance palette.*

FIGURE 7.6 *The Artboards and Layers palettes.*

Setting Document Sizes

When designing for the web, make sure you're using the right dimensions for your layout. Like the workspace arrangement, Illustrator comes with a set of document sizes that reflect browser and mobile width and height measurements.

Desktop Site Design

When opening a new document, select File > New Blank Document to pull open the New Document dialog box (**FIGURE 7.7**).

From the Profile menu, select Web (**FIGURE 7.8**) to set the dimensions of the document.

Hardware is always getting faster and better. The same is true for desktop monitors. While the pre-populated options like 1024 x 768 and 1280 x 800 are good starting places, you might want to try manually entering a larger size such as 1366 x 768 (**FIGURE 7.9**).

> **! CUSTOMIZING ILLUSTRATOR DOCUMENTS FOR RETINA**
>
> Illustrator doesn't have dimensions for Apple's Retina or high-density pixel displays. Thankfully, Retina displays are in multiples of two. So, for iPhone Retina displays, the dimensions would be 640 × 960. The Retina iPad's dimensions are 1536 × 2048. For more information on images for mobile design, see Chapter 13, "Images for Responsive Web Design."

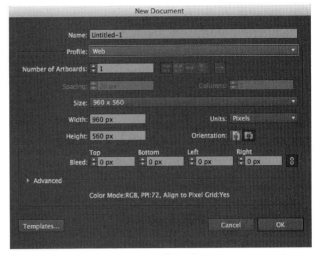

FIGURE 7.7 *The New Document dialog box.*

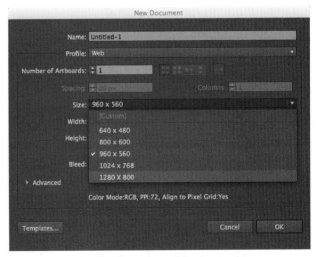

FIGURE 7.8 *Select the dimensions of the document.*

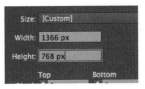

FIGURE 7.9 *Setting custom dimensions for the document.*

Mobile Browser Design

For smaller sizes, you're best served by designing for mobile and tablet dimensions. Illustrator, as it happens, has a set already built in. Select Devices from the Profile menu (**FIGURE 7.10**).

In the Size dropdown, there are dimensions for iPad, iPhone, Fire/Nook, Galaxy S, and Xoom.

Checking Site Dimensions

Check out your site's statistics through Google Analytics (Chapter 4, "Challenges in Web Design," goes into this in detail). When logged into Google Analytics, click on Content > In-Page Analytics (**FIGURE 7.11**).

Then select the Browser Size (**FIGURE 7.12**) and adjust the Web users percentage slider to show how many site visitors can see that uncovered portion of your web page (**FIGURE 7.13**).

> **! NO BLEEDS ON THE WEB**
>
> Since the web has no need for bleeds (a print term meaning portion of the design that covers the edges of the printed piece), leave those set to zero.

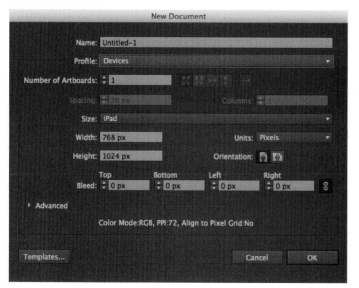

FIGURE 7.10 *Select Devices profile for mobile device dimension.*

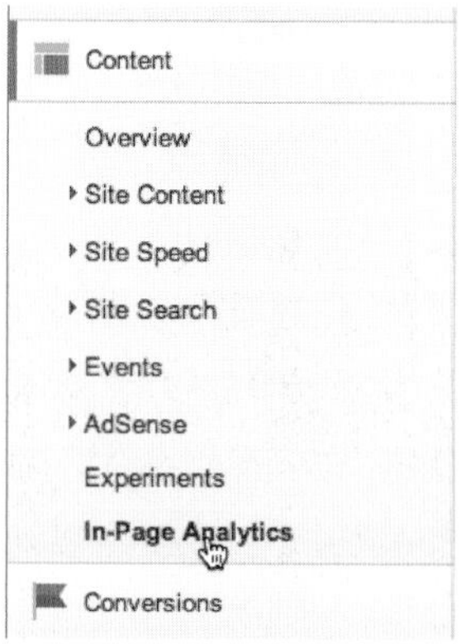

FIGURE 7.11 *Select the option to see In-Page Analytics.*

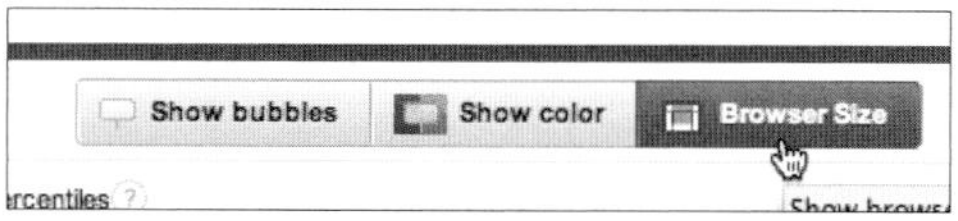

FIGURE 7.12 *Picking the option for Browser Size.*

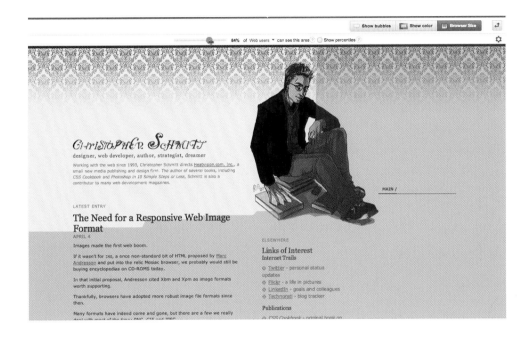

FIGURE 7.13 *Google Web Analytics masks portions of a page to reflect what a specified percentage of site visitors can see in their browser windows.*

Setting Up Artboards

Illustrator's artboards feature is very welcome when you want to create variations of the same type of image, for example, if you wanted to design logos for different situations like mobile, desktop, black-and-white printing, or full-color printing (**FIGURE 7.14**). A new Illustrator document begins with one artboard but you can add more.

FIGURE 7.14 *Logo variations for different dimensions and devices in the same Illustrator file.*

TO ADD MORE ARTBOARDS TO AN ILLUSTRATOR DOCUMENT, FOLLOW THESE (4) STEPS:

(1) Click on the Artboard tool in the toolbar.

(2) Click and drag a box in the document area to create a new artboard.

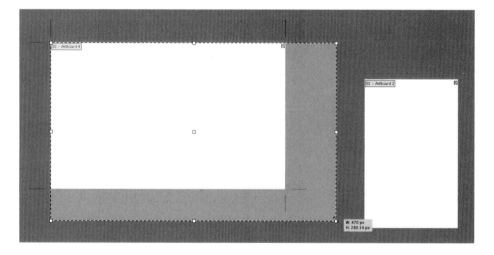

(3) To fine-tune the artboard's width and height, enter the values at the dock, in the top-right portion of the screen.

(4) Edit the name of the artboard by double-clicking on the name in the Artboard palette.

Choosing Pixel Precision

To preview how the image appears as a raster-based image, select View > Pixel Preview (**FIGURE 7.15**).

Exporting an image from vector to raster means there's a translation process. Even though the source image is vector based, the new raster image may have a halo artifact around it (**FIGURE 7.16**).

To reduce these unwanted pixels around the image, select View > Snap to Pixel (**FIGURE 7.17**). Then resize the image up or down a nudge to align the image to more pixel precision (**FIGURE 7.18**).

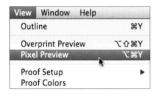

FIGURE 7.15 *Checking out how the raster image appears with Pixel Preview.*

FIGURE 7.16 *Comparing the vector- and raster-based images.*

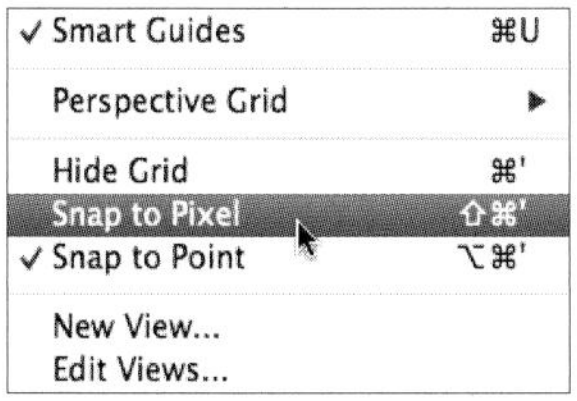

FIGURE 7.17 *Making edges rest on full pixel by selecting Snap to Pixel.*

FIGURE 7.18 *Resizing images to make them crisper.*

Exporting Raster Images

Illustrator has a robust export feature for saving image files for web delivery.

Isolating Images for Export

When you want to export an image to a web format, select File > Save for Web. If the image is smaller than the artboard, then the surrounding white space gets exported as part of the image—making for a rather large image (**FIGURE 7.19**).

To export just the image on the artboard, uncheck Clip to Artboard in the Image Size field set (**FIGURE 7.20**), and then click Apply.

FIGURE 7.19 *The large amount of white space that would be saved with the image.*

FIGURE 7.20 *Release the export constraint from the artboard to be only the image elements on the artboard itself.*

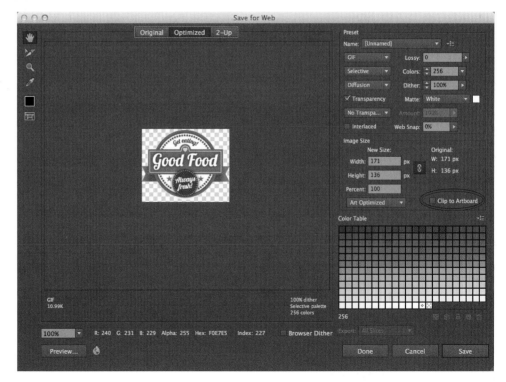

TO SAVE RASTER IMAGES FOR THE WEB OUT OF ILLUSTRATOR, FOLLOW THESE ⑥ STEPS:

① With an image ready, go to File > Save for Web to bring up a dialog box.

② In the upper-right corner, select the image format you want: GIF, JPEG, or PNG-8. As mentioned in Chapter 6, "Images for the Web," PNG-24 generally creates a larger file than a comparable JPEG, but PNG-8 is an option where a GIF would be used.

③ Adjust the settings for each format, if needed.

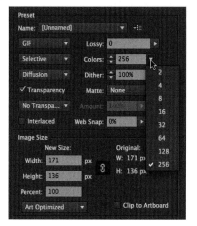

④ Compare different image formats with the 2-up or 4-up view, checking for image quality and file size.

⑤ When ready to save to a web image format, check the preferred image and click Save.

⑥ In the Save Optimized As dialog box, name the file , and click Save.

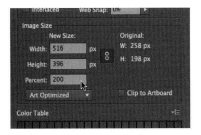

FIGURE 7.21 *Change the percentage to resize the exported image.*

Exporting Images at Twice the Size

Since Apple is doubling the resolution of its screens, we need to deliver images that are twice as large (200%) as the originals. With vector-based artwork, scaling images to correspond with Apple's Retina screens is easy.

In the Save for Web dialog box, set the Percent value to 200 (**FIGURE 7.21**) and then click out of the input box.

Exporting Vector Images from Illustrator

In addition to exporting raster images from Illustrator, we can export vector files into the SVG format. This preserves the vector data—allowing resizing of the image either up or down without any loss of visual quality.

TO GET ARTWORK OUT OF ILLUSTRATOR INTO A VECTOR WEB GRAPHIC, FOLLOW THESE ⑥ STEPS:

① If you need to reduce the amount of white space around the image, select Object > Artboards > Fit to Artwork Bounds. This step trims the space around an image.

② Select File > Save As... from the menu to bring up the Save As dialog box.

④ If you have text in your image, select Only Glyphs Used to help reduce file size.

③ Pick the SVG (svg) option from the Format drop-down menu.

⑤ For Decimal Places, the lower the number results in lower image quality. A higher value improves the image quality, but at a cost of higher file sizes. Acceptable values are from 1 to 7.

⑥ Click OK to save the SVG file.

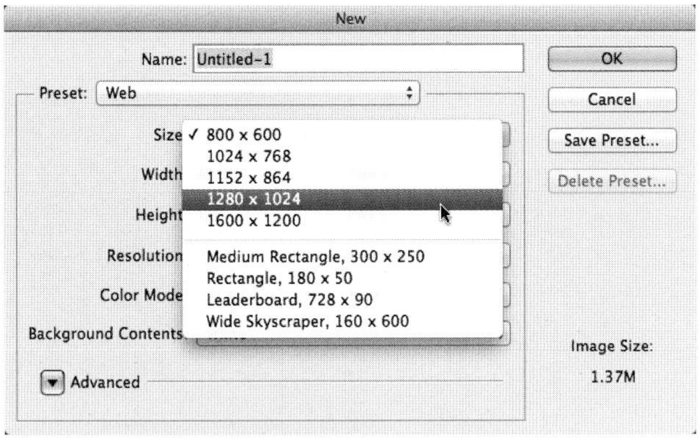

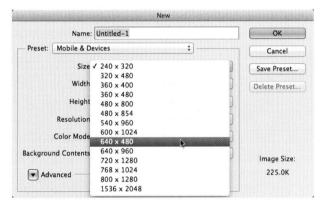

FIGURE 7.22 *The New dialog box.*

FIGURE 7.23 *Mobile presets in Photoshop.*

OTHER TOOLS BESIDES PHOTOSHOP

Photoshop isn't the only digital imaging program out there. For example, Adobe Fireworks was the first such stand-alone tool built specifically for creating and optimizing web graphics.

WORKING IN PHOTOSHOP

Even before the web existed, Photoshop was the industry standard for creating and editing images. It's still the best for image editing, with built-in tools for working with images destined for web delivery.

Setting Up a New Document

When creating a new image, select File > New to bring up the New dialog box (**FIGURE 7.22**).

Select Web from the Preset dropdown menu. Depending on your project, you can select from predetermined sizes for website designs or ad banners.

If you want to design for a mobile site, select the Mobile & Devices preset. As shown in **FIGURE 7.23**, there are options for Retina and regular displays.

Exporting Raster Images

Once you have an image such as a logo or photo ready to be processed for the web, the next step is to convert it into the web image format. Let's walk through how to get images ready for the web.

TO EXPORT WEB IMAGES FROM PHOTOSHOP, FOLLOW THESE ⑦ STEPS:

① With an image ready, go to File > Save for Web & Devices to bring up a large dialog box.

② In the upper-right corner, select the image format you want: GIF, JPEG, or PNG-8. Read more about PNG-24 in Chapter 8, "Transparency and Shadow."

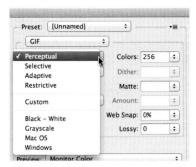

③ Adjust the settings for each format, if needed.

④ Compare different image formats with the 2-up or 4-up view, checking for image quality and file size.

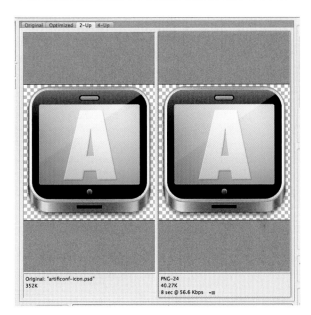

⑤ Check the rate at which the image will download by clicking the Select Download Speed dropdown.

⑥ When you're ready to save to a web image format, select the optimized version of the image you prefer, and click Save.

⑦ In the Save Optimized As dialog box, name the image file, and then click Save.

NAMING WEB IMAGE FILES

When naming an image, do so with purpose. Here are six tips for creating a filename:

Make the filename as descriptive as possible. Naming a file **picture_1** does not make it easy to search for and serves no purpose for your site. Be as specific as possible. For example, use **water-lilies** as opposed to **flowers**. Being explicit in naming photos with keywords helps with Google ranking.

Begin the filename with a letter rather than a number. Ideally, the filename should lead with the description, as this enables not only easier searching, but also easier indexing of your own files. Dates or other numbers should follow the description.

Use only letters, numbers, and dashes in the filename. This keeps the format simple and easily accessible by any web browser; special characters inserted into the filename can make it harder to identify based on typical searches.

Write dates as a four-digit year, followed by a two-digit month and a two-digit day: YYYY-MM-DD. This allows for easier searching and chronological sorting. For example, all January dates will be sorted before all March dates, within each year.

BATCH PROCESSING

If you find yourself needing to convert multiple image files from one format to another, Photoshop has a great feature called Actions.

You *record* the sequence you want performed by the software, then set the Action to be applied to a folder of images and press Start. If everything works right, your images will be converted for you.

Don't get too frustrated if there's a little trial and error. This is an automated process and computers need very explicit instructions.

Keep the filename short. Common abbreviations, like **info** for information or **gov** for government, help create shorter filenames.

Remember that the filename will end with an extension that describes the file type, such as **.gif**, **.jpg**, **.png**, or **.svg**. Thus, a GIF file containing a logo for General Motors might read **gm_logo_2012.gif**, while a photograph taken last year might bear the filename **water_lilies_2011-03-04.jpg**.

Following these conventions ensures easy identification on a computer as well as maximum searchability on web browsers.

REDUCING IMAGE FILE SIZE

While Adobe Photoshop is great for exporting images to different web-friendly formats, it doesn't always make the file sizes as low as they can be.

Compressing Raster Images

A Macintosh OS tool for optimizing images for the lowest possible format is ImageOptim (http://imageoptim.com) (**FIGURE 7.24**).

Simply drag your image files into the ImageOptim window and eight different compression tools begin to work on them (**FIGURE 7.25**). Don't worry: Compression is lossless and won't degrade the image's visual integrity.

After the compression, no new or duplicate files are created. ImageOptim replaces the old images with the new optimized ones. (But don't worry, it only processed your exported web images, not your original source files.)

Windows OS users can use PNGGauntlet (http://pnggauntlet.com), which handles more than just PNG (**FIGURE 7.26**).

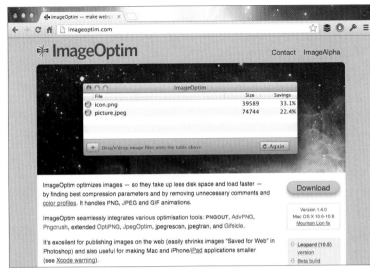

FIGURE 7.24 *The ImageOptim website.*

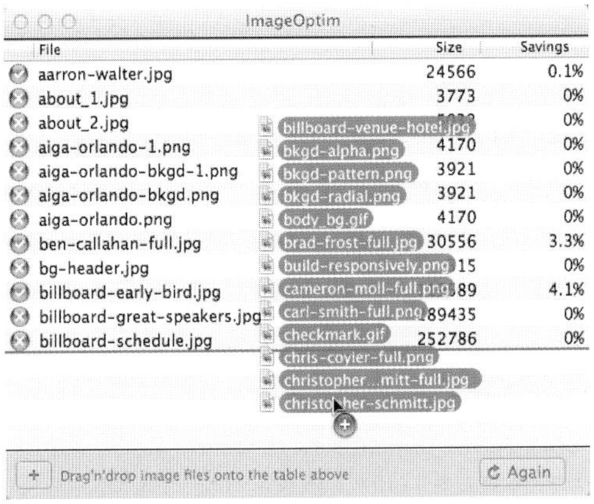

FIGURE 7.25 *Dragging image files into the ImageOptim window automatically starts the compression tools.*

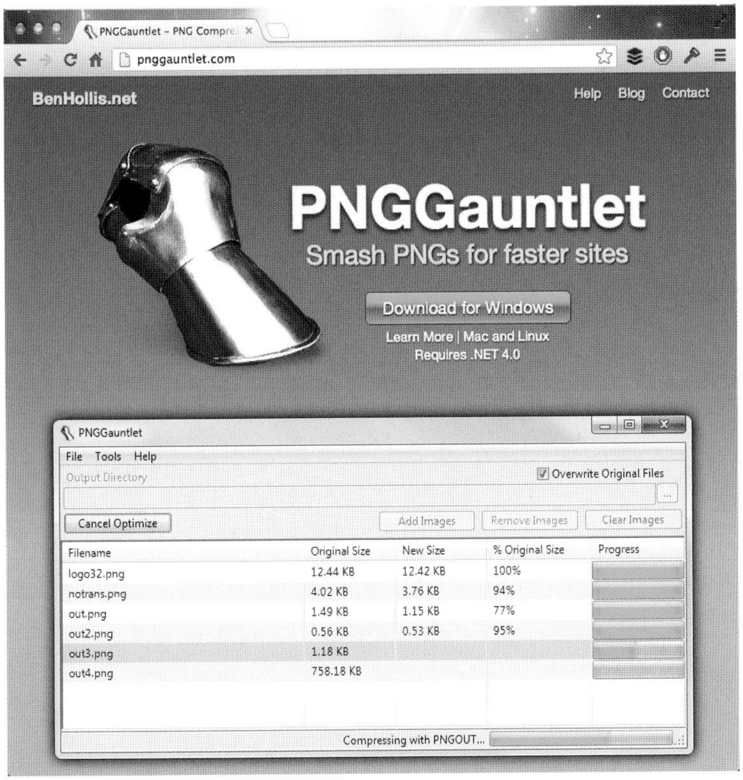

PHP, HTML, AND GZIP

If you use PHP for your site, add this line to the top of your PHP files:

```
<? ob_start("ob_gzhandler"); ?>
```

This compresses the HTML files for faster delivery.

FIGURE 7.26 *The PNGGauntlet website.*

Using HTTP Compression

Keeping file sizes as small as possible means we can deliver a faster experience for site visitors. So it's worthwhile to apply another level of compression called HTTP Compression. Before a file is sent over the Internet from your web server to the site visitor's machine, the server compresses the file further still with a software tool called gzip. Then, before the file opens at the browser, the file is decompressed.

Checking for gzip

You might already be using gzip, or perhaps a coworker or colleague has it installed. To find out, go to http://gzipwtf.com and enter your site's URL (**FIGURE 7.27**).

FIGURE 7.27 *The gzipWTF website.*

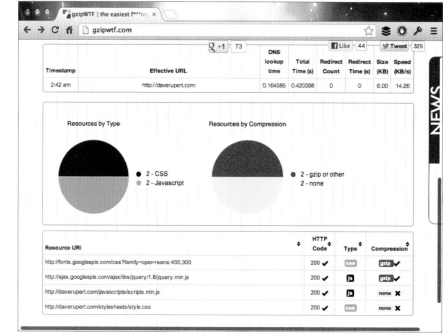

Setting Up gzip

If you're not using gzip, first check your web host's technical support documents or ask technical customer support staff for the best way to implement it. Chances are they already have this material written out with step-by-step instructions.

ABSENT ANY TECH SUPPORT, YOU CAN ADD GZIP YOURSELF USING THESE ⑥ STEPS:

① Go to the HTML5 Boilerplate at http://html5boilerplate.com.

② Click the Source Code link at the top of the page to go to https://github.com/h5bp/html5-boilerplate.

CAN YOUR SITE BEAT THE TWO-SECOND CUSTOMER?

Akamai is a company that helps clients such as Twitter and Facebook deliver web pages as quickly as possible no matter where users are around the world. According to Akamai, the standard for delivering complete web pages is two seconds (http://www.akamai.com/html/about/press/releases/2009/press_091409.html).

③ Select the **.htaccess** file in the file listing (https://github.com/h5bp/
html5-boilerplate/blob/master/.htaccess).

④ Select and copy all the text in the file that deals with gzip compression.
Note in this example the relevant chunk starts at line 152. You may have to
scroll down to find the section of text you need.

⑤ Paste the file into the bottom of your **.htaccess** file.

⑥ Upload the edited **.htaccess** file to your web server at the root level of your site. Boom. You're done.

IN CONCLUSION

Throughout this chapter we looked at how industry tools like Illustrator and Photoshop work with web and mobile images. Working efficiently means using the tools of the trade effectively. This includes creating images, getting them out of digital imaging applications looking their best, and ensuring that they're compressed and delivered quickly to site visitors. Next, we'll look at images with transparency or shadow.

Chapter 8

TRANSPARENCY AND SHADOW

For practical purposes, let's think of pixels as squares. Images made up of these square building blocks can only have edges with right angles, and can only have smooth-looking edges when they're rectangles. Working with rectangles leads to boxy layouts.

Web designers use transparency to break out of this boring, boxy mentality; with transparency, they can fake many things they normally can't have, like round and custom image shapes that rest on background colors in the browser.

CREATING TRANSPARENCY WITH GIFS

We discussed creating images in Chapter 7, "Creating Images for the Web." When you need custom shaped or textured images, transparency ensures that they rest cleanly on top of a background image or color (**FIGURE 8.1**). A GIF can have up to 256 colors, and one of those colors can be set to transparent.

TO CREATE A GIF IMAGE WITH TRANSPARENCY IN PHOTOSHOP, FOLLOW THESE ⑥ STEPS:

① Finalize the image preparations by making sure the background Photoshop pattern is visible. The checkerboard grid appears when the image is a layered image file. This grid represents the transparent part of the image.

FIGURE 8.1 *A textured image for transparency.*

LAYERS IN PHOTOSHOP

If you're new to Photoshop, the concept of **layers** might also be new. Layers first appeared nearly 20 years ago in Photoshop 3 and they made updating images easier and faster.

Layers are images stacked on top of one another in the same way a sandwich is really a stack of bread, lunchmeat, lettuce, condiments, and whatever else you want.

Just as sandwiches can be quickly modified to customers' personal tastes ("no mayo, please"), we can edit an image.

To experiment with layers, go to Windows > Layers to bring up the Layers palette. An image without layers is said to be **flattened**.

② Select File > Save for Web & Devices.

③ In the Save for Web & Devices dialog box, select GIF from the fieldset legend.

④ Check the Transparency option.

⑤ Select the matte color that closely matches the background color where the image is used. For now, we'll use white.

⑥ Click the Save button to export the image to your computer.

FIGURE 8.2 *The mugshot works well across two different colors.*

FIGURE 8.3 *White jaggies at the bottom of the image are caused by the white matte color showing against the dark background.*

Matting

You might have a design where an image overlaps two fields, as shown in **FIGURE 8.2**.

If the image is square or rectangular, it's quite easy. But what if we want the image to be a circle instead (**FIGURE 8.3**)? Remember that we just chose white as the matte color for our transparent GIF. A matte in a color that's too different from the background causes visible artifacts and a rough edge (**FIGURE 8.4**).

When we uncheck the matting option in the Save for Web & Devices dialog box, the transparent image's edges lose their halo (**FIGURE 8.5**).

However, the transparency is only 1-bit (on or off), so while the halo is removed, the edges of the image are still coarse and jagged (**FIGURE 8.6**).

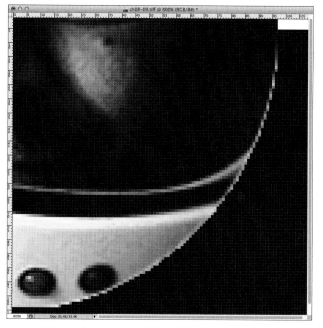

FIGURE 8.4 *A close-up look at the white halo.*

FIGURE 8.5 *An image that fits better across two different color sections.*

FIGURE 8.6 *The edges of a 1-bit transparent GIF image are very rough anyplace they aren't perfectly horizontal or vertical.*

TRANSPARENCY WITH PNGS

Whereas the GIF format only allows one color to be transparent, the PNG file format allows for multiple pixels to be transparent or in an alpha channel.

Pixels in an alpha channel can be partially transparent for smoother transitions between the image and any background colors or background textures.

8-bit PNG

To make a PNG-8 transparent image in Photoshop, follow the same rules for GIFs, making sure to select PNG-8 (**FIGURE 8.7**).

As with GIFs, you can set the matting for the image and transparency. However, the transparency will have a rough edge, just like a GIF (**FIGURE 8.8**).

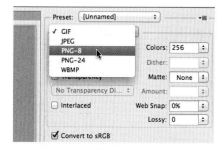

FIGURE 8.7 *Selecting the PNG-8 option in Photoshop's Save for Web & Devices dialog box.*

FIGURE 8.8 *Using a PNG-8 image in place of a GIF image.*

24-bit PNG

With 24-bit PNGs, you can specify if an image is opaque or transparent (on or off) as well as 254 settings of transparency in between. To make a PNG-24 transparent image in Photoshop, follow the same rules for GIFs, making sure to select PNG-24 (**FIGURE 8.9**).

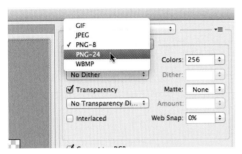

FIGURE 8.9 *Selecting the PNG-24 option in Photoshop's Save for Web & Devices dialog box.*

FIGURE 8.10 *Alpha transparency allows for smoother clipping of images.*

The result is a smoother transition (**FIGURE 8.10**) between the image and the background design elements (**FIGURE 8.11**).

> **! PNG-24 FILE SIZE**
>
> A problem with 24-bit PNGs is that their file sizes are larger than other images. In this astronaut head example, the GIF and PNG-8 images each are 24k and the PNG-24 image is 96k. Be sure to use 24-bit PNG images judiciously and to optimize your images with products like ImageOptim or PNGGauntlet, as explained in Chapter 7, "Creating Images for the Web."

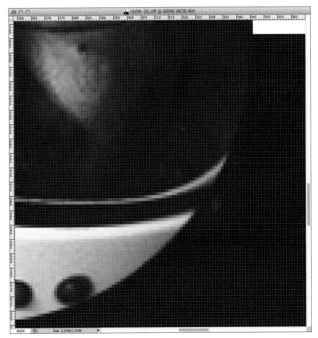

FIGURE 8.11 *Different levels of transparency in the pixels around the circular image.*

CSS TRANSPARENCY

CSS is another way that designers can tap into transparency. With the judicious use of a CSS property here or a CSS value there, you can create unique design elements without having to open up Photoshop.

FIGURE 8.12 *Making rounded corners without touching Photoshop.*

FIGURE 8.13 *Making a circle out of a square image with CSS.*

Rounding Corners

With CSS, you can round off the edges of an image. Use the **border-radius** property and set the value to 1em for an example (**FIGURE 8.12**):

```
img {
  border-radius: 1em;
}
```

Going further with the value, you can create the illusion of a circle out of a square (**FIGURE 8.13**):

```
img {
  border-radius: 100px;
}
```

Image Masking

The PNG-24 image merges the alpha channel and the image information into one file. There's a way to apply an image mask onto an image through the browser; this lets you keep the main image file (**FIGURE 8.14**) while letting browsers that support the feature (currently only Safari and Chrome) apply the effect.

FIGURE 8.14 *The image as it resides in the web page.*

TO CREATE AN IMAGE MASK, FOLLOW THESE ⑦ STEPS:

① Select the Magnetic Lasso tool from the Tool palette in Photoshop.

② Select around the main areas of the image. In this case, it's the people.

③ With the selection complete, create a new layer by clicking on the new layer icon.

DID YOU KNOW? In Photoshop, the keyboard shortcut for creating a new layer in Windows OS is Shift+Ctrl+N. To create a new layer in Macintosh OS, press Shift+Command+N.

④ Fill in the selection with a flat color like black.

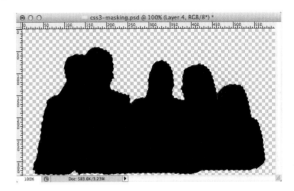

⑤ Adjust the selection to cover parts of the image you want to keep to complete the mask.

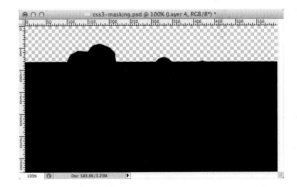

⑥ Export the mask as a PNG-24 image.

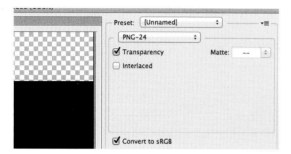

⑦ Apply the **-webkit-mask-box-image** property, setting the value to the mask image URL location.

```
img {
 display: block;
 margin: 0 auto;
 border-radius: 10px;
 -webkit-mask-box-image: url(css3-masking-mask.
png);
 background-clip: padding-box;
}
```

Element Opacity

With CSS, you can set whole elements to be transparent or partially transparent. Using the opacity property, you can set an element and its contents to be transparent (**FIGURE 8.15**):

```
.letter-c {
  background-color: yellow;
  opacity: .5;
}
```

To fully hide an element, set the opacity value to zero (**FIGURE 8.16**).

FIGURE 8.15 *The letter C circle is set to 50% transparency.*

FIGURE 8.16 *With the opacity set to zero, the element disappears completely.*

❗ HIDDEN CHILDREN

Children or descendants of elements that have been made transparent or hidden with the opacity property cannot become more opaque than their parents.

TRANSPARENCY IN OLDER INTERNET EXPLORER BROWSERS

To enable transparency in older versions of IE, use the zoom and filter property:

```
.letter-c {
background-color: yellow;
zoom: 1;
filter: alpha(opacity=50);
opacity: 0.5;
}
```

The **zoom** filter triggers a hasLayout feature found only in IE. Having hasLayout switched on, in turn, allows transparency through IE's own **filter** property.

Background Color Transparency

To control the transparency of only the background color in an element, you can use the RGBa method of citing colors (**FIGURE 8.17**):

```
.letter-c {
border-color: rgba(153,153,153,.6);
background-color: rgba(255,255,0,.5);
}
```

For more information on assigning colors, see Chapter 5, "Color for the Web."

FIGURE 8.17 *The background color behind the letter C is set to 50% transparency.*

Text Shadow

Through the use of the text shadow, you can apply a little contrast to improve text legibility (**FIGURE 8.18**):

```
div {
text-shadow: 0 2px grey;
}
```

The first value for text shadow tells the browser the distance the shadow should move horizontally or on an x-axis. The second value tells the browser how far to extend the shadow vertically or on the y-axis. The third value, color, can be a color keyword, RGB, RGBa, or HSL value.

FIGURE 8.18 *Adding a small text shadow aids text legibility, especially with light text colors on light background colors.*

FIGURE 8.19 *Some 3D text effects created using CSS's* **text-shadow** *property.*

3D Text Shadow

The text shadow can also take multiple values. By combining it with a few RGBa values, you can create three-dimensional text effects that blend well into the background (**FIGURE 8.19**):

```
.first {
color: #fff9d6;
text-shadow: 0px 0px 0px rgb(104, 104, 104),
  1px 1px 0px rgb(89, 89, 89),
  2px 2px 0px rgb(75, 75, 75),
  3px 3px 0px rgb(60, 60, 60),
  4px 4px 0px rgb(46, 46, 46),
  5px 5px 0px rgb(31, 31, 31),
  6px 6px 0px rgb(17, 17, 17),
  7px 7px 6px rgba(0, 0, 0, 0.6),
  7px 7px 1px rgba(0, 0, 0, 0.49),
  0px 0px 6px rgba(0, 0, 0, 0.2);
}

.second {
color: #fff9d6;
text-shadow:0px 0px 0 rgb(231,231,231),
  0px 1px 0 rgb(216,216,216),
  0px 2px 0 rgb(202,202,202),
  0px 3px 0 rgb(187,187,187),
  0px 4px 0 rgb(173,173,173),
  0px 5px 0 rgb(158,158,158),
  0px 6px 0 rgb(144,144,144),
  0px 7px 6px rgba(0,0,0,0.6),
  0px 7px 1px rgba(0,0,0,0.5),
  0px 0px 6px rgba(0,0,0,0.2);
}
```

Christopher Schmitt is not an astronaut, but likes the helmet anyway.

FIGURE 8.20 *A simple drop shadow on an element.*

Box Shadow

Similar to **text-shadow**, an element can accept a shadow through the **box-shadow** property (**FIGURE 8.20**):

```
img {
 box-shadow: 0 0 20px black;
}
```

Applying multiple values for **box-shadow**, you can introduce a rainbow effect (**FIGURE 8.21**):

```
box-shadow: 0 0 20px black,
    20px 15px 30px rgba(255,255,0,0.8),
    -20px 15px 30px rgba(0,255,0,0.8),
    -20px -15px 30px rgba(0,0,255,0.8),
    20px -15px 30px rgba(255,0,0,0.8);
}
```

Combining **border-radius** with the box shadows produces *circular* shadows (**FIGURE 8.22**):

```
box-shadow: 0 0 20px black,
    20px 15px 30px rgba(255,255,0,0.8),
    -20px 15px 30px rgba(0,255,0,0.8),
    -20px -15px 30px rgba(0,0,255,0.8),
    20px -15px 30px rgba(255,0,0,0.8);
border-radius: 100px;
}
```

IN CONCLUSION

Not all image formats provide the same level of transparency. In this chapter, we explored the GIF and PNG formats and how we can use each one to provide transparency. The key issue for transparent images is file size. Keeping file sizes low is especially important as mobile surfing increases. To keep your designs speedy, use CSS properties for simple drop shadows and transparency effects. Next we'll look at ways to bring visuals outside of the browser window with favicons and mobile bookmarks.

FIGURE 8.21 *Assigning multiple drop shadows to a single element.*

FIGURE 8.22 *Drop shadows match the shape of the borders.*

Chapter **9**

FAVICONS AND MOBILE BOOKMARKS

A website's brand goes beyond inserting an **img** element in the top left corner of the page. The logo can also be placed throughout a visitor's browser or mobile device in the form of a favicon, a small image or icon often found in the URL bar that represents the website.

To get the icon to show up in these places, though, means that images need to be scaled down to a handful of pixels. In this chapter, we review steps to push our logo beyond web pages as well as how to reduce images while maintaining optimal quality and crispness.

WHERE FAVICONS ARE FOUND

Due to their ubiquity, favicons are a great way for website owners to extend their brand. Favicons are commonly displayed in the browser's address bar next to the web URL (**FIGURE 9.1**) and, if it's supported, in the browser's tabs (**FIGURE 9.2**).

Favicons can also be seen long after a visitor has visited a web page. As shown in **TABLE 9.1**, browsers can display favicons for later viewing, tucking them away in the bookmarks section, links, or even in the icons that are grabbed to drop onto computer desktops (**FIGURES 9.3**, **9.4**, and **9.5**).

> **! FAVICONS DROPPED FOR SECURITY**
>
> Firefox has stopped including favicons in address bars. Instead, they're using generic icons to represent different types of unsecured and secured websites (https://msujaws.wordpress.com/2012/04/23/an-update-to-site-identity-in-desktop-firefox/).

FIGURE 9.1 *A favicon in an address bar.*

FIGURE 9.2 *A favicon in a browser tab.*

TABLE 9.1 *Favicon Support*

Browser	Favicons Displayed In:				
	Address Bar	Links Bar	Bookmarks	Tabs	Dragged to Desktop
Firefox	N	Y	Y	Y	N
Chrome	N	Y	Y	Y	Y
IE	Y	N	N	N	N
Safari	Y	N	Y	N	N
Opera	Y	Y	Y	Y	Y

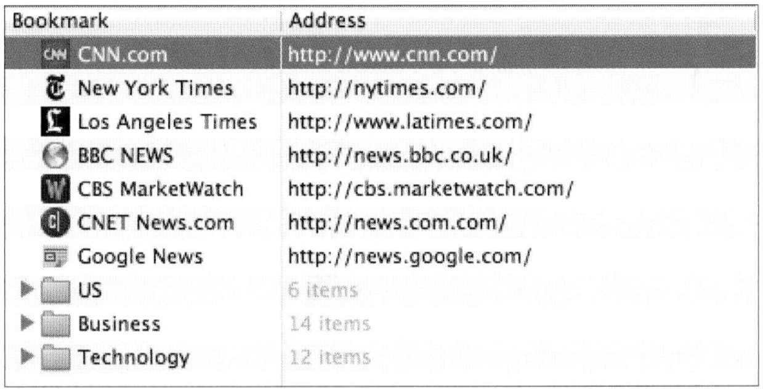

FIGURE 9.3 *Favicons in a bookmarks list.*

FIGURE 9.4 *A favicon in a links bar.*

FIGURE 9.5 *In Internet Explorer, you can click-drag the address bar's icon onto the desktop.*

IMAGE FORMATS FOR FAVICONS

Internet Explorer 5 launched favicons, but it supported only the ICO image file format that was introduced by the Windows 1.0 operating system. Since then, other browsers have widely adopted favicons and have grown to support more file formats. All browsers aside from IE support GIF, JPEG, and PNG files. All except IE, Firefox, and Safari also support SVG files.

Despite growing support for other image formats, *it's best to use the ICO file format* for favicons to provide the widest possible browser support.

INTERNET EXPLORER STILL STUCK ON ICO

Even with greater adoption of other image formats by other browsers, Internet Explorer currently supports only ICO.

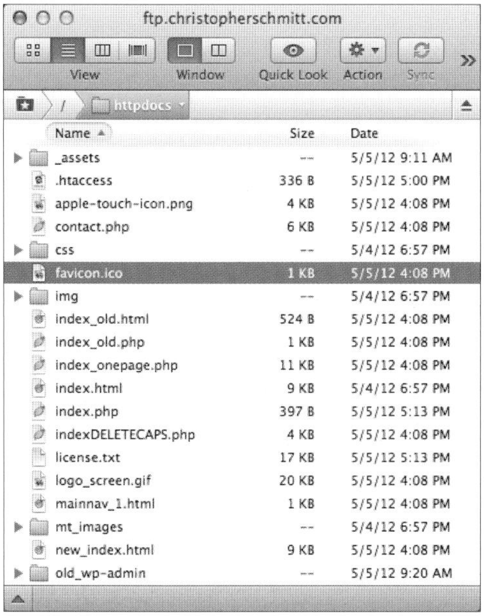

FIGURE 9.6 *Placing the favicon in the root folder.*

INSERTING FAVICONS INTO A WEBSITE

To have your image show up as a favicon, place the image in the root folder of your website. Typically that's the location where the index or main page of the site is stored on your web server (**FIGURE 9.6**).

If you're using a third-party blogging service like Tumblr and are unable to upload to the root folder, you can tell the browser to look elsewhere for the favicon. Insert a **link** element in the head portion of the web page:

```
<head>
  <link rel="shortcut icon" href="http://www.example.com/
myicon.ico"/>
  <title>My Website</title>
</head>
```

Favicons for Your Subsite

If you have a subsite or a mini-site in a subdirectory of your domain for marketing or a side project, you can have a separate favicon. For those pages, link to a different favicon:

```
<head>
  <link rel="shortcut icon" href="/assets/side-project/
side-project.ico"/>
  <title>Side Project</title>
</head>
```

For sites that are on a subdomain, the browser looks for the favicon in the root folder of that subdomain.

Spread Your Favicons Around

If a favicon is not listed with a **link** element, the browser searches for it in the root of your website's directory. As a precaution, it's best to leave a copy of the **favicon.ico** file in the root directory in case the HTML **link** reference accidentally gets removed. If you do have access to the root folder, it's a good idea to provide *both* favicon locations to the browser.

CREATING FAVICONS FOR WEB PAGES

The most straightforward way to create an ICO file is to make a 16 × 16px image in your digital imaging software. If you can export it as an ICO file, then great—we're done here. However, most common digital imaging applications don't have that option. To get around that, you can use an online generator:

TO MAKE YOUR CUSTOM FAVICONS, FOLLOW THE NEXT ③ STEPS:

① Generate a 16 × 16px graphic by creating or placing an icon or logo in your digital imaging application of choice.

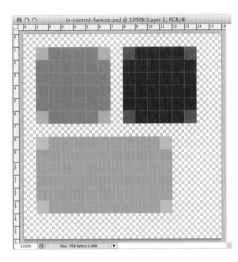

② Save or export the image as a GIF or PNG, for example through Photoshop's Save for Web and Devices interface.

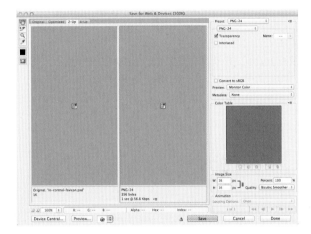

③ Upload the image to an online generator like www. convertico.com to convert it to an ICO file.

ONLINE FAVICON GENERATOR

If you don't have digital imaging software, you can make an ICO file by *drawing in the web browser* at http://favicon.cc (**FIGURE 9.7**). Once you've finished your icon masterpiece, a 16 × 16px ICO file is generated.

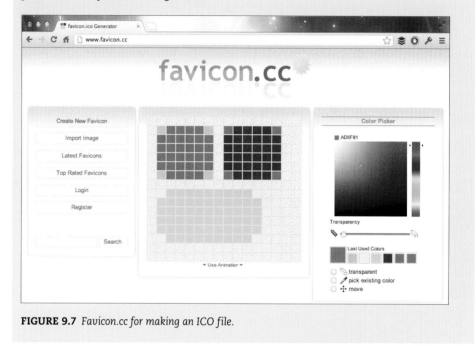

FIGURE 9.7 *Favicon.cc for making an ICO file.*

Building Retina-Ready Favicons

One advantage of using an ICO file for the favicon over other image formats is that the ICO file can become a **storage locker** of images. This is beneficial since displays are increasing in size or, in the case of Apple's Retina displays, in pixel density, and a 16 × 16px graphic doesn't contain all that much visual information.

By building different-size ICO files into a wrapper ICO file, you can provide different images for browsers on different displays as well as different scenarios. For example, a browser might display a 16 × 16px favicon in the address bar, but use a 32 × 32px image for the bookmark that the user drags to the desktop.

To build a ICO file storage locker, use Icon Slate (www.kodlian.com/apps/icon-slate), available in the Mac App Store. Icon Slate takes your preexisting images and assembles them into an ICO file.

TO CREATE A 16 × 16PX GRAPHIC AND EXPORT IT AS A PNG IMAGE, FOLLOW THESE ⑩ STEPS:

① Open your logo (or other branding element) in Photoshop, making sure that the image rests on top of a transparent layer.

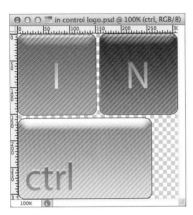

② Resize the image to a little less than 256 × 256px, making sure to constrain the proportions of the image and leave some space around the edges.

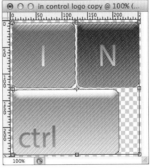

USE VECTORS WHEN POSSIBLE

If you have vector files on hand, it's better to *place* the brand element into a blank Photoshop file that's already 256 × 256 px so there's no danger of interpolation.

! **DON'T SCALE UP**

If you have a small image, don't resize the image to larger sizes. The image editor can only extrapolate or guess the image information when it's asked to add pixels.

SERIOUS ABOUT ICONS?

Want a more feature-rich icon tool for either Photoshop or Fireworks that works on PC or Mac? Try Iconfactory's IconBuilder (http://iconfactory.com/software/iconbuilder/).

③ Export the image as a GIF from Photoshop with transparency (as you learned in Chapter 8, "Transparency and Shadow"), and save it with a unique filename such as **my-web-site-favicon-256x256.gif**.

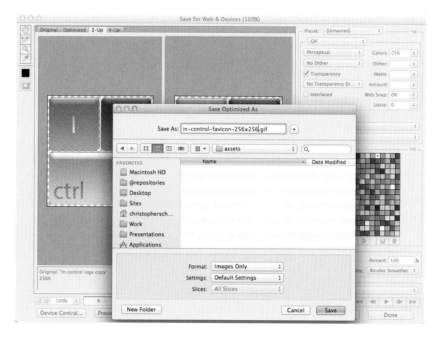

④ Select Image > Adjustments > Brightness/Contrast.

(5) Adjust the levels to +3 for both Brightness and Contrast.

(6) Click Image > Image Size and adjust the image dimensions to 128 × 128px.

(7) Once again, click Image > Adjustments > Brightness/Contrast and adjust the levels to +3 for both Brightness and Contrast to give the colors a little boost.

(8) Select Filter > Sharpen > Sharpen.

(9) Export the image from Photoshop as a GIF with transparency and save it as **my-web-site-favicon-128x128.gif**.

MULTIPLE-STEP RESIZING TECHNIQUE

This Photoshop technique is extremely handy for making images ready for desktop and mobile devices. Boosting the colors before and after you resize an image gives you greater detail and repairs some of the loss of color quality that occurs when shrinking images. You can download the Photoshop Action at the book site, http://dwmgbook.com.

10 Repeat Steps 4 through 9 for exporting images with 64 × 64px, 48 × 48px, 32 × 32px, 24 × 24px, and 16 × 16px dimensions, or for as many sizes as the logo is legible.

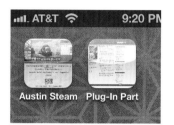

11 When you reach smaller sizes like 16 × 16px, the image may become illegible or excessively blurry. You might find the need to recreate the icon pixel by pixel! With that little visual real estate, you might opt to go with an abstract reproduction of the logo (as shown with blocks of color) or isolate a detail from the logo.

MOBILE BOOKMARKS

Mobile Safari often uses less-than-great-looking screenshots of what you're viewing as the icon for the home screen bookmark (**FIGURE 9.8**).

iPhones and iPads offer another opportunity to take your brand beyond the desktop. This is where mobile bookmarks start to differentiate from favicons. Unlike favicons, mobile bookmarks can't rely on just *one* image for all devices (**TABLE 9.2**). With different devices and high-resolution or Apple Retina displays, you need to create a handful of icons.

FIGURE 9.8 *Mobile Safari's Add to Home Screen command can create less than ideal mobile bookmarks.*

TABLE 9.2 *Web Clip Icon Sizes*

Device	Dimensions
iPhone	57 × 57px
iPhone Retina	114 × 114px
iPad	72 × 72px
iPad Retina	144 × 144px

File Format

The first difference you'll notice between mobile bookmarks and favicons is the use of PNGs over ICOs.

Naming Conventions

Another difference is that unlike favicons, where the filename can be almost anything you like, the filenames of the web clip icons need to be exact or the browser will skip over them. Here's a list of images needed to support iOS devices and the names they need to be:

■ apple-touch-icon-72x72.png

■ apple-touch-icon-114x114.png

■ apple-touch-icon.png

Automating Graphic Treatment

Another difference between mobile bookmarks and favicons is that iOS devices automatically apply three design effects to the icons (**FIGURE 9.9**): rounded corners, drop shadows, and reflective shine.

This is a helpful feature if you want to make sure your icons look more like the other icons on the mobile home screen. If you want to stop this automatic graphic treatment, you can rename the image files with "precomposed" affixed at the end (**FIGURE 9.10**):

■ apple-touch-icon-72x72-precomposed.png

■ apple-touch-icon-114x114-precomposed.png

■ apple-touch-icon-precomposed.png

FIGURE 9.9 *iOS adds its own graphic treatments to mobile bookmarks.*

FIGURE 9.10 *Adding a suffix of "precomposed" prevents iOS from adding its own graphic treatment to your mobile bookmark.*

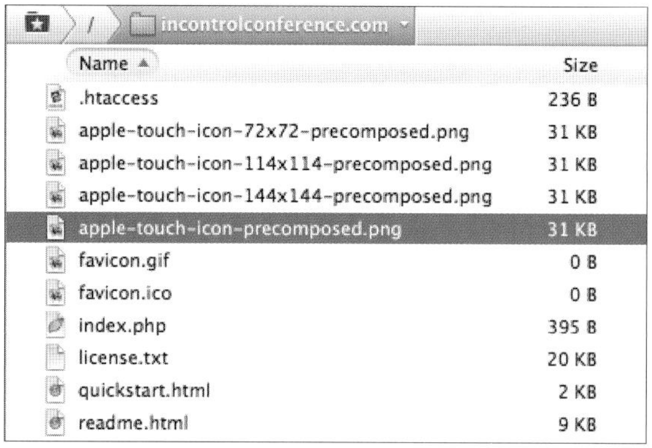

FIGURE 9.11 *Favicon and mobile bookmark files in the root folder.*

CUSTOMIZING A MOBILE BOOKMARK LABEL

By default, iOS takes the contents of the page's title element as the label for the mobile bookmark, which might not be the most apt—such as when it includes navigation identifiers or time-sensitive information like the current date. To set a custom bookmark label, place this meta tag in the head of your web pages:

```
<meta name="apple-mobile-web-app-
title" content="TITLE HERE">
```

In place of TITLE HERE, set the bookmark label to your own text, making sure to restrict the title to 12 characters. Additional characters past the 12-character limit are ignored.

LOTS OF CODE   If this looks like a lot of code, remember that you don't need to cite all the references in the HTML as long as you can deposit the image files in the root folder of your website.

Inserting Icons as Mobile Bookmarks

As with the favicons, placing mobile bookmark files in the root folder of your website is all you should need to do (**FIGURE 9.11**).

However, if you're publishing through a third-party software system, you may not be able to upload the mobile bookmark icons to the root folder. To get around this, you can mirror the favicon approach and use the **link** element to instruct the mobile browser to pull in the right icon for the right device. To add a bookmark icon for high-resolution display iPads, use this line:

```
<link rel="apple-touch-icon-precomposed"
sizes="144x144"
href="apple-touch-icon-144x144-precomposed.png" />
```

To add a bookmark icon for high-resolution display iPhones, use this line:

```
<link rel="apple-touch-icon-precomposed"
sizes="114x114"
href="apple-touch-icon-114x114-precomposed.png" />
```

To add a bookmark icon for first- and second-generation iPads, use this line:

```
<link rel="apple-touch-icon-precomposed"
sizes="72x72"
href="apple-touch-icon-72x72-precomposed.png" />
```

To add a bookmark icon at a smaller size, use this line:

```
<link rel="apple-touch-icon-precomposed"
href="apple-touch-icon-precomposed.png" />
```

To ensure backward compatibility with older devices, insert the largest icon first in the order. The system will scan down the list until it finds the larges size it can handle. The general rule is to cite the largest icon first and work down to the smallest.

COMBINING FAVICONS AND MOBILE BOOKMARKS

Once you have your favicons and mobile iOS bookmark icons ready, you can set them using the following lines of code (**FIGURE 9.12**):

```
<head>
    <link rel="apple-touch-icon-precomposed" sizes="144x144"
href="apple-touch-icon-144x144-precomposed.png" />
    <link rel="apple-touch-icon-precomposed" sizes="114x114"
href="apple-touch-icon-114x114-precomposed.png" />
    <link rel="apple-touch-icon-precomposed" sizes="72x72"
href="apple-touch-icon-72x72-precomposed.png" />
    <link rel="apple-touch-icon-precomposed"
href="apple-touch-icon-precomposed.png" />
    <link rel="shortcut icon" href="/assets/img/favicon.ico" />
    <title>My Website</title>
</head>
```

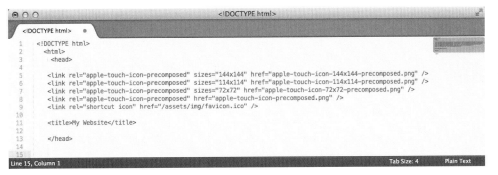

FIGURE 9.12 *Add mobile bookmark code in the head section to support different combinations of iOS and Apple devices.*

IN CONCLUSION

And with that, you've successfully set up brand-extending icons for your site! Web design is usually thought of as existing on the web, but our icons and bookmark graphics can extend to the desktop and home screen.

In the next chapter we'll look at more ways to use icons and other small vector graphics.

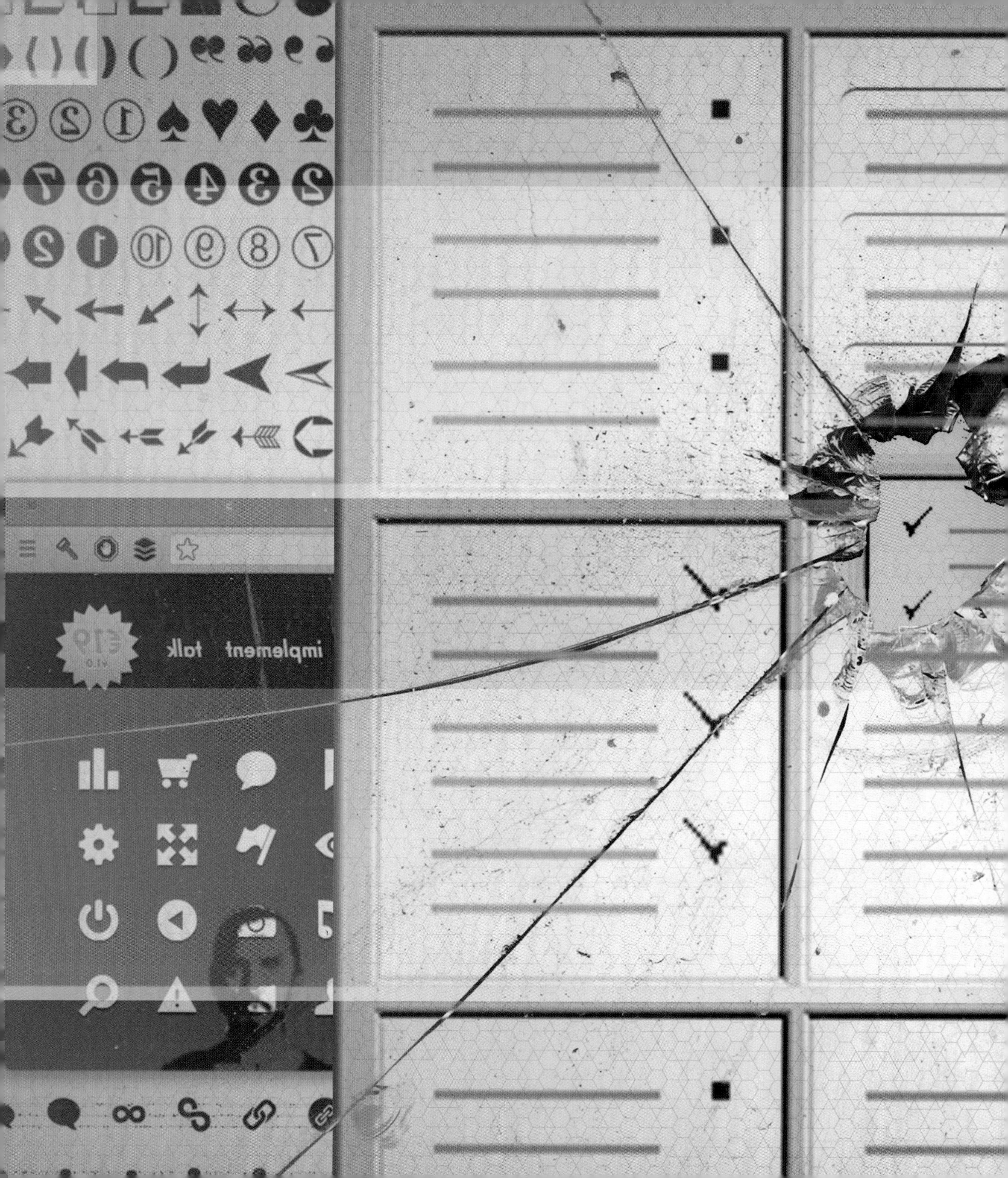
implement
talk

Chapter **10**

LISTS AND ICON FONTS

People seldom read the web. Studies have found that people skim. Visitors to your website are experts at scoping out a web page. Their eyes dart from one corner to another looking for words and high-contrast imagery to determine if they're in the right place. They look for what user experience researcher Jared Spool calls "the scent of information."

To aid their hunt, it's good to create bullet points and icons of key messages on your web page. In this chapter, we look at how to craft lists and incorporate icons for both web and mobile delivery.

List of Public Domain Movies

The following is a list of movies in the public domain due to the owners failing to renew their copyright.

- List item

Public domain allows for free movie watching. Or just watch movies on Netflix.

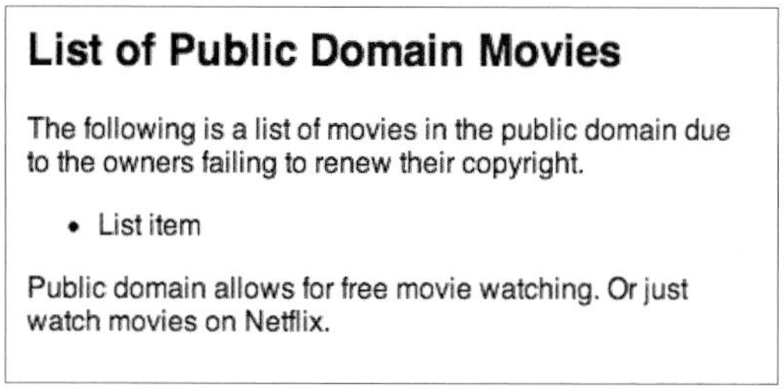

FIGURE 10.1 *The beginnings of a very basic unordered list, ready for more bullet points.*

List of Public Domain Movies

The following is a list of movies in the public domain due to the owners failing to renew their copyright.

- *A Farewell to Arms* (1932)
- *Go for Broke!* (1951)
- *His Girl Friday* (1940)
- *The Hunchback of Notre Dame* (1923)
- *The Little Princess* (1939)
- *The Little Shop of Horrors* (1960)

Public domain allows for free movie watching. Or just watch movies on Netflix.

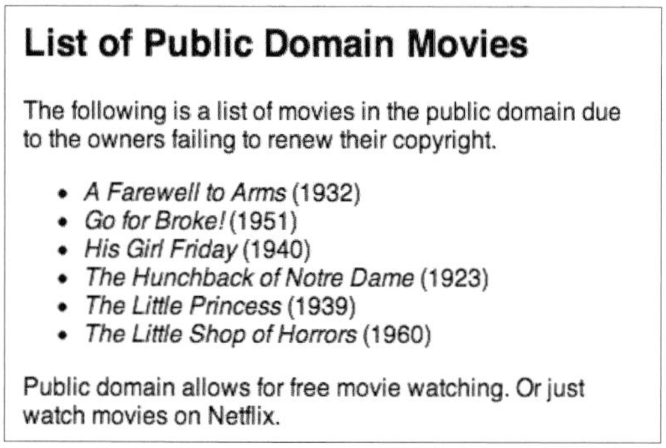

FIGURE 10.2 *An expanded unordered list using the default disc bullet.*

List of Public Domain Movies

The following is a list of movies in the public domain due to the owners failing to renew their copyright.

- *A Farewell to Arms* (1932)
- *Go for Broke!* (1951)
- *His Girl Friday* (1940)
- *The Hunchback of Notre Dame* (1923)
- *The Little Princess* (1939)
- *The Little Shop of Horrors* (1960)

Public domain allows for free movie watching. Or just watch movies on Netflix.

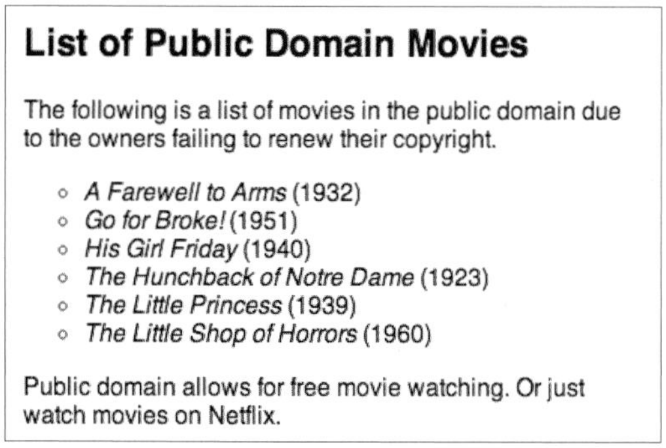

FIGURE 10.3 *Circles can be used in place of discs for list items.*

UNORDERED LISTS

To type up a bullet list in HTML, use the unordered list element. The list is wrapped in a **ul** element and each list item gets an **li** tag (**FIGURE 10.1**):

```
<ul>
 <li>List item</li>
</ul>
```

Combined with content, an unordered list coded properly is fairly easy to expand (**FIGURE 10.2**):

```
<ul>
  <li><em>A Farewell to Arms</em> (1932)</li>
  <li><em>Go for Broke!</em> (1951)</li>
  <li><em>His Girl Friday</em> (1940)</li>
  <li><em>The Hunchback of Notre Dame</em> (1923)</li>
  <li><em>The Little Princess</em> (1939)</li>
  <li><em>The Little Shop of Horrors</em> (1960) </li>
</ul>
```

CSS List Icons

The default bullet marker is a **disc**, which is usually displayed as a solid circle (Figure 10.2). Other bullet options include **circle** and **square**. Throughout this chapter we'll refer to the bullets, numbers, or graphics next to the list items as markers.

To change the browser rendering of the list item bullet to circle, use the **list-style-type** property (**FIGURE 10.3**):

```
ul li {
  list-style-type: circle;
}
```

For a square bullet, use the **list-style-type** property (**FIGURE 10.4**):

```
ul li {
  list-style-type: square;
}
```

List of Public Domain Movies

The following is a list of movies in the public domain due to the owners failing to renew their copyright.

- *A Farewell to Arms* (1932)
- *Go for Broke!* (1951)
- *His Girl Friday* (1940)
- *The Hunchback of Notre Dame* (1923)
- *The Little Princess* (1939)
- *The Little Shop of Horrors* (1960)

Public domain allows for free movie watching. Or just watch movies on Netflix.

FIGURE 10.4 *Using square bullets for list items.*

List of Public Domain Movies

The following is a list of movies in the public domain due to the owners failing to renew their copyright.

- *A Farewell to Arms* (1932)
- *Go for Broke!* (1951)
- *His Girl Friday* (1940)
- *The Hunchback of Notre Dame* (1923)
- *The Little Princess* (1939)
- *The Little Shop of Horrors* (1960)

Public domain allows for free movie watching. Or just watch movies on Netflix.

FIGURE 10.5 *Pulling in a custom graphic for the bullet point.*

Inserting Custom Icons

CSS provides a way to overwrite the default marker icons for lists through the **list-style-image** property. This method lets us use our own bullet icons in place of the default bullets (**FIGURE 10.5**):

```
ul li {
  list-style-image: url(bullet-icon.gif);
}
```

This assumes that the image is in the same directory as the CSS file. If not, you must include the path from the CSS file to the graphic as discussed in Chapter 1, "Understanding HTML." While this method allows easy placement of bullet points, it requires some vigilance. There are no CSS methods to control the size of the bullet point. So, the sizing of the bullet needs to be done in digital imaging software. For example, if a bullet point is rather large it forces the list items further down (**FIGURE 10.6**):

```
ul li {
  list-style-image: url(bullet-icon-xxl.gif);
}
```

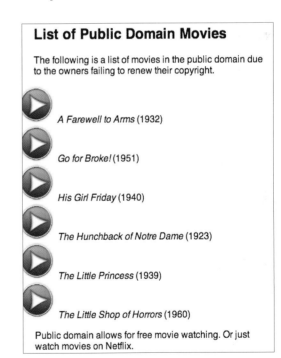

FIGURE 10.6 *There is lack of control when large icons are introduced through the* **list-style-image** *property.*

List of Public Domain Movies

The following is a list of movies in the public domain due to the owners failing to renew their copyright.

A Farewell to Arms (1932)
    The film won two Academy Awards.
Go for Broke! (1951)
    The story and screenplay by Robert Pirosh were nominated for an Academy Award in 1951.
His Girl Friday (1940)
    The film was #19 on *American Film Institute's 100 Years 100 Laughs* list.
The Hunchback of Notre Dame (1923)
    Known for its sets that reflected 15th century Paris.
The Little Princess (1939)
    A film that's about 91 minutes long.
The Little Shop of Horrors (1960)
    Shot on a budget of $30,000 in two days utilizing pre-built sets.

Public domain allows for free movie watching. Or just watch movies on Netflix.

FIGURE 10.7 *An example of a definition list used to add comments to list items.*

Where was the photo on the cover of *How To Dismantle An Atomic Bomb* taken?

In Portugal, during a photo shoot with Anton Corbijn in late April / early May of 2004.

What font is used on the *How To Dismantle An Atomic Bomb* album cover and on other tour logos and merchandise?

Clarendon (Light)

FIGURE 10.8 *Example of using a definition list as a way to code questions and answers.*

DEFINITION LISTS

Definition lists display two pieces of information: a keyword or phrase and an explanation of the meaning or, well, definition of that keyword. The dt (definition term) and dd (definition description) structure is often used to create a list of items with a comment—not necessarily a definition—for each. The definition list is wrapped in a **dl** element. Then each term and explanation are listed in **dt** and **dd** tags, respectively (**FIGURE 10.7**):

```
<dl>
   <dt><em>A Farewell to Arms</em> (1932)</dt>
    <dd>The film won two Academy Awards.</dd>
   <dt><em>Go for Broke!</em> (1951)</dt>
    <dd>The story and screenplay by Robert Pirosh were
nominated for an Academy Award in 1951.</dd>
   <dt><em>His Girl Friday</em> (1940)</dt>
    <dd>The film was #19 on <em>American Film
Institute's 100 Years 100 Laughs</em> list.</dd>
   <dt><em>The Hunchback of Notre Dame</em> (1923) </dt>
    <dd>Known for its sets that reflected 15th century
Paris.</dd>
   <dt><em>The Little Princess</em> (1939)</span></dt>
    <dd>A film that's about 91 minutes long.</dd>
   <dt><em>The Little Shop of Horrors</em> (1960) </dt>
    <dd>Shot on a budget of $30,000 in two days
utilizing pre-built sets.</dd>
</dl>
```

Because of the pairing of keyword/definition elements and the semantic power of the list, web builders have used definition lists as building blocks for Frequently Asked Questions (FAQs). Mark up questions with the **dt** element and answers with the **dd** element (**FIGURE 10.8**):

```
<dl>
   <dt>Where was the photo on the cover of <em>How to
Dismantle an Atomic Bomb</em> taken?</dt>
    <dd>In Portugal, during a photo shoot with Anton
Corbijn in late April / early May of 2004.</dd>
   <dt>What font is used on the <em>How to Dismantle an
Atomic Bomb</em> album cover and on other tour logos and
merchandise?</dt>
    <dd>Clarendon (Light)</dd>
</dl>
```

ORDERED LISTS

To number list items, use the **ol** tag. The browser auto-matically appends a number sequentially in place of a bullet. This time the entire list is wrapped in **ol** with the usual **li** tag for each item (**FIGURE 10.9**):

```
<h3>Introduction to the world of web
standards</h3>
<ol>
  <li><a href="http://dev.opera.com/articles/
view/2-the-history-of-the-internet-and-the-w/"
title="web history article">The history of the
Internet and the web, and the evolution of web
standards</a>, by Mark Norman Francis. </li>
  <li><a href="http://dev.opera.com/articles/
view/3-how-does-the-internet-work/" title="how
does the internet work explanation">How does
the internet work?</a>, by Jonathan Lane.</li>
  <li><a href="http://dev.opera.com/articles/
view/4-the-web-standards-model-html-css-a/"
title="web standards intro article">The Web
standards model—HTML, CSS and JavaScript</a>,
by Jonathan Lane</li>
  <li><a href="http://dev.opera.com/articles/
view/5-web-standards-beautiful-dream-bu/"
title="web standards reality">Beautiful dream,
but what's the reality?</a>, by Jonathan
Lane.</li>
</ol>
```

Introduction to the world of web standards

1. The history of the Internet and the web, and the evolution of web standards, by Mark Norman Francis.
2. How does the internet work?, by Jonathan Lane.
3. The Web standards model—HTML, CSS and JavaScript, by Jonathan Lane
4. Beautiful dream, but what's the reality?, by Jonathan Lane.

FIGURE 10.9 *An example of an ordered list.*

Changing the Order

For ordered lists, the browser automatically starts the numbering sequence with the number one. What if we want to start with a different value? To do that, add the **start** attribute to the **ol** tag with the numerical value you want the list to start with (**FIGURE 10.10**):

```
<h3>The beginning</h3>
<ol>
  <li><a href="http://dev.opera.com/articles/
view/1-introduction-to-the-web-standards-
cur/">Introductory material</a>, by Chris
Mills</li>
</ol>
<h3>Introduction to the world of web
standards</h3>
  <ol start="2">
  <li><a href="http://dev.opera.com/articles/
view/2-the-history-of-the-internet-and-the-w/"
title="web history article">The history of the
Internet and the web, and the evolution of web
standards</a>, by Mark Norman Francis. </li>
  ...
</ol>
```

The Web Standards Curriculum Table of Contents
The beginning

1. Introductory material, by Chris Mills

Introduction to the world of web standards

2. The history of the Internet and the web, and the evolution of web standards, by Mark Norman Francis.
3. How does the internet work?, by Jonathan Lane.
4. The Web standards model—HTML, CSS and JavaScript, by Jonathan Lane
5. Beautiful dream, but what's the reality?, by Jonathan Lane.

FIGURE 10.10 *Beginning an ordered list with a specific numeral.*

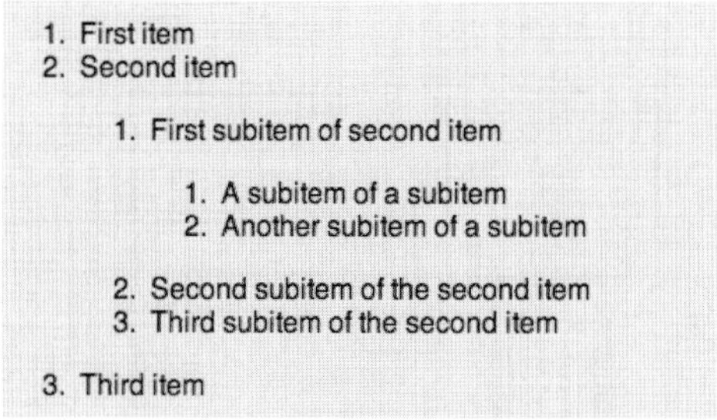

FIGURE 10.11 *An example of nested ordered lists.*

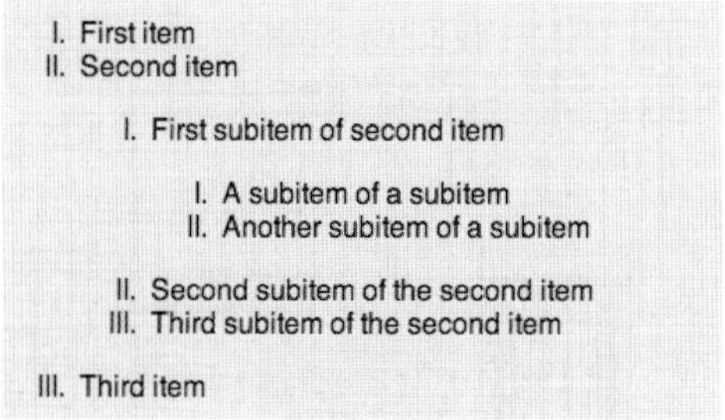

FIGURE 10.12 *Changing the markers to Roman numerals.*

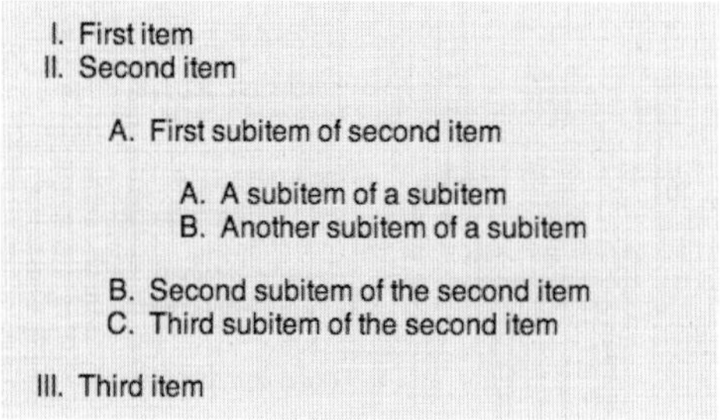

FIGURE 10.13 *Modifying the markers of nested ordered lists.*

Setting up a Table of Contents

Taking ordered lists one step further, we can create a detailed table of contents. The first step is to create nested lists that reflect the table of contents (**FIGURE 10.11**):

```
<ol>
  <li>First item</li>
  <li>Second item
  <ol>
    <li>First subitem of second item
    <ol>
      <li>A subitem of a subitem</li>
      <li>Another subitem of a subitem</li>
    </ol>
    </li>
    <li>Second subitem of the second item</li>
    <li>Third subitem of the second item</li>
  </ol>
  </li>
  <li>Third item</li>
</ol>
```

Next, set a style for using upper case Roman numerals for the list markers (**FIGURE 10.12**):

```
ol li {
  list-style-type: upper-roman;
}
```

Remember from Chapter 2, "Styling with CSS," that descendant selectors match an element that is an immediate sibling, in other words, a nested element like **ol** that is one level deep! That simplifies writing a CSS rule to specify the next level of ordered list items. To differentiate from the first level, set the markers to appear as uppercase letters (**FIGURE 10.13**):

```
ol li {
  list-style-type: upper-roman;
}
ol > ol li {
  list-style-type: upper-alpha;
}
```

Continuing to the next or third level of list elements is also easy. In this level, set the markers to be lowercase roman numerals by setting the value to **lower-roman** (**FIGURE 10.14**):

```
ol li {
  list-style-type: upper-roman;
}
ol > ol li {
  list-style-type: upper-alpha;
}
ol > ol > ol li {
  list-style-type: lower-roman;
}
```

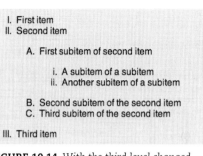

FIGURE 10.14 *With the third level changed, this now appears as a proper outline or table of contents.*

Another Way to Add List Markers

Using the methods discussed so far, the approach to adding ordered lists is fairly straightforward. There's another way to add markers to lists: the CSS **counter-increment** property.

To start, assign a reset counter to the element to which you want to apply the marker. The content renders normally since we haven't told the browser to adjust the default markers yet as shown in **FIGURE 10.15**.

```
ol {
  counter-reset: li;
}
```

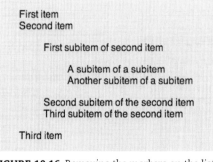

FIGURE 10.15 *Starting with the default rendering of nested ordered lists.*

Next, we need to remove the automatic numbering the browser appends to list items (**FIGURE 10.16**):

```
ol {
  counter-reset: li;
}
ol > li {
  list-style:none;
}
```

FIGURE 10.16 *Removing the markers on the list items.*

DEEP DIVE INTO COUNTERS For more information on counters, read the blog post at http://www.456bereastreet.com/archive/201105/styling_ordered_list_numbers/ by Roger Johansson.

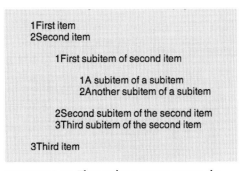

FIGURE 10.17 *The markers appear next to the list items.*

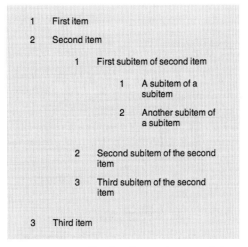

FIGURE 10.18 *Adjusting the spacing around the list items and markers.*

Then using the **content** generation property through the **:before** pseudo property, we can tell the browser to count the number of **li** elements. When the browser finds a new **li** element, it increments the number as shown in **FIGURE 10.17**:

```
ol {
  counter-reset: li;
}
ol > li {
  list-style:none;
}
ol > li:before {
  content:counter(li);
  counter-increment:li;
}
```

Adding a few CSS rules to move the list items to the right and adjust the markers to the left, we can give the text some breathing room (**FIGURE 10.18**):

```
ol {
  counter-reset: li;
}
ol > li {
  list-style:none;
  position: relative;
  margin: 0 0 6px 2em;
  padding: 4px 8px;
}
ol > li:before {
  content:counter(li);
  counter-increment:li;
  position:absolute;
  left:-2em;
}
```

EFFECTIVE LIST DESIGN

Why would we want to add CSS on top of HTML's default **ul** or **ol** tags? The main thing is that CSS allows greater design control of the markers than HTML.

For example, taking what has been built so far, place a border and background on the list items to create a banner (**FIGURE 10.19**):

```
ol {
  counter-reset: li;
}
ol > li {
 list-style:none;
 position: relative;
 margin: 0 0 6px 2em;
 padding: 4px 8px;
 border-top: 2px solid #666;
 background: #f6f6f6;
}
ol > li:before {
 content:counter(li);
 counter-increment:li;
 position:absolute;
 left:-2em;
}
```

Then extend the border at the top of the list item (**FIGURE 10.20**):

```
ol {
  counter-reset: li;
}
ol > li {
 list-style:none;
 position: relative;
 margin: 0 0 6px 2em;
 padding: 4px 8px;
 border-top: 2px solid #666;
 background: #f6f6f6;
}
ol > li:before {
 content:counter(li);
 counter-increment:li;
 position:absolute;
 left: -2em;
 top: -2px;
 width: 2em;
 margin-right: 8px;
 padding: 4px;
 border-top: 2px solid #666;
}
```

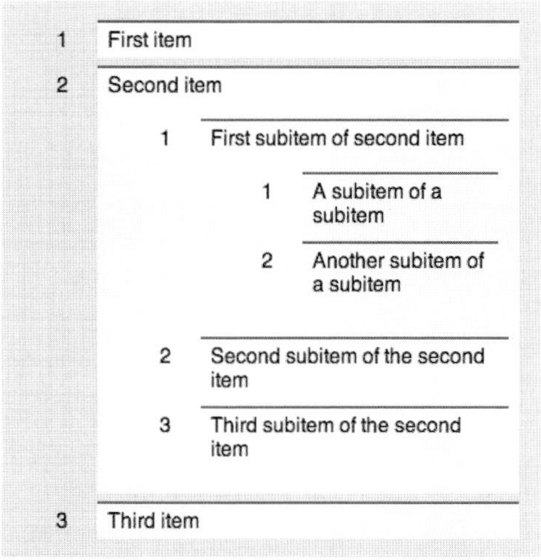

FIGURE 10.19 *Placing banners on the list items.*

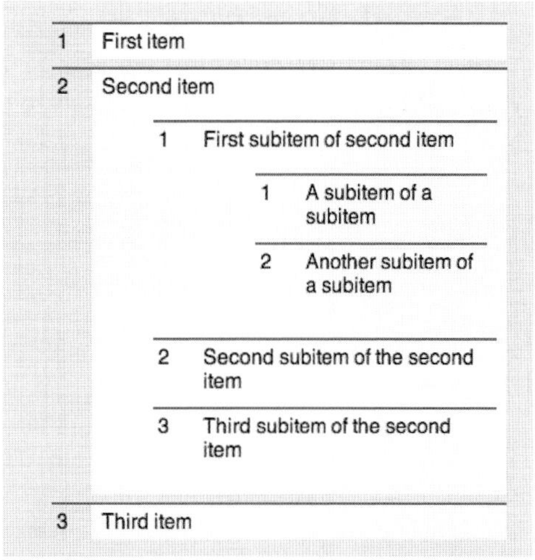

FIGURE 10.20 *Extending the border to the markers.*

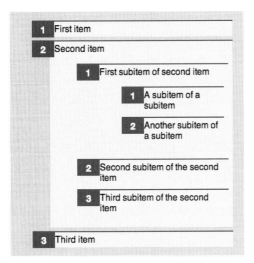

FIGURE 10.21 *Inverting the color of the list markers.*

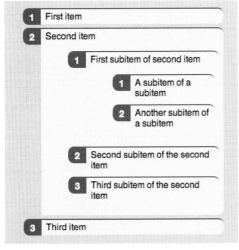

FIGURE 10.22 *Rounding the corners of the list items and markers.*

Center the markers and give them a bolder presence through typography (**FIGURE 10.21**):

```
ol {
  counter-reset: li;
}
ol > li {
  list-style:none;
  position: relative;
  margin: 0 0 6px 2em;
  padding: 4px 8px;
  border-top: 2px solid #666;
  background: #f6f6f6;
}
ol > li:before {
  content:counter(li);
  counter-increment:li;
  position:absolute;
  left: -2em;
  top: -2px;
  width: 2em;
  margin-right: 8px;
  padding: 4px;
  border-top: 2px solid #666;
  color: #fff;
  background: #666;
  font-weight: bold;
  font-family: "Helvetica Neue", Arial, sans-serif;
  text-align: center;
}
```

Next, round off the corners of each element. Whereas **border-radius** lets us apply one set of values to all four corners of one element, we have to deal with two elements. Since there are two elements—the marker and the list item—we need to specifically round the right corners of the list item and the left corners of the marker (**FIGURE 10.22**):

```
ol {
  counter-reset: li;
}
ol > li {
  list-style:none;
  position: relative;
  margin: 0 0 6px 2em;
```

```
  padding: 4px 8px;
  border-top: 2px solid #666;
  background: #f6f6f6;
  border-top-right-radius: 10px;
  border-bottom-right-radius: 10px;
}
ol > li:before {
  content:counter(li);
  counter-increment:li;
  position:absolute;
  left: -2em;
  top: -2px;
  width: 2em;
  margin-right: 8px;
  padding: 4px;
  border-top: 2px solid #666;
  color: #fff;
  background: #666;
  font-weight: bold;
  font-family: "Helvetica Neue", Arial, sans-serif;
  text-align: center;
  box-sizing:border-box;
  border-top-left-radius: 10px;
  border-bottom-left-radius: 10px;
}
```

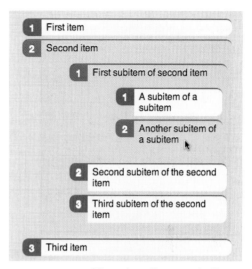

FIGURE 10.23 *Adding color rollovers to the list items.*

Then we can create a little hover effect for when the user rolls the mouse over a list item (**FIGURE 10.23**):

```
ol li:hover {
  background: rgba(255,204,204,.33);
  text-shadow: 0 -1px white;
}

ol li:hover:before {
  background: #fcc;
  text-shadow: 0 -1px grey;
}
```

Of course, this approach to designing lists isn't reserved for ordered lists. Try using it on unordered lists, a series of images, or wherever you have a number of similar elements in a row.

ICON FONTS

Another way to bring icons into a list is to use an icon or dingbat font, which uses ornaments or special shapes in place of alphanumeric characters. Dingbat fonts range from the classic Zapf Dingbats font designed in 1978 (**FIGURE 10.24**) to a fan-made Superman font (**FIGURE 10.25**).

FIGURE 10.24 *Characters from the Zapf Dingbats typeface.*

FIGURE 10.25 *Marks from a fan-made Superman dingbat font.*

COMMERCIAL ICON FONTS

- Fico (US $30, 52 characters)
  http://fico.lensco.be/
- Tipogram (US $18, 90 characters)
  http://css-tricks.com/flat-icons-icon-fonts/
- CleanIcons (US $10, 57 characters)
  http://cleanicons.com/
- ClickBits (US $12–49, 390+)
  http://www.fonthead.com/fonts/ClickBits
- IcoMoon (US $35, 500+ characters)
  http://keyamoon.com/icomoon/#toHome
- Pictos (US $19–249, 600+ characters)
  http://pictos.cc/
- iconSweets2 (US $8, 1,000+ characters)
  http://iconsweets2.com/

FREE ICON FONTS

- Foundation Icons (47+ characters)
  http://www.zurb.com/playground/
  foundation-icons
- Ecqlipse 2 (116 system; 165 app dock icons)
  http://chrfb.deviantart.com/art/
  quot-ecqlipse-2-quot-PNG-59941546
- Heydings Icons (60 characters)
  http://www.heydonworks.com/
  a-free-icon-web-font
- PulsarJS (73 characters)
  http://xperiments.es/blog/en/
  free-pulsarjs-fontface-iconfont/
- Entypo (100+ characters)
  http://www.entypo.com/
- Raphaël (110+ characters)
  http://icons.marekventur.de/
- Erler Dingbats (110+ characters)
  http://www.ffdingbatsfont.com/erler/index.html
- Font Awesome (150+ characters)
  http://fortawesome.github.com/Font-Awesome/

Selecting an Icon Font

To start, find and download one of the many icon fonts available on the web (**FIGURE 10.26**). With so many to choose from, there will undoubtedly be one that fits your budget and design sensibilities.

> **! FONT SIZE WARNING**
>
> Font files are notoriously large due to the fact that they contain a lot of information for each character. If you include an entire typeface, the file size for the typeface by itself can outweigh the HTML and probably most images for a web page.
>
> To keep files snappy, be sure to use gzipping as discussed in Chapter 4, "Challenges in Web Design."

FIGURE 10.26 *Entypo, Pictos, and Fico are a few of the icon fonts available on the web.*

Highlighting a Word or Phrase

This example draws attention to a specific heading on a website.

TO ENHANCE A HEADING WITH AN ICON, FOLLOW THESE ⑦ STEPS:

① To start using icon fonts, first download an icon font to your computer and store it with your web page's other assets, such as images and CSS files. In this example, we use the Pictos typeface.

```
@font-face {
  font-family: 'Pictos';
  src: url('/fonts/pictos-web.eot?#iefix')
format('embedded-opentype'),
  url('/fonts/pictos-web.woff') format('woff'),
  url('/fonts/pictos-web.ttf')
format('truetype'),
  url('/fonts/pictos-web.svg#PictosWeb')
format('svg');
  font-weight: normal;
  font-style: normal;
}
```

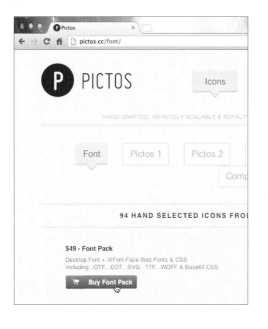

② Follow the steps discussed in Chapter 3, "Web Typography," for embedding a web font into a web page. This step brings the icons as an asset to be pulled through CSS and HTML in the next steps.

```
<h2>
 <span></span>
 Links <span class="preposition">of</span>
Interest
</h2>
```

③ To add flair to a word or the start of the heading, add an empty span element before the word or heading text.

```
<h2>
 <span data-icon="l"></span>
 Links <span class="preposition">of</span>
Interest
</h2>
```

Links *of* **Interest**

④ Insert a **data-icon** attribute set to the character of the icon. In this example, the list item icon is set to the lowercase letter l.

```
<h2>
 <span data-icon="l" aria-hidden="true"></span>
 Links <span class="preposition">of</span>
Interest
</h2>
```

⑤ Add an **aria-hidden** attribute to the span tag. This keeps screen readers from reading out the character l.

```
[data-icon]:before {
  font-family: 'Pictos';
  content: attr(data-icon);
  -webkit-font-smoothing: antialiased;
}
```

6 Using an attribute selector combined with a **:before** pseudo selector to pick out the HTML element with the icon information, instruct the browser to use the Pictos family font, and the letter from that is listed as the data-icon attribute's value.

```
[data-icon]:before {
 font-family: 'Pictos';
 content: attr(data-icon);
 -webkit-font-smoothing: antialiased;
 font-weight: normal;
 font-size: 1.4em;
 text-shadow: white 0px 2px 0px;
 color:  #0cc;
 padding-right: .25em;
}
```

≡ **Links** *of* **Interest**

7 Adjust the CSS rules to create a visual style that suits your taste.

≡ **Links** *of* **Interest**

ICON FONTS AND RETINA   Another advantage of using icon fonts is that they're vector-based, so they work great on both regular and retina or high-definition displays and monitors. For more information on retina and images, see Chapter 13, "Images for Responsive Web Design."

Making a Stand-alone Link Icon

To make an icon clickable and introduce an icon font, we follow similar steps as we did with the heading by embedding the Pictos font into the web page (see Chapter 3, "Web Typography").

```
<a href="play.html"
 Play
</a>
```

TO MAKE ICONS CLICKABLE, FOLLOW THESE ⑦ STEPS:

1 Start with a basic HTML link.

```
<a href="play.html"
 <span data-icon="9"></span>
 Play
</a>
```

Play

2 Add a **span** attribute that includes the **data-icon** attribute. Inside the value of the **data-icon** attribute, place the corresponding letter for the icon you want.

```
<a href="play.html"
 <span aria-hidden="true" data-icon="9"></span>
 Play
</a>
```

▷ Play

③ Add the **aria-hidden** attribute to keep screen readers from reading that letter.

```
<a href="play.html"
 <span aria-hidden="true" data-icon="9"></span>
 <span class="hidden">Play</span>
</a>
```

④ Wrap a span element with a special class attribute.

```
.hidden {
  position: absolute;
  top: -9999px;
  left: -9999px;
}
```

⑤ The purpose of the **span** attribute is to apply a CSS rule that keeps the text from being seen on the screen, but eligible to be read by screen readers.

```
[data-icon]:before {
font-family: 'Pictos';
  content: attr(data-icon);
  font-weight: normal;
  -webkit-font-smoothing: antialiased;
font-size: 2em;
text-shadow: white 0px 2px 0px;
color:  red;
padding-right: .25em;

}
```

SUPPORT FOR OLDER VERSIONS OF INTERNET EXPLORER

If you need to deliver icon fonts for browsers like IE7, use class attributes instead of the newer HTML5 **data-icon** attribute.

⑥ Use CSS rules to adjust the style of the font to your liking.

```
<a href="#" class="icon alone">
 <span aria-hidden="true" data-icon="8"></span>
 <span class="hidden">Rewind</span>
</a>
<a href="#" class="icon alone">
 <span aria-hidden="true" data-icon="6"></span>
 <span class="hidden">Stop</span>
</a>
<a href="#" class="icon alone">
 <span aria-hidden="true" data-icon="9"></span>
 <span class="hidden">Play</span>
</a>
```

⑦ Add additional icons.

Since icon fonts are based in typography, you can do to them whatever you can do with typography:

- Increase icon sizes with font-size property.
- Change color with the color property.
- Apply shadows with the text-shadow property.

IN CONCLUSION

In this chapter we looked at additional ways to help you catch your site visitor's eye. By using markers and icon fonts, you help people see the key messages of your content and drive them to dive deeper into your site. Next we'll learn a way to add multiple interactions to a single image with image maps.

Chapter **11**   IMAGE MAPS

Putting basic link tags around an image makes the entire image
a link. Alternatively, an *image map,* created by web pioneer Kevin
Hughes in 1993, allows for multiple links at predefined areas within
an image.

Back then, you had to use server-side programming to get image
maps to work. Eventually, though, the browser vendors programmed
the browser to handle the workload—as long as the HTML contained
a *map* that specified the coordinates of the links within the image.

Today, for simplicity and accessibility, server-side image maps are
the only ones still used.

MAKING IMAGE MAPS

The predefined areas of an image map are written up as a small piece of HTML that lets the browser know which regions of an image are clickable (**FIGURE 11.1**). The value of the **usemap** property of the image must correspond exactly to the map **ID**.

```
<map id="treasure_map" name="treasure_map">
 <area shape="rect" coords="186,139,217,170"
href="http://en.wikipedia.org/wiki/X_mark" />
</map>
<img usemap="#treasure_map" src="treasure_map.
png" alt="Treasure Map" />
```

While it's a bit time consuming, creating a basic image map is fairly straightforward and can be done with almost any digital imaging software application.

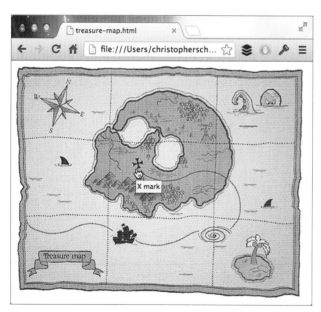

FIGURE 11.1 *An example of an image map.*

Basic Hand-coding

For this example, we'll use Photoshop's Info palette to help determine the coordinates of our hotspots.

TO CREATE AN IMAGE MAP, FOLLOW THESE ⑫ STEPS:

① Open the image in Adobe Photoshop.

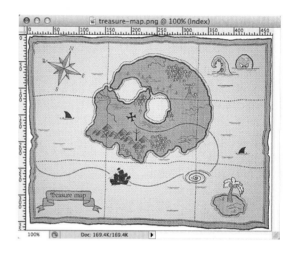

② Open the Info palette and locate the display of the x and y coordinates for the cursor.

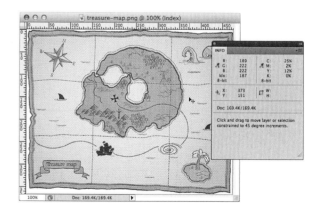

3 For square or rectangular hotspots, move the cursor to determine the upper-left position.

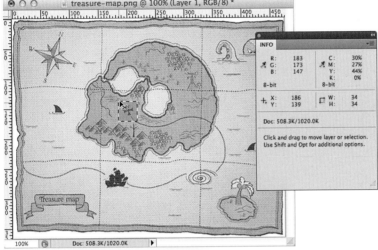

4 Make a note of the lower-right position.

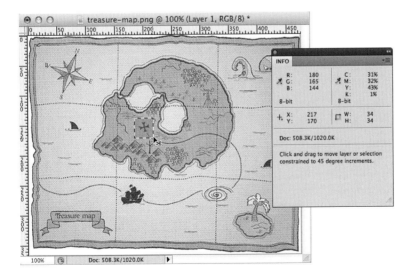

(5) Write the **map** element, using the **id** and **name** attributes:

```
<map id="treasure_map" name="treasure_map">
</map>
```

(6) Insert an **area** element with the **shape** attribute set to **rect** value. Add a **coords** attribute placing the upper-left pair first. So the sequence is: top-left x, top-left y, bottom-right x, bottom-right y. Be sure to also insert the URL to which this hotspot will link in using the usual **href** property:

```
<map id="treasure_map" name="treasure_map">
 <area shape="rect" coords="186,139,217,170" href="http://en.wikipedia.org/
wiki/X_mark" />
</map>
<img usemap="#treasure_map" src="treasure_map.png" alt="Treasure Map" />
```

(7) For circular hotspots, make note of the coordinates where you want the center point and what the radius (half the diameter) of your circle will be. Because the whirlpool on the map is about 102px across, the radius of this hotspot will be 51.

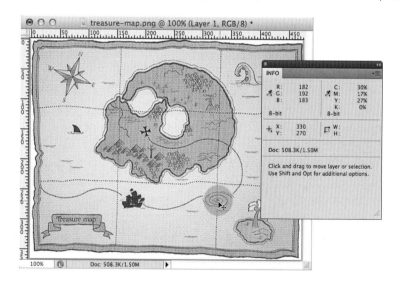

⑧ Insert HTML for a new area element inside the map element. Set the **shape** attribute to **circle** and add the coordinates as center x, center y, and radius, and then enter your link:

```
<map id="treasure_map" name="treasure_map">
 <area shape="rect" coords="186,139,217,170" href="http://en.wikipedia.org/
wiki/X_mark" />
  <area shape="circle" coords="330,270,51" href="http://en.wikipedia.org/wiki/
Whirlpool" />
</map>
<img usemap="#treasure_map" src="treasure_map.png" alt="Treasure Map" />
```

⑨ To create a complex shape like a polygon, use Photoshop's Info palette to determine each point.

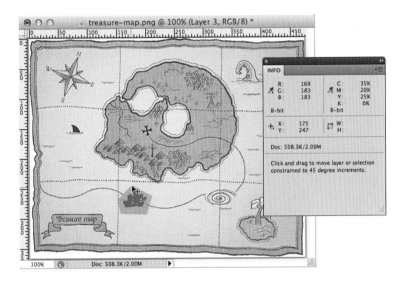

⑩ Add a new **area** element with the **shape** attribute set to **poly**. Insert each set of x,y coordinates in a clockwise fashion, and don't forget your link:

```
<map id="treasure_map" name="treasure_map">
 <area shape="rect" coords="186,139,217,170" href="http://en.wikipedia.org/
wiki/X_mark" alt="X mark" title="X mark" />
 <area shape="circle" coords="330,270,51" href="http://en.wikipedia.org/wiki/
Whirlpool" alt="whirlpool" title="whirlpool" /> <area shape="poly"
coords="175,247,212,266,201,294,156,293,151,272" href="http://en.wikipedia.
org/wiki/Pirate_ship_(ride)" />
</map>
<img usemap="#treasure_map" src="treasure_map.png" alt="Treasure Map" />
```

(11) Add **alt** and **title** attributes to each **area** tag for better accessibility and usability:

```
<map id="treasure_map" name="treasure_map">
 <area shape="rect" coords="186,139,217,170" href="http://en.wikipedia.org/
wiki/X_mark" alt="X mark" title="X mark" />
 <area shape="circle" coords="330,270,51" href="http://en.wikipedia.org/wiki/
Whirlpool" alt="whirlpool" title="whirlpool" />
 <area shape="poly" coords="175,247,212,266,201,294,156,293,151,272"
href="http://en.wikipedia.org/wiki/Pirate_ship_(ride)" alt="pirate ship"
title="pirate ship" />
</map>
<img usemap="#treasure_map" src="treasure_map.png" alt="Treasure Map" />
```

(12) Test the image map in the browser.

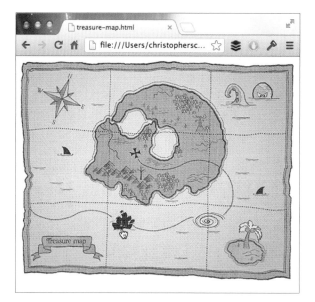

Using Fireworks

Coding up an image map by hand is a time-consuming task. Thankfully, software applications like Adobe Fireworks can speed up the process.

TO CREATE AN IMAGE MAP WITH ADOBE FIREWORKS, FOLLOW THESE ⑨ STEPS:

① Open your image in Adobe Fireworks.

② Select and hold the Polygon Hotspot tool. (Circle and Rectangle Hotspot tools are also available.)

(3) Click to set the key points that will define the area of the hotspot.

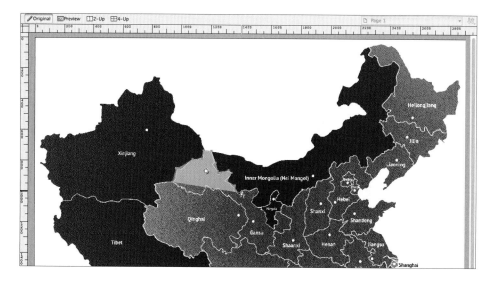

(4) After marking the hotspot, rename the sublayer to help you identify the hotspot in case you need to edit it later.

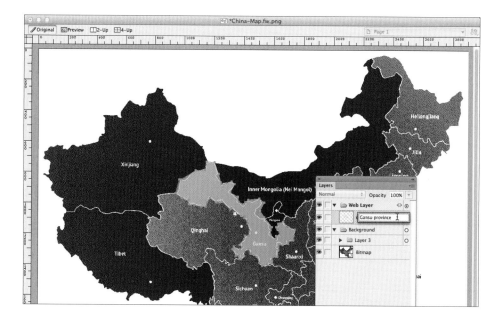

(5) If you need to refine the selection, use the pointer and subselection tools from the Tools palette.

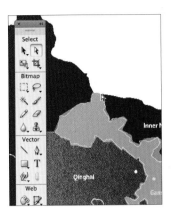

(6) Go to Windows > URL to open up the URL palette. For each hotspot, add the URL where users will be taken when they click. If the link is external, add **http://** to the beginning of the link.

(7) Add **alt** text to the link through the Properties palette.

⑧ To export the image, along with the HTML, select File > Export. (Make sure Export HTML File is selected next to the HTML option.) Here's the result. Aren't you glad you didn't do it by hand?

```
<img name="ChinaMap" src="China-Map.jpg" width="2901" height="2371"
id="ChinaMap" usemap="#m_ChinaMap" alt="" />
<map name="m_ChinaMap" id="m_ChinaMap">
<area shape="poly" coords="942,934,962,889,976,847,1086,782,1139,782,1150,
731,1198,737,1223,818,1243,863,1246,878,1319,855,1339,872,1311,925,1358,956,
1367,987,1401,1001,1432,973,1502,965,1536,993,1508,1046,1538,1088,1589,1150,
1578,1173,1578,1198,1609,1226,1617,1207,1637,1198,1640,1178,1626,1167,1617,
1150,1628,1131,1659,1114,1685,1148,1741,1167,1733,1207,1733,1235,1693,1243,
1696,1257,1657,1268,1628,1263,1628,1283,1628,1299,1626,1342,1592,1344,1586,
1364,1586,1384,1555,1395,1524,1403,1502,1384,1485,1342,1465,1333,1446,1325,
1432,1294,1401,1311,1403,1336,1378,1358,1364,1336,1347,1336,1322,1294,1333,
1277,1373,1294,1389,1283,1370,1266,1403,1226,1406,1209,1429,1207,1440,1178,
1423,1131,1420,1111,1401,1091,1401,1077,1381,1080,1313,1027,1308,1035,1254,
987,1235,990,1212,990,1176,959,1153,996,1142,1021,1117,1021,1069,1010,1032,
1007,1027,982,984,965,942,934" href="http://en.wikipedia.org/wiki/Gansu"
alt="" /></map>
```

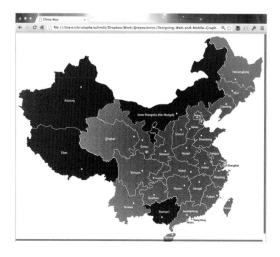

⑨ Load the exported HTML file in the browser to make sure all the hotspots work.

RESPONSIVE IMAGE MAPS

In modern web development, images need to be adaptive. An image that was once okay with fixed, pixel-based widths might need to be set with percentages or em units.

To work around that issue, we use a JavaScript through jQuery to power the changes in the hotspot. As the image resizes—shrinks or expands—we can use a jQuery plugin to check the dimensions of the image and then scale the coordinates as needed.

TO CREATE FLEXIBLE IMAGE MAPS, FOLLOW THESE ⑥ STEPS:

① So that the image adjusts to the width of the browser, set the **max-width** property to **100%**. (Using an attribute selector to work off the **usemap** attribute for image maps, we can have the CSS rule affect only images used for image maps.)

```css
img[usemap] {
  border: none;
  height: auto;
  max-width: 100%;
  width: auto;
}
```

② Include a reference to jQuery in the HTML file:

```html
<script src="http://code.jquery.com/jquery-latest.min.js "></script>
```

③ Download the Responsive Image Maps jQuery Plugin from the GitHub page at https://github.com/stowball/jQuery-rwdImageMaps.

④ Add a reference to the jQuery plugin below the jQuery file:

```html
<script src=" http://code.jquery.com/jquery-latest.min.js "></script>
<script src="jquery.rwdImageMaps.min.js"></script>
```

(5) Activate the plugin to work on any image with an image map:

```
<script src=" http://code.jquery.com/jquery-latest.min.js "></script>
<script src="jquery.rwdImageMaps.min.js"></script>
<script>
$(document).ready(function() {
 $('img[usemap]').rwdImageMaps();
});
</script>
```

(6) Resize the page in the browser or load the page in a smartphone or tablet and make sure it works.

IN CONCLUSION

Image maps are perfect for those situations when you want to display a map and ask people to pick a location visually. Image maps are also a great way to provide more information or interaction in a small amount of space. This is ideal when designing for mobile devices where real estate is less than ample. In the next chapter we'll look at laying out pages to make use of the various image formats we've learned about.

> "I'd been painting rats for three years
> before someone said, 'that's clever. It's
> an anagram of art,' and I had to pretend
> I'd known that all along."
>
> — *Banksy, Wall and Piece*

Chapter 12   LAYING OUT PAGES

For designers, the abundance of web access devices creates an abundance of opportunities for potentially awkward interpretations of our web pages.

Luckily, CSS floats, CSS frameworks, and responsive layouts enable us to separate the presentation of a web page (what it looks like) from the content (images and text). That's a good thing. When content and presentation are separated, web pages can be processed more easily and consistently by different browsers, mobile devices, and accessibility technologies. Using CSS for presentation can save a lot of time in production: website redesigns are simpler to roll out when you don't have to muck around in the HTML.

In this chapter, we look at ways to harness CSS to make attractive and functional layouts that work smoothly across platforms.

FIGURE 12.1 *The default rendering of an image in layout.*

FIGURE 12.2 *The same document, but this time we added a left float rule to the image element.*

FLOAT BEHAVIOR

The **float** property enables you to create fluid page layouts. You can use CSS to "float" any block-level element on a web page. The float property performs a deceptively simple task: it takes an element out of its normal flow to allow other content to flow—or wrap—around it. Despite its humble function, the **float** property can be used to create a number of impressive effects on a page, ranging from standard column design to floated navigation bars to image grids.

Float Property

Let's take a moment to explore how browsers render floats. The **float** property takes one of three values: left, right, or none.

When an element is floated, it's taken out of the document's normal flow and shifted as far to the left or right as it can go on the current line. Content that appears after the float wraps around the floated element.

To demonstrate the basic behavior of floats, let's float a simple image. Suppose we have the following markup:

```
<p>Lorem ipsum dolor sit amet...</p>
  <img src="tulips.jpg" alt="" />
<p>Pellentesque nec felis...</p>
```

By default the browser would render this as a block-level element, with a line break before and after the image (**FIGURE 12.1**).

In the CSS, we add a float property to the image rule, along with some padding to create a little space between the image and the wrapped text:

```
img {
float: left;
padding: 15px;
  }
```

Up until to the floated image, the document is rendered normally. Then, because of our CSS, the browser plucks the image out of normal flow and moves it all the way to the left on the current line. The text that follows it in the markup (**FIGURE 12.2**) wraps around the image.

Multiple Floats

But what happens if two floats appear consecutively in the markup? Suppose we have a series of small paragraphs, which we style like so:

```
p {
    float: left;
    width: 250px;
    background-color: #eee;
    margin: 10px;
}
```

Floats move as far to the right or left as possible on the current line, until they hit the edge of the containing element or run into another float. If the float can't fit on the current line, the floated element moves to the next line.

In this example, the first paragraph in the markup shifts all the way to the left edge of the containing element (**FIGURE 12.3**). The second paragraph shifts as far left as

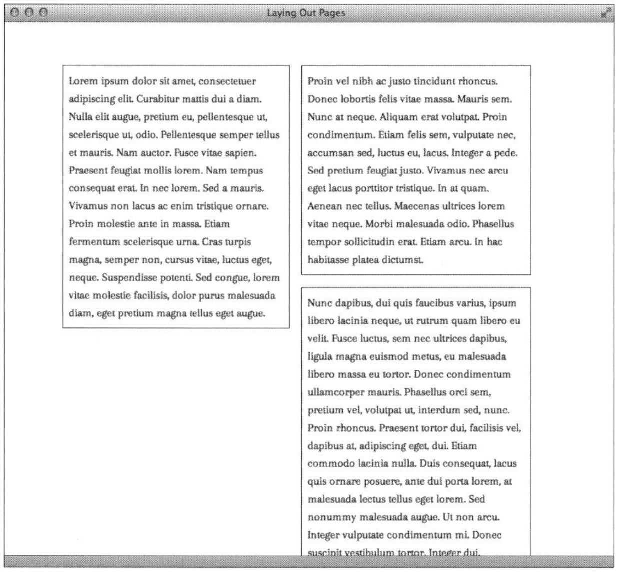

FIGURE 12.3 *A group of three paragraphs, each floated left. If you had a big enough monitor and expanded the window, all of the paragraphs would be on the same line and not wrap.*

possible on that same line—that is, it settles next to the previous floated paragraph.

This is true only if there is room within the containing element. If there is no room, it moves down line by line until there is enough space to fit. Here, the second paragraph can fit next to the first, while the remaining paragraph is forced onto the next line.

If the containing element is stretched—when the browser window is made larger—more floated paragraphs fit next to one another. Similarly, if the browser is made narrow, all the paragraphs stacked up one below the other.

This behavior lets you create page layouts that are **fluid**—layouts that make ideal use of the browser window width by including all and only those elements that fit within a horizontal space.

In order to be used for layout, *all floats need a defined width*. Some floated elements, like images, already have a particular width. For all other floated elements, you need to set the **width** property.

```
p {
    width: 250px;
}
```

Otherwise, your floats will behave unpredictably—depending on the browser, the floated element either takes up the entire width of the containing element, or becomes very, very tiny, shrinking to the width of a single character or word.

Clear Property

Floats are all very well, but sometimes you want to prevent content from wrapping around floated elements. To do this, add the **clear** property to a rule to prevent any elements from floating next to the element. Using **clear: right** stops anything from floating to the right of the element, while **clear: left** stops anything from floating to the left. Or, just use **clear: both** to prevent anything from floating on either side.

LAYING OUT PAGES WITH FLOATS

Controlling the layout of a page using CSS helps us distinguish between presentation and content. We can structure our content into logical sections within the HTML document, and then use CSS to manipulate the size, shape, and position of those sections in the browser window.

While floats were not originally intended to be building blocks for page layouts, they work very well for the task. As the floating paragraphs example shows, you can use floats to create columns of content. Floated elements can then be used to create two, three, or more columns in making up a page layout.

To explore constructing multicolumn layouts with floats, let's take a moment to create a properly structured web page.

Page Structure

To properly structure an HTML document, you want to divide your document into sections based on function: header, footer, navigation bar, and so on. Thankfully, we have HTML elements for most of these common divisions including header, footer, nav, and aside. (For more on HTML5, read Bruce Lawson and Remy Sharp's *Introducing HTML5*.)

Start a new HTML document now with the usual basic markup (**html**, **head**, **body**, and so on). Make sure you're up to date and using an HTML5 doctype. Within the body, we will use a mixture of **div**s and HTML5 elements to build up our page structure.

For this example, we're making a blog page with a header, navigation section, "about" section, and main section for our blog post. Notice the sections in the code below and take note of which sections are nested in others.

```
<!doctype html>
<html>
<head>
<meta charset="UTF-8">
<title>Untitled Document</title>
</head>

<header>
    <h1>you're soaking in it</h1>
</header>

<div id="sidebar">
    <nav>
        <div id="menu">
            <ul>
```

```
            <li><a href="/archives" id="archives">archives</a></li>
            <li><a href="/portfolio" id="portfolio">portfolio</a></li>
            <li><a href="/contact" id="contact">contact me</a></li>
            <li><a href="/colophon" id="colophon">colophon</a></li>
        </ul>
    </div>
</nav>

<div id="about">
    <img src="images/profile.jpg" alt="Mark" />
            [...]
        </p>
    </div><!--end about-->
</div><!--end sidebar-->

<div role="main">
    <h2>An Afternoon in Cummer Gardens</h2>
    <h3>September 2, 2012</h3>
            [...]
        </p>
</div><!--end main-->
```

With this structure in place, we can start styling our page by adding a basic CSS style sheet that tweaks the fonts, color, and other features of the body element. You can create your own basic styles for the body if you like. Here are mine:

```
body {
  font-family: Verdana, sans-serif;
  font-size: 76.5%;
  line-height: 1.5;
  color: #333;
}
```

Connect that document to the HTML file by creating an embedded style sheet within the HTML header and using the "import" at-rule to pull in the CSS file. You can see the result in **FIGURE 12.4**.

```
<head>
    [...]
    <style type="text/css">
        @import url("basic.css");
    </style>
</head>
```

CODE EXAMPLES

Note that the [...] you see in this and other code samples throughout the chapter stands for additional content within the **div**s.

When you're building a multiple page website that needs consistent styles across pages, remember that it's a good practice to keep your style sheets and HTML documents separate, so you can make site-wide changes quickly and easily by just changing the one CSS file.

Now that you've gotten a refresher on page structure and applying basic styles, and we've reviewed some fundamentals about normal flow and floats, we can put all of this together to create various layouts for this blog page using CSS. You'll note that some of these are *fluid* layouts and some are *fixed*. The differences will be apparent as we go through them, and then we'll return to the fixed versus fluid topic when we talk about responsive layouts.

Two-Column Fluid Layout

Let's apply some more CSS to turn this into a two-column fluid layout using floats (**FIGURE 12.5**). When a layout is fluid, the widths of the columns stretch and shrink according to the width of the containing element (usually the browser viewport). So, as the user resizes the browser window, the width of the columns make ideal use of the browser space. The disadvantage is that it gives you less control over layout.

FIGURE 12.5 *Our fluid two-column layout will look like this when we're through.*

Our HTML is mostly divided up as we need it into **div**s. Note how we've contained the **nav** element and "about" **div**—which make up the left-hand column—inside another **div** called "sidebar":

```
<div id="sidebar">
    <nav>
    [...]
    </nav><!--end nav-->
    <div id="about">
    [...]
    </div><!--end about-->
</div><!--end sidebar-->
```

Also, let's add a footer for good measure:

```
<footer>
    <p>&copy; Mark Schmedley. All Rights Reserved. | <a
href="mailto:markschmedley@example.com">Email Me</a></p>
</footer>
```

To turn this into two fluid columns, all you need to do is float the sidebar **div** to the left in the CSS, and set its width in percentages:

```
#sidebar {
    float: left;
    width: 27%;
    margin-top: 0;
    padding: 10px 15px;
}
```

We'll also add some padding to the **div**, providing some space on either side of the column. The "main" **div** needs little special treatment other than the desired margins, padding, and so on:

```
div[role="main"] {
    margin-top: 0;
    border-top: 0;
    padding: 15px;
}
```

This **div** just wraps around the floated main **div**. Since the content in this section is longer than the floated sidebar, we want to create the illusion of a proper column by adding a substantial margin to the left-hand side. That way, the text won't wrap around the sidebar (**FIGURE 12.6**).

```
div[role="main"] {
    margin-top: 0;
    margin-left: 31%;
    border-top: 0;
    padding: 15px;
}
```

Finally, you want to make sure that the footer appears below (not next to) the floated **div**. By using the **clear** property, we prevent anything from floating on either side of the footer (**FIGURE 12.7**).

```
footer {
 clear: both;
 width: 100%;
 padding: 5px 0 5px 5px;
}
```

One thing to keep in mind with this layout, as well as any layout created with floats, is that if the browser viewport is too narrow for the columns to fit, then one or more columns will move down below the preceding columns. This behavior may or may not be desired, but it is important to keep in mind when creating layouts with floats. You may not be able to ensure that all of the columns fit on a page, but you might want to size them so that they fit within certain standard browser window sizes.

FIGURE 12.6 *The two column layout is almost finished, but the footer is in the wrong place.*

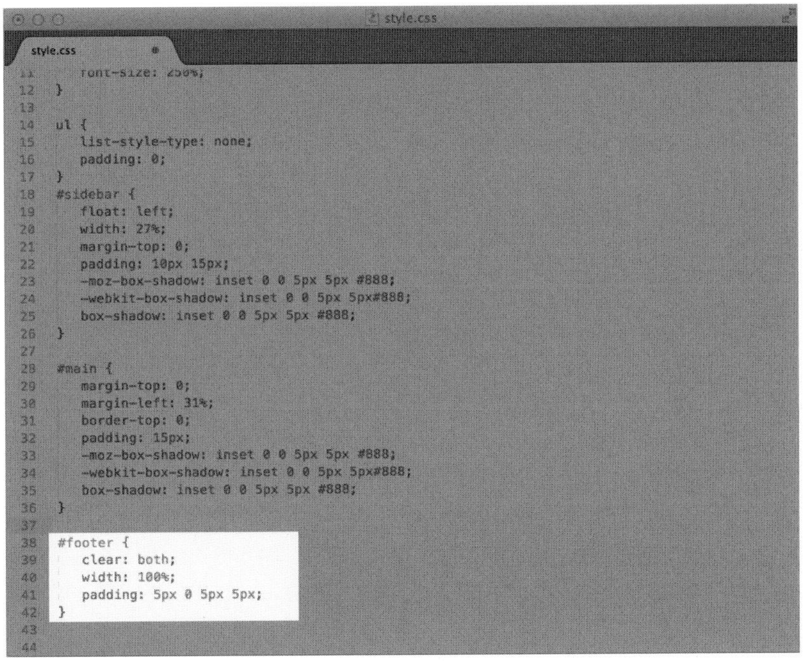

FIGURE 12.7 *Adding the CSS* **clear** *property to push the footer below the columns.*

FIGURE 12.8 *Two-column fixed layout.*

FIGURE 12.9 *Setting the boundary of the page.*

Two-Column Fixed Layout

Next, let's build a fixed two-column layout using floats. When a layout is fixed, the width of the columns is static—the columns remain the same size no matter what the size of the browser window. Fixed layouts give you more control over the way the page looks, but it may mean that not all of the content fits in a user's browser window, forcing the user to scroll horizontally to see the rest of the page.

When we're finished creating our fixed two-column layout, it will look like **FIGURE 12.8**.

Using the same approach to the HTML markup, we're going to start styling the page by applying a width to the body element (**FIGURE 12.9**).

```
body {
    width: 800px;
    margin: 20px 0 0 20px;
}
```

Then, we float the sidebar div to the left while applying a specific width in pixels (**FIGURE 12.10**).

```
#sidebar {
    float: left;
    width: 250px;
    margin-top: 0;
    padding: 10px 15px;
}
```

As in the fluid layout, we have to make sure to add a left-hand margin to the main **div** that's large enough to accommodate the sidebar column (so it doesn't wrap around the shorter navigation column). Our column is 250 pixels wide, so we'll set the margin to 290 pixels to add a bit of space between the columns:

```
div[role="main"] {
    margin-top: 0;
    margin-left: 290px;
    border-top: 0;
    padding: 15px;
}
```

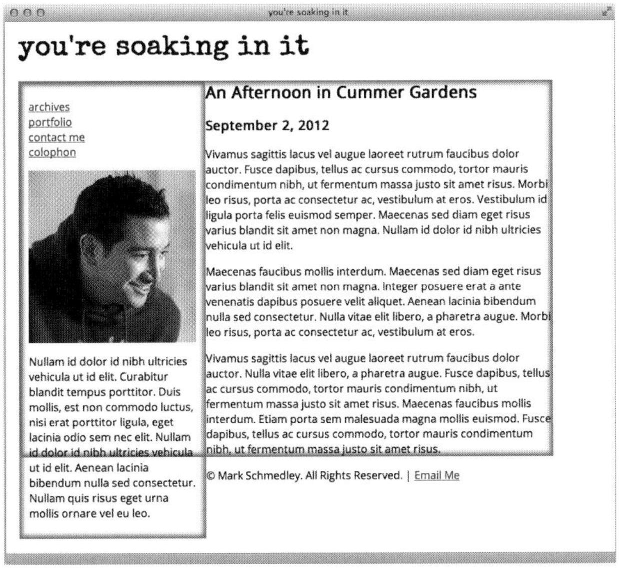

FIGURE 12.10 *Setting up the first column.*

Finally, like the last example we set the clear property of the **footer** to **both**:

```
footer  {
    clear: both;
    width: 100%;
    height: 30px;
    padding: 5px 0 10px 0;
}
```

Three-Column Fluid Layout

Next, we're going to make a fluid three-column layout using floats as shown in **FIGURE 12.11**. For this example, we'll separate the **nav** element and the "about" **div** into two separate columns, one on the left, and one on the right-hand side of the main **div**.

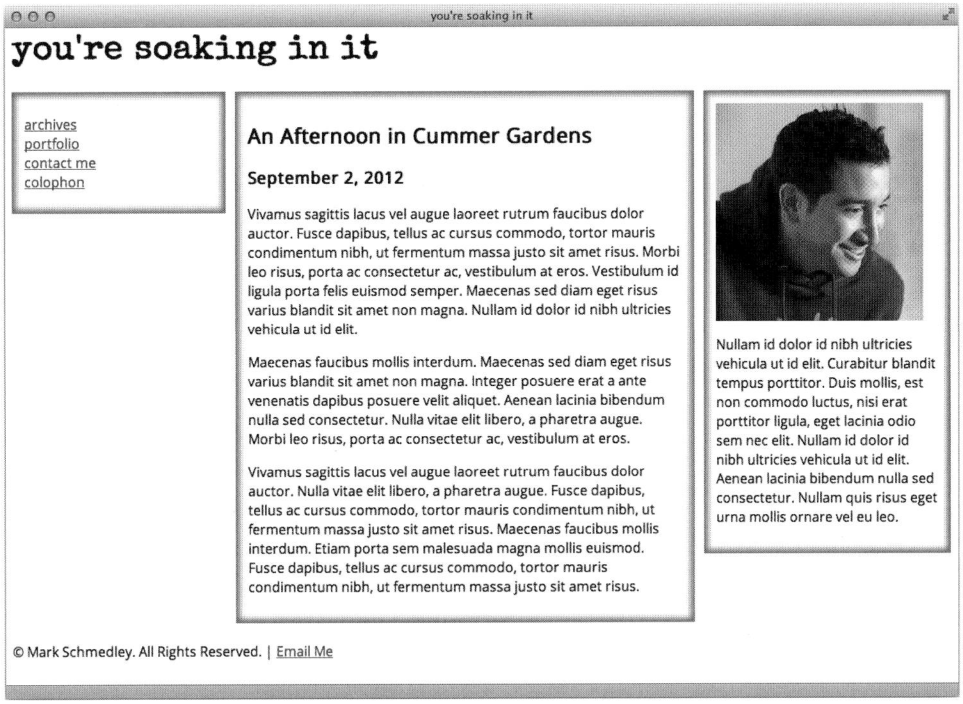

FIGURE 12.11 *A three-column fluid layout.*

In order to do this with floats, we must rearrange the **divs** within the HTML markup so that the "about" div is below the "main" **div**. That way, the "about" **div** floats next to the right of the "main" div. Note that we've removed the "sidebar" **div** (**FIGURE 12.12**).

```
<nav>
    [...]
</nav><!--end nav-->

<div role="main">
    [...]
</div><!--end main-->

<div id="about">
    [...]
</div><!--end about-->
```

Then, style the columns by floating the column elements to the left and applying widths in percentages.

FIGURE 12.12 *The three basic elements in the order they appear in the HTML.*

Note that the width of all of the columns (plus any margin and padding) should add up to 100%—if they exceed 100%, then one or more of the columns will wrap below their predecessors. Indeed, given the discrepancy among browsers, it is probably safest if your columns add up to a little under 100% to avoid breaking the browser's *float tolerance*.

```
div[role="main"]{
    float: left;
    width: 46%;
    margin: 0 1% 0 0;
    padding: 15px;
}

nav {
    float: left;
    width: 20%;
    margin: 0 1% 0 0;
    padding: 10px 15px;
}

aside {
    float: left;
    width: 24%;
    padding: 15px
}
```

Notice in the above code that the percentages add up to 92% just to be safe. You might also check the results of small changes to the margins, padding, and borders of each **div** to better understand how all of these display properties work together.

Three-Column Fixed Layout

Finally, let's make a three-column fixed layout using floats. After wrapping each column in its own respective HTML element, wrap the first two columns in another **div** (here, called "wrapper"). Finally, enclose the entire layout (including the header and footer) in a **div** (here labeled "container") as shown in **FIGURE 12.13**.

```
<div id="container">
  <header>
  [...]
  </header>
  <div id="wrapper">
    <nav>
    [...]
    </nav>
    <div role="main">
    [...]
    </div>
  </div><!--end wrapper-->
  <div id="sidebar">
  [...]
  </div>
  <footer>
  [...]
  </footer>
</div><!--end container-->
```

For the CSS, assign a width (in pixels) to the "container" **div**. The width of the three columns (plus any margins and padding) should add up to the container width (**FIGURE 12.14**).

```
#container {
    width: 875px;
    margin-left: 20px;
}
```

FIGURE 12.13 *The start of a fixed-width three-column layout.*

FIGURE 12.14 *Setting the containing element to 875 pixels.*

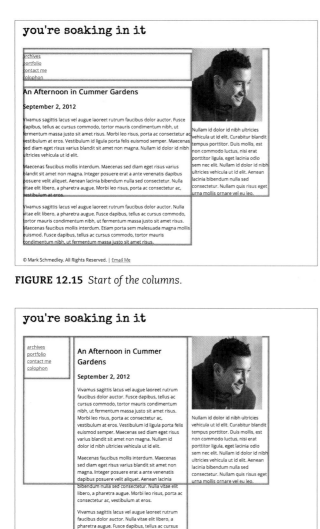

FIGURE 12.15 *Start of the columns.*

FIGURE 12.16 *Three columns start to appear.*

Float the "wrapper" **div** to the left. Its width should be the total width of the first two columns that it encloses (taking into account padding and margins) as shown in **FIGURE 12.15**.

```
#wrapper {
    width: 600px;
    float: left;
}
```

Float the first two columns to the left, assigning their widths in pixels as shown in **FIGURE 12.16**.

```
div[role="main"]{
    float: left;
    width: 380px;
    margin-top: 0;
    border-top: 0;
    padding: 15px;
}

nav {
    float: left;
    width: 137px;
    margin-top: 0;
    padding: 10px 15px;
}
```

Finally, float the last column to the right, assigning it the approximate remaining width as shown in **FIGURE 12.17**.

```
aside {
    float: right;
    width: 245px;
    margin-top: 0;
    padding: 10px 15px;
}
```

Test out the result in the browser to make sure it's fixed width.

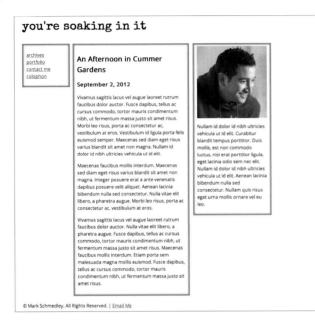

FIGURE 12.17 *Finishing the three columns.*

Pros and Cons of Layouts with Floats

Floats may not be appropriate for every layout. There are distinct pros and cons with regard to using floats to lay out a page. One of the main advantages of floats is that they allow you to clear elements that follow them. This permits you, for instance, to create a footer at the bottom of a layout. If you were to use absolute or relative positioning (as discussed in Chapter 2, "Styling with CSS)," this becomes more tricky. To position a footer below other positioned elements, you have to know the length of the other columns beforehand (as positioning would require exact placement down the length of the page).

One of the main disadvantages of using floats is that they generally require **div**s to be placed in a certain order in the markup: if you want a certain **div** to be the left-hand column of a page, it has to come first in the markup. This violates the principle of content and presentation separation.

Ideally, content should be completely separated from presentation. You should be able to semantically structure and order the sections in the HTML considering accessibility, reuse, and search optimization. Then, you should be able to manipulate them with CSS to appear wherever you want in the design. But using floats with **div** tags means that if you ever want to, say, switch the right- and left-hand columns on a page, you have to go into the markup and move the content around. This can be time consuming for a large site.

There is a way to use floats to display columns in whatever order you'd like, regardless of their order in the markup. This involves the use of negative margins, a technique which we won't explore in detail here, but which involves yanking a floated column behind preceding columns. But this method is quite complicated, unfortunately, in contrast to the relative ease of using floats in most other contexts.

CSS FRAMEWORKS

While simple layouts are easy to construct with floats, complex layouts can quickly become quite hairy, and that's where a CSS framework can come in handy.

A *CSS framework* is a predefined set of files that includes (among other things) a layout system that makes it easy to quickly construct complex multi-column layouts. Rather than having to build your CSS from scratch every time, you can implement the framework to jumpstart your web projects.

CSS frameworks include not only a layout system, but also, depending on how robust the framework is:

- CSS reset
- Basic typographic and element styling (such as typography, buttons, tabs, forms, and media queries)
- JavaScript libraries like jQuery, YUI3, Dojo, and Modernizr

This set of commonly used code and libraries is supposed to save the designer the headache and time of having to research and set up these files for every new web project. And, indeed, the majority of these frameworks are thoughtfully crafted and represent current best design and coding practices.

So, let's take a look at how these frameworks use floats to create a CSS abstraction that can be used to create an endless variety of multicolumn layouts.

Grid Systems

Most frameworks use a grid system: the layout comprises a grid made up of a number of same-sized columns, which serve as building blocks for constructing sections of the web page. You build the layout by specifying each section as being a number of these blocks.

Blueprint Framework

To better understand this, let's take a look at the Blueprint framework (**FIGURE 12.18**). It's a 24-column system (950 pixels in width), where each column is 30 pixels in width, with a 10-pixel gutter (the gutter is the space between the columns).

I want to divide my layout into four parts: a header that spans the width of the container, a first and last sidebar that spans 6 columns, and the middle content area that spans eight columns. The HTML would look like this:

```
<div class="container">
    <div class="span-24">
        <h1>My Title</h1>
    </div>
    <div class="span-6">
        [...]
    </div>
    <div class="span-12">
        [...]
    </div>
    <div class="span-6 last">
        [...]
    </div>
</div>
```

After adding a background color to the header section, our page appears as shown in **FIGURE 12.19.**

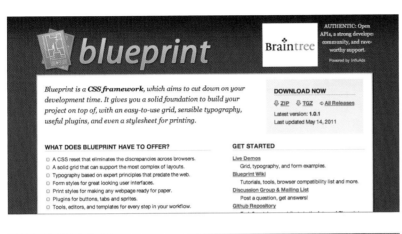

FIGURE 12.18 *Blueprint framework site (blueprintcss.org).*

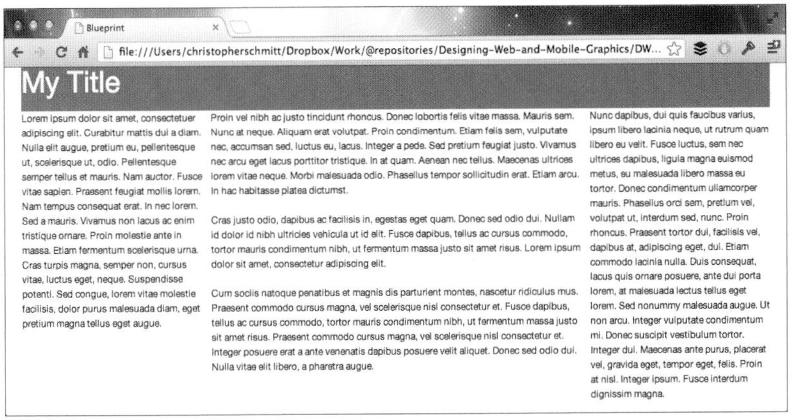

FIGURE 12.19 *An example of a three-column layout with a framework.*

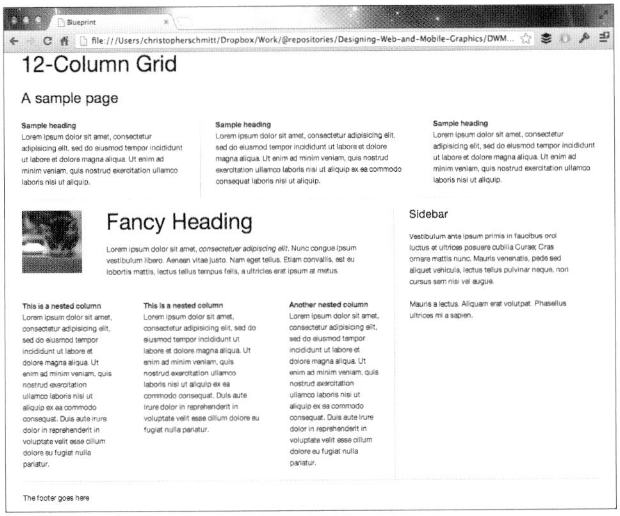

FIGURE 12.20 *Spanning columns in a 12-column grid in a variety of combinations.*

To understand how Blueprint is constructing this layout, let's take a look at its CSS. The container class houses the building blocks (the "span" classes) that make up the layout. It is 950 pixels wide. All "span" classes (**.span-1** to **.span-24**) are floated to the left. And all but **.span-24** have a 10 pixel right margin (or gutter). (**.span-24** doesn't need a gutter, as no other columns fit next to it.)

```
.span-1  {width:30px;}
.span-2  {width:70px;}
.span-3  {width:110px;}
.span-4  {width:150px;}
.span-5  {width:190px;}
.span-6  {width:230px;}
.span-7  {width:270px;}
.span-8  {width:310px;}
.span-9  {width:350px;}
.span-10 {width:390px;}
.span-11 {width:430px;}
.span-12 {width:470px;}
.span-13 {width:510px;}
.span-14 {width:550px;}
.span-15 {width:590px;}
.span-16 {width:630px;}
.span-17 {width:670px;}
.span-18 {width:710px;}
.span-19 {width:750px;}
.span-20 {width:790px;}
.span-21 {width:830px;}
.span-22 {width:870px;}
.span-23 {width:910px;}
.span-24 {width:950px;margin-right:0;}
```

The first span class (**.span-1**) is 30 pixels wide. Each subsequent class increases its width by 40 pixels. So, **.span-2** is 70 pixels wide, **.span-3** is 100 pixels wide, and so on, to **.span-24**, which is 950 pixels. So long as the "span" suffix numbers add up to 24 or less, they float next to one another within the 950-pixel container.

Note the **.last** class added to the final column in the HTML? What's that all about? The last (rightmost) column in the layout doesn't need a gutter. The **.last** specifies a margin of 0, thus removing the 10-pixel gutter of any column it is tacked onto.

```
.last {margin-right:0;}
```

So, in our layout: our two sidebars are 230 pixels wide, and our main content column is 470 pixels. That plus our two 10-pixel gutters yield 950 pixels, which fits beautifully into the container **div**.

With this simple building block construct, building multi-column layouts is a breeze, as is stacking different column spans on top of each other (**FIGURE 12.20**).

960 Grid System

Let's briefly contrast Blueprint with another popular grid-based framework system: the 960 Grid System (**FIGURE 12.21**). The 960 Grid System uses a 12 or 16-column grid (depending on your preference). In the 12-column grid, the columns are 60 pixels wide; the 16-column grid has 40-pixel columns. The 960 Grid System works much like Blueprint. You build your layout by encapsulating each column in a **div** labeled with a **class** (**.grid-1**, **.grid-2**, and so on), and putting all of those columns in a containing **div** (**.container-12** or **.container-16**). The container is 960 pixels wide (hence the name).

However, in contrast to Blueprint, each column has a right- and a left-hand margin of 10 pixels, yielding a 20-pixel gutter and 10-pixel padding within the containing element. The upshot of this method is that you wouldn't need to add anything like a **.last** class to the rightmost column in your layout (**FIGURE 12.22**).

FIGURE 12.21 *The 960 Grid System (960.gs).*

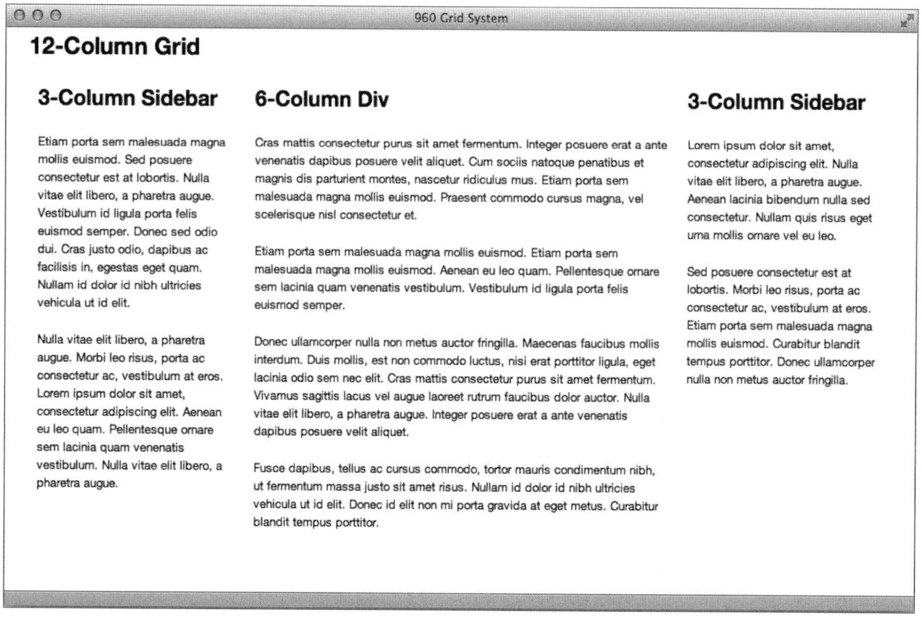

FIGURE 12.22 *An example of a 12-column grid using the 960 Grid System.*

Final Look at Frameworks

Blueprint and the 960 Grid System are great representatives of grid-based frameworks, though note that there are quite a few popular frameworks, each with their own collection of CSS files and libraries. With a few exceptions, however, most share a similar method of creating layouts. Admittedly, they're quite useful for quickly constructing complex layouts, but they are not without their disadvantages.

Class names such as span-1 or grid-12 are not semantic: that is, they describe the width of the **div**, rather than its function (such as "header" or "article"). While this makes it easy to quickly put together a web page, you set yourself up for trouble down the line. Say you want to change the width of all your sidebars. You would have to go in and change all of the relevant class names within your HTML, rather than just tweak a line in your CSS.

Also, depending on how light the framework is, you can also run into the problem of code bloat. While you may use many of the features within your framework, there will undoubtedly be libraries, or CSS class or id names, that you either won't use or will have to style over.

This means you end up bloating your web page with unneeded code, wasting bandwidth. There is virtue in using only the code that you need and nothing else.

That being said, it's certainly arguable that the convenience and ease of creating web documents with a framework overrides any disadvantages, and it's up to you whether they are worth it. Another option, of course, is once you understand how such grid-based systems work, you can build your own framework that is tailored to your method of styling web pages.

RESPONSIVE LAYOUTS

One of the biggest challenges in multicolumn layout is ensuring that it will work on a variety of screen sizes. One approach, popularized by Ethan Marcotte, is called *responsive* web design. In the simplest terms, this is about developing a website or app design where text, images, and other media work together seamlessly in almost any browser experience—mobile, desktop, or some future device.

With a mobile browser in a smartphone, websites can be viewed in a much smaller screen the same way they look on a desktop, especially if they're built to web standards. But to focus on a single column of text or a photo on a small screen, you'd have to double tap the area of the page you want to see (**FIGURE 12.23**).

This hunt and peck method of trying to find and act on the content in those pages isn't the best user experience—especially for people who are mobile and using their device.

With the rise of features and smartphones carrying web browsers, it's important that a web presence be adaptive. Rather than building a site around the dimensions of desktop browser windows and letting them be rendered smaller on mobile browsers, we can give a site the ability to change the size and layout of its elements depending on the device it's being rendered in.

ONE SITE FOR EACH DEVICE

One approach would be to build independent or siloed versions of a website, such as m.example.com, and send it directly to each device and browser it was intended for.

However, that's really not practical.

Given the fragmentation of mobile operating systems and differences in devices, that would mean customizing one website design with over 1,000 variations. And that's just the design. Not all mobile and desktop browsers are built the same way, so you would have to factor in development costs to code in workarounds for any browser bugs.

So, let's not follow this idea.

FIGURE 12.23 *Double tapping on the article's photo brings it forward to the user.*

MEDIA TYPES AND CSS FOR PRINTING

In CSS2, we had the the ability to deliver specific CSS tailored for different media types, like print, speech, and screen. By default the medium of a web page is considered to be the screen. Another useful and popular media type is print, which creates a separate design that's optimized for the printed page. By changing the value of the media attribute from screen to print, we can tell the browser to deliver CSS rules just for printing:

```
<link rel="stylesheet" href="print.css" type="text/css" media="print" />
```

When going from web browser to the printer, here are some areas to optimize to make sure content is legible:

- Remove background images.
- Remove main navigation links.
- Reformat the header and footers to be more streamlined.
- Change text and link colors to black and white.
- Set font size to print-based unit like points, for example, **12pt**.
- Set links in text to bold.
- Auto-print URLs with the **content** property:

```
a:link:after {
  content: " (" attr(href) ") ";
}
```

- Expand the content area to take advantage of the printed page.

For more information about styling for print, see my *CSS Cookbook* from O'Reilly.

Adapting to Media Queries

CSS3 extends the concept of media types to check for particular screen sizes so style sheets can be more precise in making a design fit. To send a set of CSS rules to mobile devices with a small screen, for example, set those CSS declarations with an @media rule that sets both screen delivery with viewport sizes:

```
<style type="text/css">
// regular, default CSS rules go here for browsers that don't understand
basic layout.

@media screen and (min-width: 480px) {
 // CSS rules go here
}
</style>
```

In this manner, we can tell the browser to deliver the CSS rules to the browser only if the viewport or browser window is at least 480 pixels wide.

To set up rules for multiple types of screens from mobile to desktop screens:

```
<style type="text/css">
@media screen and (min-width: 480px) {
 // CSS rules go here
}
@media screen and (min-width: 600px) {
 // CSS rules go here
}
@media screen and (min-width: 768px) {
 // CSS rules go here
}
@media screen and (min-width: 910px) {
 // CSS rules go here
}
</style>
```

This leads to the ability to set different flavors of the same design for different viewports, as shown in **FIGURE 12.24**.

DIFFERENCE BETWEEN ADAPTIVE AND RESPONSIVE

There are distinctions between the two words *adaptive* and *responsive* in web design. The adaptive approach to design is to generate specific, tailored designs for different breakpoints. These breakpoints usually accommodate the big items like desktop, tablet, and mobile devices. Responsive web design follows the same approach, but introduces fluid layouts to adjust to the size of the browser.

Fluid Layouts

When we were creating the two-column and three-column layouts earlier in this chapter, we did versions that were fixed and versions that were fluid. Now, we'll look more closely at the differences with respect to responsive design, and the advantages of fluid layouts.

While breakpoints give us the ability to group our designs into ranges of currently common viewport widths, we can actually take it further by giving our elements proportional widths so that they flow into the exact viewport they're being rendered on.

FIGURE 12.24 *Mediaquri.es showcases what's possible when designing separate experiences.*

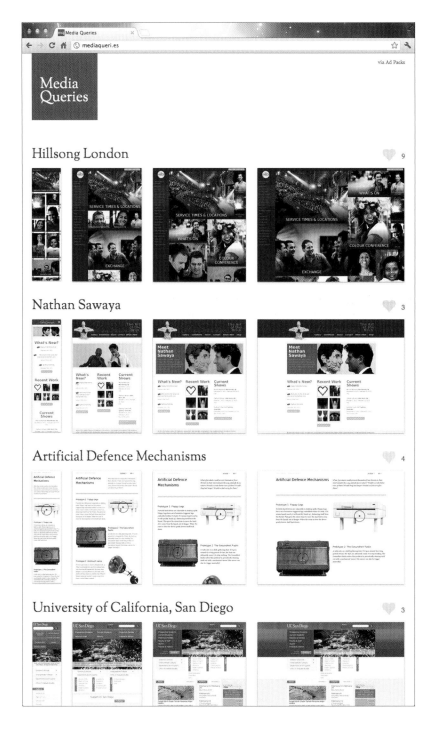

Since a new medium is often dictated by the elements of the previous media, print designers come to web design with the idea of setting up fixed, precise layouts like in print projects.

```
div.container {
  margin: 0 auto;
  width: 960px;
}
div.main {
  width: 600px;
  float: left;
}
div.aside {
  width: 300px;
  float: right;
}
```

A basic two-column structure is demonstrated in **FIGURE 12.25**.

Widths are usually built with pixel units to define the widths of containing elements. To revise our existing designs for a fluid approach, we use basic mathematics: division.

For example, take the main column width in our fixed width design and divide it by the container or context it's in:

```
600px ÷ 960px = 0.625
```

Then we translate the result into percentages:

```
0.625 x 100 = 62.5%
```

Why a percentage? Because while pixels are an absolute unit, percentages are a relative unit. As the browser window expands, the columns' widths expand as shown in **FIGURE 12.26**. The rules for the new layout is now set up for fluid delivery:

```
div.container {
  margin: 0 auto;
  width: 100%;
}
div.main {
  width: 62.5%;
  float: left;
}
div.aside {
  width: 31.25%;
  float: right;
}
```

MATH SPEAK

The first value in a division problem is called the *dividend*. It's then divided by what's called the *divisor* to get the result, which is called the *quotient*.

If division isn't your strength, there are calculators all around us. They come installed on PC and Mac computers, smartphones, and even websites.

RatioSTRONG (http://ratiostrong.com/) is an online calculator geared toward finding the precentage used for responsive web design.

FIGURE 12.25 *Fixed- width columns will always be the same width, no matter the browser or device.*

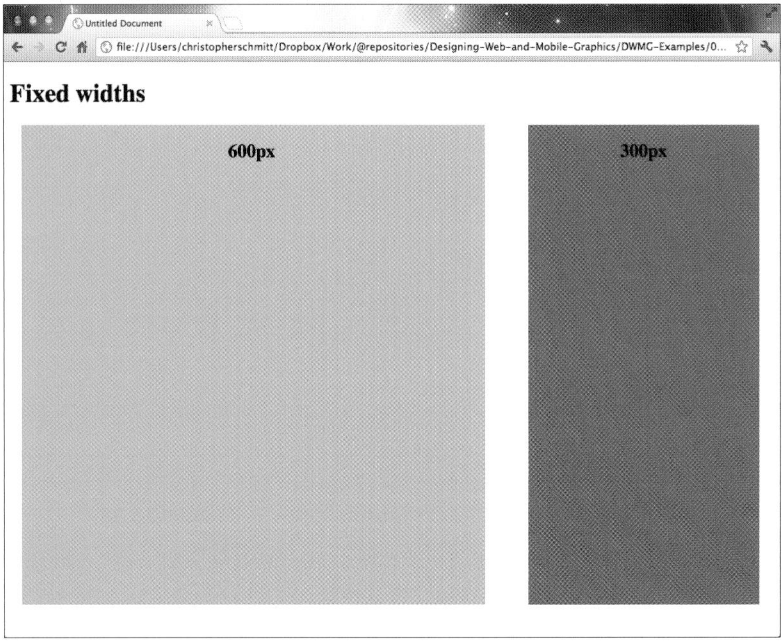

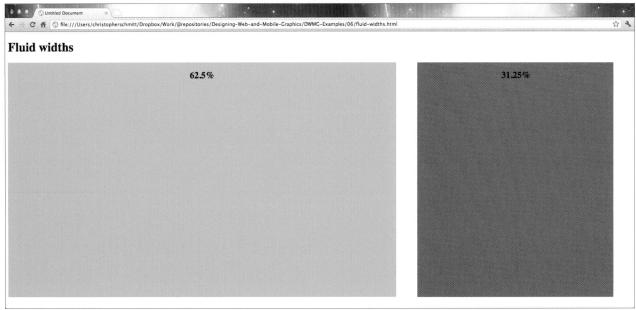

FIGURE 12.26 *Columns now fit the container they are displayed in.*

The next step is to wrap the media rule around the specified rules:

```
@media screen and (min-width: 910px) {
  div.container {
    margin: 0 auto;
    width: 100%;
  }
  div.main {
    width: 62.5%px;
    float: left;
  }
  div.aside {
    width: 31.25%;
    float: right;
  }
}
```

Then rinse and repeat for each breakpoint you want to support.

Text Reflow

Text reflows easily into new container shapes. As the columns expand, the length of each line changes, and all looks good no matter the size or width. When text changes to fill a flexible container, there's no worry about text stretching, distorting, or becoming illegible. As shown in **FIGURE 12.27**, the same amount of text in each column shows the differing line lengths and height.

OPTIMUM LINE LENGTH

There is an always ongoing discussion, though, as to what is the optimum number of characters or words to stuff into a line for legibility. For more discussion on this issue, check out Viget's great looking blog post at http://viget.com/inspire/the-line-length-misconception.

One trick to know if there is too much text on a line is to follow this general rule: keep about 66 characters on one line. To do a quick test, place a special character like a carat (^) every 45 and 75 characters. As long as *one* carat is on *one* line, the line length is acceptable.

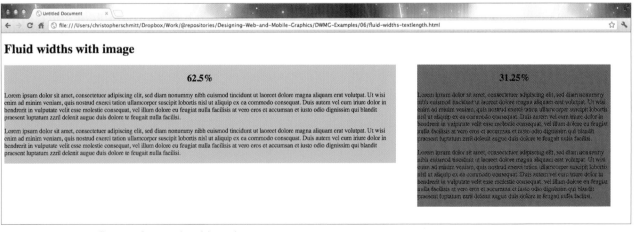

FIGURE 12.27 *Text flows to the container it's set in.*

Media Queries in Action

To see media queries in action, let's create a simple layout that we can adapt for desktops and smartphones. While there are many strategies for creating responsive layouts, a straightforward method is to create a fluid grid for the desktop version, and then alter the CSS minimally for mobile browsers.

For this layout, we're going to include the basics: a header, navigation menu, main content section, and sidebar. We'll also stick an image in there for good measure.

```
<div id="container">
    <header>
        <h1>Responsive Layout</h1>
    </header>

    <nav>
        <ul>
            <li><a href="">Archives</a></li>
            <li><a href="">About</a></li>
            <li><a href="">Portfolio</a></li>
            <li><a href="">Hire Me</a></li>
            <li><a href="">Contact Me</a></li>
            <li><a href="">Colophon</a></li>
        </ul>
    </nav>

    <div id="content">
        [...]
        <img src="images/savannah.jpg"
alt="Savannah, Georgia"/>
        [...]
    </div>

    <div id="sidebar">
        <h2>Sidebar</h2>
        [...]
    </div>
</div>
```

Now let's create the CSS for the desktop version of our site. I'm not going to include all of the CSS for this site in the snippet below, just the bit relevant to the layout.

```
nav {
    width: 100%;
    padding: 10px 0;
    border-top: 1px solid #aaa;
    border-bottom: 1px solid #aaa;
}

nav ul {
    list-style-type: none;
    position: relative;
    top: -17px;
    padding: 0;
    border-bottom: 0;
}

nav ul li {
    width: auto;
    float: left;
    margin-right: 30px;
    padding: 0;
    border-top: 0;
}

#content {
    width: 70%;
    margin-right: 3%;
    float: left;
}

#sidebar {
    width: 27%;
    float: left;
}

img {
    float: right;
    margin-left: 3%;
    border: 1px solid #ccc;
}
```

What have we done here? We've created a horizontal navigation bar and a fluid two-column layout. Our image is floated within our content to the right. We've also specified some things that don't exist on this layout, such as top borders above our list items. This is to ensure that our regular layout won't inherit styles from the phone version we're going to make a little later—you'll see how this works when we explain the CSS for the phone layout. On our desktop, the page looks as shown in **FIGURE 12.28**.

This layout is great for a desktop, which has a lot of screen real estate. But for a mobile device, squeezing a horizontal navigation menu and two columns within 320 pixels or so makes the site quite difficult to read. So we have to change the layout for mobile devices by doing the following:

- Change the horizontal navigation menu to a vertical one, preferably one in which the clickable areas, or buttons, are fat enough to be finger-friendly.

- Change the two-column layout to a one-column: let's drop the sidebar below the main content section.

- Our image is too big to float, and too big to fit, horizontally, within a mobile browser's window. We have to fix that.

First, we're going to add the following line within the head section of the HTML page:

```
<meta name="viewport" content="width=device-
width; initial-scale=1.0">
```

What is this for? This line is to correct iPhone's attempt to rescale our website. When displaying a site, iPhones (with the greatest of intentions) "shrink" the site so that pages designed for desktops can fit into iPhone's tiny screen.

While this is great for sites not optimized for mobile devices, we don't want the iPhone shrinking our page elements! So this line resets the scale to the actual size of the page elements.

FIGURE 12.28 *Our responsive layout on a desktop with plenty of screen space.*

Creating Media Queries

Next, we need to create the media query in our style sheet. This can get complicated, as there are hundreds of mobile devices out there, each a specific size and screen resolution. We could make a separate media query for several common mobile devices, but the simplest strategy would be to create one media query that captures nearly all smartphones, and make the layout flexible enough to adapt to all of them. So we're going to target our media queries to devices that are, at maximum, 480 pixels wide. This targets most smartphones in portrait and landscape mode. (Note that we're excluding tablet devices here, such as the iPad. We would probably want to create a separate media query for such devices. For simplicity's sake, we're sticking to mobile phones in this example.)

So, let's create our media query. You'll want to put this section of CSS after the styles for your regular layout:

```
@media screen and (max-width: 480px) {
    /* Smartphone Specific Styles */
}
```

Now, we're going to put all of the CSS targeted to smartphones within these brackets. Let's begin with the navigation menu:

```
nav {
    padding: 0;
    border: 0;
}

nav ul li {
    float: none;
    margin: 0;
    border-top: 1px solid #aaa;
    padding: 3% 0 3% 5%;
}

nav ul {
    border-bottom: 1px solid #aaa;
    top: 0;
}
```

First, we've gotten rid of the borders on the top and bottom of the navigation section, as well as the padding. Again, we're turning the horizontal "bar" into a vertical series of "buttons." For the navigation list items, we've added a top border to our navigation buttons, echoing the styling we had for the horizontal bar. We've also set the float property to none, as we want the buttons to be below one another rather than next to one another. We've added some padding to fatten them up a bit. Finally, for the list itself, we've added a bottom border and readjusted the positioning tweaks we had to do when it was a horizontal bar.

As you can see, we didn't want our regular layout to have the things we've added here (top borders and so forth), which is why we "pre-removed" those in our default CSS. When creating layouts with media queries, it's very important to pay attention to how your styles cascade and keep track of what styles might get inherited.

Now, let's move on to our two columns. We want our two columns to be stacked vertically, and we want each column to take up the width of the mobile screen:

```
#content {
    width: 100%;
}

#sidebar {
    width: 100%;
    clear: both;
}
```

How simple was that? Note that we've kept the fluidity of the original layout. Since we're targeting a variety of smartphones, we don't want to set the column to a specific width; we want the layout to adapt to a myriad of possible device widths. So, we've just set the width at 100%. Also, we've cleared our floats by setting **clear** to both for the sidebar.

Finally, let's style our image:

```
img {
    margin: 0 0 10px 0;
    max-width: 100%;
}
```

Besides setting a small bottom margin to our image, the only thing of note that we've done is set the max-width at 100%. That's so the size of the image doesn't exceed the width of the device screen, which would require the user to scroll horizontally to view the entire image.

Now, let's see how our page looks on an iPhone (**FIGURE 12.29**). Now, our page is easily readable on our mobile browser, and our navigation menu is easy to manipulate with a thumb or finger!

Custom Media Queries

We looked at designing one alternative design for smartphones that went along with our desktop display. With the spread of smartphones and tablets, these two designs won't serve a majority of devices. So, we need to deliver multiple media queries with different flavors of our site design.

Prolific web designer Chris Coyier has a reference list of media queries for multiple devices (http://css-tricks.com/snippets/css/media-queries-for-standard-devices/):

```
/* Smartphones (portrait and landscape) ----------- */
@media only screen
and (min-device-width : 320px)
and (max-device-width : 480px) {
/* Styles */
}

/* Smartphones (landscape) ----------- */
@media only screen
and (min-width : 321px) {
/* Styles */
}

/* Smartphones (portrait) ----------- */
@media only screen
and (max-width : 320px) {
/* Styles */
}
```

RESPONSIVE LAYOUT

Archives

About

Portfolio

Hire Me

Contact Me

Colophon

Lorem ipsum dolor sit amet, consectetuer adipiscing elit. Curabitur mattis dui a diam. Nulla elit augue, pretium eu, pellentesque ut, scelerisque ut, odio. Pellentesque semper tellus et mauris. Nam auctor. Fusce vitae sapien. Praesent feugiat mollis lorem. Nam tempus consequat erat. In nec lorem. Sed a mauris. Vivamus non lacus ac enim tristique ornare. Proin molestie ante in massa. Etiam fermentum scelerisque urna. Cras turpis magna, semper non, cursus vitae, luctus eget, neque. Suspendisse potenti. Sed congue, lorem vitae molestie facilisis, dolor purus malesuada diam, eget pretium magna tellus eget augue.

Pellentesque nec felis nibh ac justo tincidunt rhoncus. Donec lobortis felis vitae massa. Mauris sem. Nunc at neque. Aliquam erat volutpat. Proin condimentum. Etiam felis sem, vulputate nec, accumsan sed, luctus eu, lacus. Integer a pede. Sed pretium feugiat justo. Vivamus nec arcu eget lacus porttitor tristique. In at quam. Aenean nec tellus. Maecenas ultrices lorem vitae neque. Morbi malesuada odio. Phasellus tempor sollicitudin erat. Etiam arcu. In hac habitasse platea dictumst.

SIDEBAR

Aenean eu leo quam. Pellentesque ornare sem lacinia quam venenatis vestibulum. Vivamus sagittis lacus vel augue laoreet rutrum faucibus dolor auctor. Etiam porta sem malesuada magna mollis euismod. Curabitur blandit tempus porttitor. Nullam quis risus eget urna mollis ornare vel eu leo.

FIGURE 12.29 *Responsive layout for a mobile device.*

```
/* iPads (full and mini; portrait and
landscape) ----------- */
@media only screen
and (min-device-width : 768px)
and (max-device-width : 1024px) {
/* Styles */
}


/* iPads (landscape) ----------- */
@media only screen
and (min-device-width : 768px)
and (max-device-width : 1024px)
and (orientation : landscape) {
/* Styles */
}


/* iPads (portrait) ----------- */
@media only screen
and (min-device-width : 768px)
and (max-device-width : 1024px)
and (orientation : portrait) {
/* Styles */
}


/* Desktops and laptops ----------- */
@media only screen
and (min-width : 1224px) {
/* Styles */
}


/* Large screens ----------- */
@media only screen
and (min-width : 1824px) {
/* Styles */
}


/* iPhone 4 and 5 ----------- */
@media
only screen and (-webkit-min-device-pixel-ratio
: 1.5),
only screen and (min-device-pixel-ratio : 1.5)
{
/* Styles */
}
```

While this is a fairly comprehensive list of devices, it also means that there are a lot of different flavors of one site to support. So, it's better not to go down the path of supporting every type of popular device lest you be caught updating your site for every device ad infinitum.

In fact, Chris Coyier's approach is based on an old fairy tale, Goldilocks and the Three Bears (http://css-tricks.com/media-queries-sass-3-2-and-codekit/).

Instead of delivering numerous versions of the same site, Coyier produces three versions:

- **Papa Bear**—site designs for screens wider than 1600px
- **Mama Bear**—site designs for screens 650px to 1600px wide
- **Baby Bear**—site designs for small screens up to 650px wide

The media queries for this approach would look something like this:

```
@media only screen and (max-width: 1600px) {
... /* papa bear size  */
}
@media (max-width: 1250px) {
... /* mama bear size */
}
@media (max-width: 650px)  {
... /* baby bear size */
}
```

Of course, you can add device specific media queries, if you feel the need (or your customer wants them). But the focus should be about testing your design and adding media queries at points along the width where the design gets covered up by the browser or collapses.

Responsive Framework

If you want to use a framework to get up and running quickly, but also want the flexibility of responsive design, check out 960's responsive CSS at http://adapt.960.gs.

While they have a JavaScript for delivering media queries (ostensibly for older browsers that don't handle dynamic style sheet switching), you can download the various style sheets with all the relevant CSS rules to power the framework.

The additional style sheets available for downloading:

- `mobile.css`—site designs for small screens below 760px

- `720.css`—site designs for small screens from 760px to 980px

- `960.css`—site designs for small screens from 980px to 1280px

- `1200.css`—site designs for small screens from 1280px to 1600px

- `1560.css`—site designs for small screens from 1600px to 1940px

- `1920.css`—site designs for small screens from 1940px to 2540px

- `2520.css`—site designs for small screens above 2540px

IN CONCLUSION

As mentioned throughout this chapter, being able to float elements is important. It's nice to be able to design a web page, float an image to the right, and have the text wrap around the image. You can also use floats to make fluid or fixed multiple column layouts, as well as horizontal and vertical menus. For more complex layouts, you might consider a CSS framework.

Floats and media queries are a good way to start your designs toward adaptability, but there is a lot more to explore when it comes to making web pages look good across multiple devices.

In our next chapter, we look at images for responsive web design.

"So, I said to the gym instructor, 'Can you teach me to do the splits?' He said, 'How flexible are you?' I said, 'I can't make Tuesdays.'"

—Tim Vine

Chapter 13 IMAGES FOR RESPONSIVE WEB DESIGN

We are in a time where the web browser is ubiquitous. People now have many devices connected to the Internet and each one with their own browser and screens for browsing.

This multiple user experience is bringing up more challenges for crafting images than ever before.

SCALING IMAGES AND MEDIA

As our designs are resized to adapt to different devices, we need our images to do the same thing: change sizes. However, raster-based image formats can only create images that have fixed widths and heights.

Thanks to CSS, we can scale images down for use in responsive web design. If they were to be scaled up, they would lose image quality, so we begin by setting the **max-width** property for images to 100%:

```
img {
  max-width: 100%;
  height: auto;
}
```

In **FIGURE 13.1**, we place the same 600 by 600 pixel kitten photo in the left and right columns. Since the image is less wide than the left column, it displays just fine. On the right, however, the image is wider than the column. Using CSS rules, we tell the image to scale down and keep the same proportions.

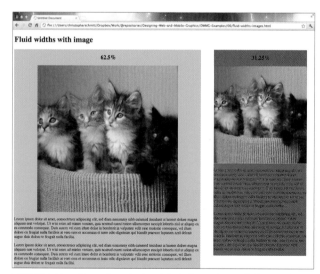

FIGURE 13.1 *Even though the right column image is larger than its container, the CSS rules tell it to resize down.*

We can use the same technique for videos. We build on the **img** element CSS rule but simply add **video** selector (as well as **object** for Flash video):

```
img, video, object {
  max-width: 100%;
  height: auto;
}
```

BACKGROUND IMAGES ARE DIFFERENT

For this discussion, we're focusing on the images that go with the content on the web page: the *inline* images. With media queries, images set in the background of HTML elements by CSS can be delivered easily depending on the context, but that's not the case with *inline* images.

! FLEXIBLE IMAGES IN OLDER IE BROWSERS

If you're supporting Internet Explorer 7 or IE6, check out Ethan Marcotte's "Fluid Images" blog post at http://unstoppablerobotninja.com/entry/fluid-images/ for a piece of JavaScript that keeps resized images looking sharp.

Be sure to use conditional comments to make sure only that piece of JavaScript gets delivered to older IE versions.

THE PROBLEM WITH SCALING IMAGES

The ability to scale images down with CSS solves half the problem. Raster images get their crispness from having enough pixel data for their viewing size. If they're scaled up to larger dimensions, there is no extra pixel data to add. Instead, edges get fuzzy and soft. That's why it's best to start with the image that has the largest dimension that might be needed. That could be the width of a very large monitor.

Large Images Required

At the time of this writing, Dell ships the UltaSharp U3011 that is a 30″ diagonal screen displaying at 2560 x 1600. So, our adaptive images need to accommodate screen sizes that are quite possibly that huge. (Be sure to check your site statistics as discussed in Chapter 4, "Challenges in Web Design," to see if you are getting visitors surfing on monitors that large.)

FIGURES 13.2 through **13.4** demonstrate how an increase in pixel data leads to an increase in file size.

FIGURE 13.2 *A medium-sized image at 250 x 375 pixels and 145 kb.*

FIGURE 13.4 *An extra-large image at 512 x 766 pixels and 503 kb.*

FIGURE 13.3 *A large image at 320 x 480 pixels and 223 kb.*

ADAPTIVE YOUTUBE VIDEOS

To get popular YouTube or Vimeo embeddable HTML to become adaptive takes some work. Thankfully, web developers Chris Coyier, Dave Rupert, and Thierry Koblentz put their heads together and developed a jQuery plugin called FitVids.js that makes it a breeze to set up. For a video tutorial, see http://fitvidsjs.com/.

Even Larger Images Required

While Dell's monitor is large by today's standards, there is another type of screen that packs in data in a different way: it makes the pixels smaller and more dense. Joining Apple in shipping high-density or, as Apple calls them, Retina displays will be manufacturers of hardware for Windows OS.

A high density display soaks up all that visual information and displays it in the same size as a regular monitor thanks to CSS rules like `width: max-width`. To support these displays with crisp images, we need to provide images *twice* the intended size of a regular display. Again, with more pixels comes greater file size (**TABLE 13.1**).

TABLE 13.1 *High Density and Regular Image Dimensions and File Sizes*

Size Type	Dimensions	Display Pixel Density	File Size
Extra Large	1024 × 1536	2×	1,745 kb
	512 × 768	1×	503 kb
Large	640 × 960	2×	746 kb
	320 × 480	1×	223 kb
Medium	500 × 750	2×	485 kb
	250 × 375	1×	145 kb

Even though they are "physically" larger when compared side-by-side as shown in **FIGURE 13.5**, **FIGURE 13.6**, and **FIGURE 13.7**, the larger images appear at the same size on a high-density screen as the smaller images would appear on a regular screen.

Internet Speed Concerns

As these adaptive images grow in size, their download hit might be acceptable if a visitor has broadband connection. But even the lucky ones among us don't always have the luxury of an ultrafast Wi-Fi hotspot.

When traveling to and from work or engaging in this thing called "camping" that people tell me is fun, there are times when we rely on a slower cellular Internet service to stay connected. Even though our smartphones and mobile tablets are gaining HD screens, we are still at the mercy of location and availability of Internet access.

So, if we use large images, whether HD or regular, we run the risk of forcing visitors to digest more data than they want to or can, especially if they're on a tight data plan from their Internet provider.

FIGURE 13.5 *Medium size image for high-density displays.*

FIGURE 13.6 *Large image for high-density displays.*

FIGURE 13.7 *Extra-large image for high-density displays.*

ADAPTIVE IMAGE SOLUTIONS

To deal with these large and small problems of adaptive images, there are a couple of paths we can take.

Using Alternatives

One unlikely solution is to never use raster images and rely instead on alternative image formats.

Since the issue at the heart of the problem is the file size of raster images, if we can shift our visual workload to other file formats or techniques, we can reduce or eliminate the adaptive image problem.

A couple of potential workarounds include:

- **SVG**—vector graphics are built for resizing (**FIGURE 13.8**). With greater browser support than ever before, if you have a graphic that uses flat areas of color or line art that you'd usually create as a GIF image, then SVG is a possible alternative. (For more on SVG, see Chapter 6, "Images for the Web.")

- **Icon fonts**—Fonts are vector-based like SVG, so they scale well. Using icon fonts (**FIGURE 13.9**) (discussed in Chapter 10, "Lists and Icon Fonts") is a great way to leverage the scabality of type for a visual edge.

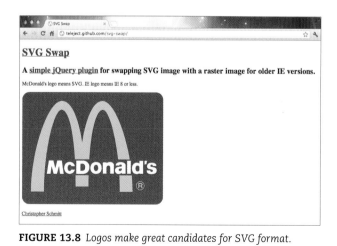

FIGURE 13.8 *Logos make great candidates for SVG format.*

While it's unlikely that we would forsake raster images altogether, utilizing alternative image methods is something to consider. You probably won't be able to unload all your raster images, but converting what images you can to SVG or icon fonts makes your site that much more ready for responsive web design.

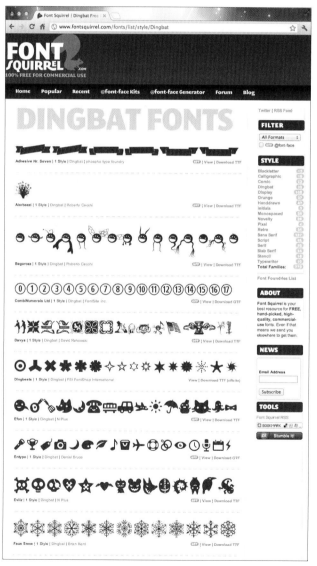

FIGURE 13.9 *Collection of dingbat fonts at Font Squirrel.*

Compressing Retina Images

When building images for the web, it's best to output them for the dimensions that they will be in the browser. For example, for a mugshot we would use a GIF image about 115 by 115 pixels when saved from Photoshop (**FIGURE 13.10**). If we made the image 1,150 by 1,150 pixels, we would force the user to download a bigger image file for very little gain.

The Secret Sauce

The curious thing, though, is that since responsive web design deals with resizing images to fill percentage-based widths, we can have an extremely large image and compress it mightily. While the resulting image does not look pretty at 100%, as shown in **FIGURE 13.11**, that doesn't matter. We're resizing the image *down* to fill the space of the column. The rough looking artifacts are covered up like so much dust under a rug.

FIGURE 13.10 *Crop and prepare to use only the parts of an image intended for a website.*

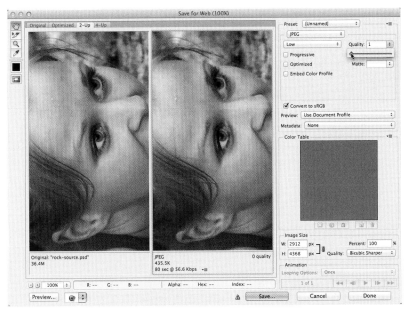

FIGURE 13.11 *Setting compression to maximum.*

For example, let's take a photo and leave it at its original dimensions of 2276 by 1400 pixels. Then compress that image to 0% quality (or 100% compression). The result is an image that comes in at 460 kb. Then take that image and compress it further with ImageOptim (as discussed in Chapter 7, "Creating Images for the Web"). The image as shown in **FIGURE 13.12** is reduced another 14 kb to a final 446 kb.

While the Extreme image doesn't beat the medium or large images for regular desktop displays on file size (**TABLE 13.2**), its usefulness for almost any device and display makes it a reasonable option well worth considering (**FIGURE 13.13**).

> **! SVG FOR OLD IE**
>
> Older versions of IE don't support SVG natively. To help work around that, use a jQuery plugin (see https://github.com/teleject/svg-swap) to swap out raster images when needed, or use Modernizr (see http://modernizr.com) to feature-detect SVG support.

FIGURE 13.12 *The large image with 0% quality preserved.*

FIGURE 13.13 *Comparison of images as seen on a Retina iPad.*

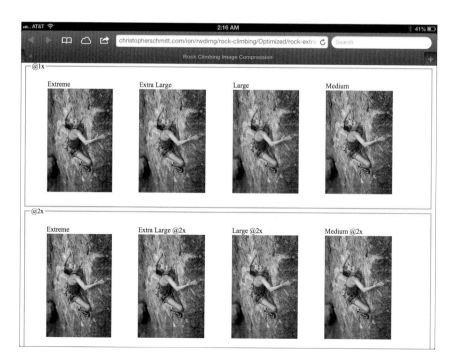

TABLE 13.2 *Comparing HD and Regular Image Sizes*

Size Type	Dimensions	Display Pixel Density	File Size
Extreme	2276 × 1400	1× & 2 ×	446 kb
Extra Large	1024 × 1536	2×	1,745 kb
	512 × 768	1×	503 kb
Large	640 × 960	2×	746 kb
	320 × 480	1×	223 kb
Medium	500 × 750	2×	485 kb
	250 × 375	1×	145 kb

Use Cautiously

This solution isn't for every image. Avoid images that have sharp and contrasting colors or long spans of gradation such as the one shown in **FIGURE 13.14**.

If the photo has large areas of gradation, compression causes banding or posterization. Sharp color changes don't play well to JPEG's compression scheme; it's hard for JPEGs to maintain smooth transitions while throwing away color data to save on file size.

FIGURE 13.14 *A high contrast photo shows artifacts from JPEG compression.*

It's best to use these techniques on photos that have an even tonal range or overall brightness. The image's histogram (**FIGURE 13.15**) should appear as a smooth "mountain range" rather than spikes and ridges (**FIGURE 13.16**).

FIGURE 13.15
Histogram for the rock climbing image.

FIGURE 13.16 *Histogram for the kayaking image.*

MANY-IMAGE SOLUTION

If you want to have more granular control over the quality of the images and assign more than one kind of image, then the **picture** element and **scrset** attribute are solutions to consider.

Picture Element

A **picture** element (**FIGURE 13.17**) proposed by the Responsive Images Community Group (http://picture.responsiveimages.org/) helps web designers assign an appropriate image for the user's viewing context:

```
<picture width="500" height="500">
 <source media="(min-width: 45em)" srcset="pizza-large-1.jpg 1x, pizza-large-HD.jpg 2x">
 <source media="(min-width: 18em)" srcset="pizza-med-1.jpg 1x, pizza-med-HD.jpg 2x">
 <source srcset="pizza-small-HD.jpg 1x, pizza-small-HD.jpg 2x">
 <img src="pizza-small-1.jpg" alt="A photo of a supreme pizza.">
 <p><a href="pizza-small-1.jpg">A photo of a supreme pizza.</a></p>
</picture>
```

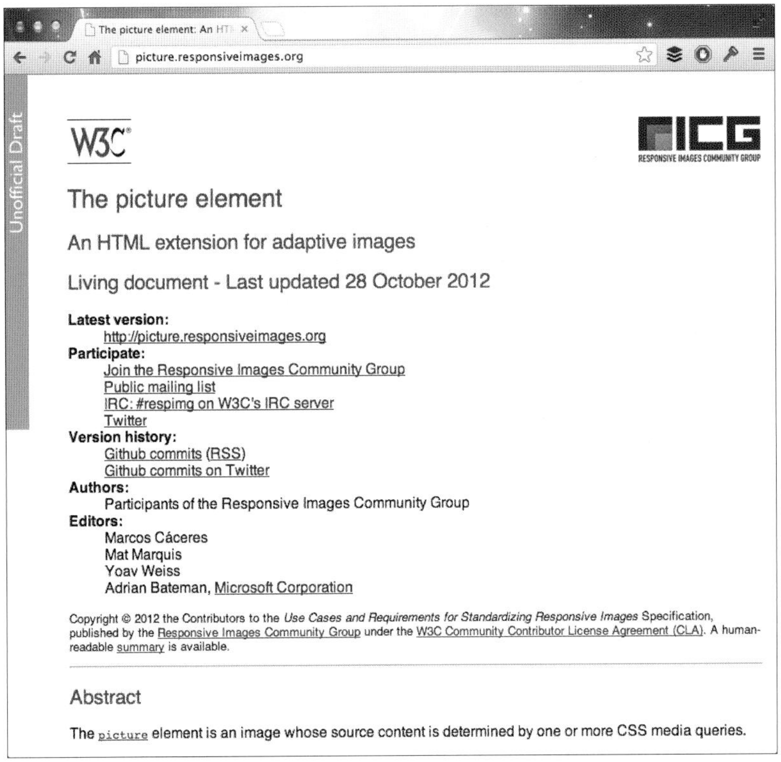

FIGURE 13.17 *Picture element specification.*

If a user is coming to our site on a large screen with HD display, we would serve them a large HD image:

```
<picture width="500" height="500">
<source media="(min-width: 45em)" srcset="pizza-large-1.jpg 1x, pizza-large-HD.jpg 2x">
<source media="(min-width: 18em)" srcset="pizza-med-1.jpg 1x, pizza-med-HD.jpg 2x">
<source srcset="pizza-small-1.jpg 1x, pizza-small-HD.jpg 2x">
<img src="pizza-small-1.jpg" alt="A photo of a supreme pizza.">
<p><a href="pizza-small-1.jpg">A photo of a supreme pizza.</a></p>
</picture>
```

If the user is surfing in on a smaller screen with a regular monitor, we would serve a smaller "medium" image in place of the larger, HD image:

```
<picture width="500" height="500">
 <source media="(min-width: 45em)" srcset="pizza-large-1.jpg 1x, pizza-large-HD.jpg 2x">
 <source media="(min-width: 18em)" srcset="pizza-med-1.jpg 1x, pizza-med-HD.jpg 2x">
 <source srcset="pizza-small-1.jpg 1x, pizza-small-HD.jpg 2x">
 <img src="pizza-small-1.jpg" alt="A photo of a supreme pizza.">
 <p><a href="pizza-small-1.jpg">A photo of a supreme pizza.</a></p>
</picture>
```

If a browser wouldn't understand the **picture** element, the old **img** element would be the fallback option:

```
<picture width="500" height="500">
 <source media="(min-width: 45em)" srcset="pizza-large-1.jpg 1x, pizza-large-HD.jpg 2x">
 <source media="(min-width: 18em)" srcset="pizza-med-1.jpg 1x, pizza-med-HD.jpg 2x">
 <source srcset="pizza-small-HD.jpg 1x, pizza-small-HD.jpg 2x">
 <img src="pizza-small-1.jpg" alt="A photo of a supreme pizza.">
 <p><a href="pizza-small-1.jpg">A photo of a supreme pizza.</a></p>
</picture>
```

Srcset Attribute

Another proposed solution (**FIGURE 13.18**) to the adaptive image problem is the **srcset** attribute (see http://dev.w3.org/html5/srcset/). The attribute would be a part of the **img** element extending to display only the appropriate image for the browser window width and display density.

```
<figure>
 <img alt="Pizza Supreme"
   src="pizza.jpeg"
   srcset="pizza-HD.jpeg 2x,
    pizza-phone.jpeg 480w,
    pizza-phone-HD.jpeg 480w 2x">
</figure>
```

The **srcset** takes multiple values. Each value comes with at least the URL reference to an image's location, and it's paired with a viewport size and optionally also a pixel density.

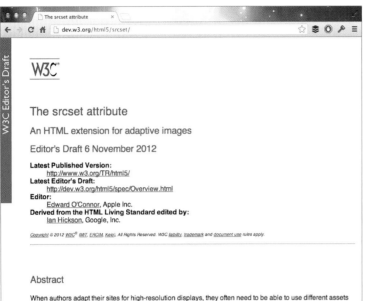

FIGURE 13.18 Srcset *attribute use.*

PROPOSING A NEW RESPONSIVE IMAGE FORMAT

Instead of preparing a slew of raster images for almost any instance in responsive web design, we need an image file format that is, in essence, a storage locker.

For example, the popular .mp3 audio file format is actually a collection of metadata information inside an audio tag. This is where iTunes finds song information like song title, artist, album title, year the song came out, and so on (**FIGURE 13.19**).

We need to have a similar file format for images. Instead of capturing meta information for the image, we store different variations of the image.

One "image" file would be able to contain a thumbnail image, a mobile friendly image, desktop friendly version, retina display version, print-friendly image, and so on. Browsers would tell the server the viewing context of a web page that is being requested and get the appropriate resolution from the image's storage locker.

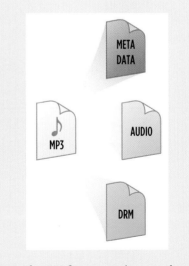

FIGURE 13.19 *The MP3 format contains more than music.*

MORE THAN ONE SOLUTION

There are other methods to deliver adaptive images for responsive web design, including using server-side methods to automate much of the process. Review Chris Coyier's post "Which responsive images solution should you use?" at http://css-tricks.com/which-responsive-images-solution-should-you-use/.

For the example value of **pizza-phone-HD.jpeg 480w 2x**, the **480w** value means that the browser's window is a maximum of 480 pixels (and *only* pixels).

The **2x** in the value sets the parameter of two device pixels per CSS pixel. This signifies a high density display.

So, taken as a whole, the value reads that if the browser display is less than 481 pixels wide *and* on an HD display, use the **pizza-phone-HD.jpeg** image.

Implementing the Picture Patch

The problem with **picture** and **scrset** is that they are merely proposed elements. They aren't native to browsers at the time of this writing.

Web developer Scott Jehl created a patch or *polyfill* called picturefill (**FIGURE 13.20**) that implements a hybrid approach utilizing the best of both **picture** and **srcset**. Yes, we can use picturefill now to deliver the appropriate images to the right display for the right viewing width.

FIGURE 13.20 *Picturefill code working to deliver different images for a large, regular desktop display and a Retina display iPad.*

TO IMPLEMENT SCOTT JEHL'S PICTUREFILL, FOLLOW THESE ⑩ STEPS:

① Go to the Picturefill polyfill's page at https://github.com/scottjehl/picturefill and download the code.

```
<head>
 <meta charset=utf-8 />
 <title>Picturefill</title>
 <script src="picturefill.js"></script>
</head>
```

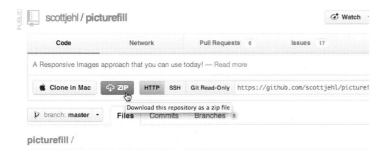

② Move **picturefill.js** to your assets folder and associate the JavaScript in the head of your document.

```
<head>
 <meta charset=utf-8 />
 <title>Picturefill</title>
 <script src="picturefill.js"></script>
 <script src="external/matchmedia.js"></script>
</head>
```

(3) Associate **matchmedia.js**, which comes within the zip download, to the head document. This bit of JavaScript is used to find out if media queries are supported on browsers, but can't easily tell you through a standard API.

```
<img src="external/imgs/pic-Small-180x111-@1x-72ppi.jpg" alt="Kayaking in
front of Sandy Spit, BVI" />
```

```
●○○                              picturefill.html

  picturefill.html          ✕

1    <!DOCTYPE html>
2    <html>
3        <head>
4          <meta charset="utf-8" />
5            <title>Picturefill</title>
6            <script src="picturefill.js"></script>
7            <script src="external/matchmedia.js"></script>
8        </head>
9        <body>
10       </body>
11   </html>
```

(4) Set the image element to a low file size, mobile-friendly version.

```
<!-- Fallback content for non-JS browsers. -->
<noscript>
<img src="external/imgs/pic-Small-180x111-@1x-72ppi.jpg" alt="Kayaking in
front of Sandy Spit, BVI" />
</noscript>
```

```
●○○                              picturefill.html

  picturefill.html          ●

1    <!DOCTYPE html>
2    <html>
3        <head>
4          <meta charset="utf-8" />
5            <title>Picturefill</title>
6            <script src="picturefill.js"></script>
7            <script src="external/matchmedia.js"></script>
8        </head>
9        <body>
10
11           <img src="external/imgs/pic-Small-180x111-@1x-72ppi.jpg" alt="Kayaking in  front of Sandy Spit,
             BVI" />
12
13       </body>
14   </html>
```

(5) Since the picturefill is powered by JavaScript, we need a contingency in case JavaScript isn't available in the user's browser. Wrap the fallback image with **noscript** tags to keep the image hidden from JavaScript aware images.

```
<div data-picture data-alt="Kayaking in  front of Sandy Spit, BVI"
title="Photo of kayakers in front of Sandy Spit, BVI"> <!-- Fallback content
for non-JS browsers. -->
 <noscript><img src="external/imgs/pic-Small-180x111-@1x-72ppi.jpg"
alt="Kayaking in front of Sandy Spit, BVI"></noscript>
</div>
```

6. Wrap the **noscript** and **img** element with a **div** element. Assign attributes **data-picture**, **data-alt**, and **title**. The **data-alt** value is provided to screenreaders like a regular **alt** attribute. Set a value for the **title** attribute if you want a tooltip to appear when the user hovers over the image.

```
<div data-picture data-alt="Kayaking in front of Sandy Spit, BVI"
title="Photo of kayakers in front of Sandy Spit, BVI">
 <div data-srcset="external/imgs/pic-Small-180x111-@1x-72ppi.jpg 1x,
external/imgs/pic-Small-360x221-@2x-72ppi.jpg 2x"></div>
<!-- Fallback content for non-JS browsers. -->
 <noscript><img src="external/imgs/pic-Small-180x111-@1x-72ppi.jpg"
alt="Kayaking in front of Sandy Spit, BVI"></noscript>
</div>
```

```
1   <!DOCTYPE html>
2   <html>
3       <head>
4        <meta charset="utf-8" />
5          <title>Picturefill</title>
6          <script src="picturefill.js"></script>
7          <script src="external/matchmedia.js"></script>
8       </head>
9       <body>
10
11          <div data-picture data-alt="Kayaking in  front of Sandy Spit, BVI" title="Photo of kayakers in
            front of Sandy Spit, BVI">
12          <!-- Fallback content for non-JS browsers. -->
13          <noscript>
14          <img src="external/imgs/pic-Small-180x111-@1x-72ppi.jpg" alt="Kayaking in  front of Sandy Spit,
            BVI" />
15          </noscript>
16          </div>
17
18       </body>
19   </html>
```

⑦ Since the **img** element is hidden behind the **noscript** element, replace the basic image with the mobile-friendly image in a **div** element with the **data-srcset** attribute. If the browser is on an HD display, the larger image displays.

```
<div data-picture data-alt="Kayaking in  front of Sandy Spit, BVI"
title="Photo of kayakers in front of Sandy Spit, BVI">
 <div data-srcset="external/imgs/pic-Small-180x111-@1x-72ppi.jpg 1x,
external/imgs/pic-Small-360x221-@2x-72ppi.jpg 2x"></div>
  <div data-media="(min-width: 25em)" data-srcset="external/imgs/pic-Medium-
375x231-@1x-72ppi.jpg 1x, external/imgs/pic-Medium-750x461-@2x-72ppi.jpg
2x"></div>
<!-- Fallback content for non-JS browsers. -->
 <noscript><img src="external/imgs/pic-Small-180x111-@1x-72ppi.jpg"
alt="Kayaking in  front of Sandy Spit, BVI"></noscript>
</div>
```

⑧ With another **div** element, set another source for larger images. Mimicking media queries, set the minimum width where the larger image appears. In this example, the minimum width of the browser window of **25em** needs to be met before the next higher image is displayed. If the monitor is HD, set the reference URL for the HD image to appear.

```
<div data-picture data-alt="Kayaking in  front of Sandy Spit, BVI"
title="Photo of kayakers in front of Sandy Spit, BVI">
 <div data-srcset="external/imgs/pic-Small-180x111-@1x-72ppi.jpg 1x,
external/imgs/pic-Small-360x221-@2x-72ppi.jpg 2x"></div>
 <div data-media="(min-width: 25em)" data-srcset="external/imgs/pic-Medium-
375x231-@1x-72ppi.jpg 1x, external/imgs/pic-Medium-750x461-@2x-72ppi.jpg
2x"></div>
 <div data-media="(min-width: 50em)" data-srcset="external/imgs/pic-Large-
480x295-@1x-72ppi.jpg 1x, external/imgs/pic-Large-960x591-@2x-72ppi.jpg
2x"></div>
 <div data-media="(min-width: 62.5em)" data-srcset="external/imgs/pic-
ExtraLarge-768x472-@1x-72ppi.jpg 1x, external/imgs/pic-ExtraLarge-1536x845-
@2x-72ppi.jpg 2x"></div>
<!-- Fallback content for non-JS browsers. -->
 <noscript><img src="external/imgs/pic-Small-180x111-@1x-72ppi.jpg"
alt="Kayaking in  front of Sandy Spit, BVI"></noscript>
</div>
```

```
1    <!DOCTYPE html>
2    <html>
3        <head>
4        <meta charset="utf-8" />
5            <title>Picturefill</title>
6            <script src="picturefill.js"></script>
7            <script src="external/matchmedia.js"></script>
8        </head>
9        <body>
10
11           <div data-picture data-alt="Kayaking in  front of Sandy Spit, BVI" title="Photo of kayakers in
                  front of Sandy Spit, BVI">
12                <div data-srcset="external/imgs/pic-Small-180x111-@1x-72ppi.jpg 1x, external/imgs/pic-Small-
                      360x221-@2x-72ppi.jpg 2x"></div>
13                <div data-media="(min-width: 25em)" data-srcset="external/imgs/pic-Medium-375x231-@1x-72ppi.
                      jpg 1x, external/imgs/pic-Medium-750x461-@2x-72ppi.jpg 2x"></div>
14                <!-- Fallback content for non-JS browsers. -->
15                <noscript>
16                <img src="external/imgs/pic-Small-180x111-@1x-72ppi.jpg" alt="Kayaking in  front of Sandy Spit,
                      BVI" />
17                </noscript>
18                </div>
19
20        </body>
21    </html>
```

ADD MANY OR FEW IMAGE SOURCES

In this example, we are demonstrating that Picturefill can handle multiple image sources. Your design solution might require fewer or more images. This is a demonstration of what's possible. It's up to you to figure out what's best for your design.

9 Continue to add browser width intervals through the **data-media** attribute and source additional images though **data-srcset** until finished.

```html
<div data-picture data-alt="Kayaking in  front of Sandy Spit, BVI"
title="Photo of kayakers in front of Sandy Spit, BVI">
 <div data-srcset="external/imgs/pic-Small-180x111-@1x-72ppi.jpg 1x,
external/imgs/pic-Small-360x221-@2x-72ppi.jpg 2x"></div>
 <div data-media="(min-width: 25em)" data-srcset="external/imgs/pic-
Medium-375x231-@1x-72ppi.jpg 1x, external/imgs/pic-Medium-750x461-@2x-
72ppi.jpg 2x"></div>
 <div data-media="(min-width: 50em)" data-srcset="external/imgs/pic-Large-
480x295-@1x-72ppi.jpg 1x, external/imgs/pic-Large-960x591-@2x-72ppi.jpg
2x"></div>
 <div data-media="(min-width: 62.5em)" data-srcset="external/imgs/
pic-ExtraLarge-768x472-@1x-72ppi.jpg 1x, external/imgs/pic-ExtraLarge-
1536x845-@2x-72ppi.jpg 2x"></div>

<!--[if (lt IE 9) & (!IEMobile)]>
 <div data-src="medium.jpg"></div>
<![endif]-->

<!-- Fallback content for non-JS browsers. -->
 <noscript><img src="external/imgs/pic-Small-180x111-@1x-72ppi.jpg"
alt="Kayaking in front of Sandy Spit, BVI"></noscript>
 </div>
```

10 If you need to support versions of IE older than IE8, which don't support media queries, use conditional comments to deliver a larger image to desktop browsers. Otherwise, the smaller image will be picked up by the older IE versions.

```
1   <!DOCTYPE html>
2   <html>
3       <head>
4           <meta charset="utf-8" />
5           <title>Picturefill</title>
6           <script src="picturefill.js"></script>
7           <script src="external/matchmedia.js"></script>
8       </head>
9       <body>
10
11          <div data-picture data-alt="Kayaking in  front of Sandy Spit, BVI" title="Photo of kayakers in
            front of Sandy Spit, BVI">
12              <div data-srcset="external/imgs/pic-Small-180x111-@1x-72ppi.jpg 1x, external/imgs/pic-Small-
                360x221-@2x-72ppi.jpg 2x"></div>
13              <div data-media="(min-width: 25em)" data-srcset="external/imgs/pic-Medium-375x231-@1x-72ppi.
                jpg 1x, external/imgs/pic-Medium-750x461-@2x-72ppi.jpg 2x"></div>
14              <div data-media="(min-width: 50em)" data-srcset="external/imgs/pic-Large-480x295-@1x-72ppi.
                jpg 1x, external/imgs/pic-Large-960x591-@2x-72ppi.jpg 2x"></div>
15              <div data-media="(min-width: 62.5em)" data-srcset="external/imgs/pic-ExtraLarge-768x472-@1x-
                72ppi.jpg 1x, external/imgs/pic-ExtraLarge-1536x845-@2x-72ppi.jpg 2x"></div>
16
17              <!--[if (lt IE 9) & (!IEMobile)]>
18              <div data-src="medium.jpg"></div>
19              <![endif]-->
20
21
22              <!-- Fallback content for non-JS browsers. -->
23              <noscript>
24              <img src="external/imgs/pic-Small-180x111-@1x-72ppi.jpg" alt="Kayaking in  front of Sandy Spit,
                BVI" />
25              </noscript>
26          </div>
27
28      </body>
29  </html>
```

Line 19, Column 13; Saved ~/Dropbox/Work/@repositories/Designing-Web-and-Mobile-Graphics/DWMG Manuscript/12 Adaptive Images/A/exa

IN CONCLUSION

Adaptive images are a big puzzle for the modern web designer. Thanks to advancements in current browsers to support embedding fonts and the use of vector graphics natively, we can offload a lot of graphic work from raster-based images, making our designs more flexible for any web device.

Until a native browser solution becomes available in all major browsers, there are workarounds and techniques we can use to deliver raster images. Next we'll look at three difficult image alignment challenges and some ways to meet them.

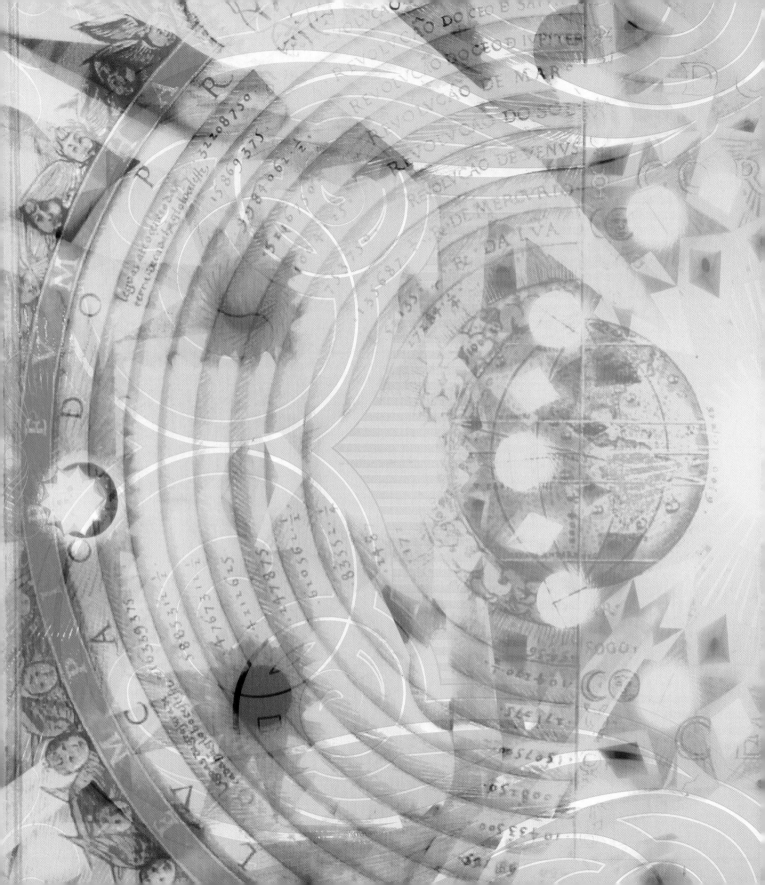

> "Sometimes you want to give up the guitar, you'll hate the guitar. But, if you stick with it, you're gonna be rewarded."
>
> —*Jimi Hendrix*

Chapter 14 ALIGNING IMAGES

Adding an image to a web page is fairly straightforward. While the **img** element has its own alignment attribute, it's now better practice to control image alignment through CSS.

You can use CSS to control where the image appears in relation to other elements using relative positioning, floats, and margins. Alternatively, you can control an image's position with respect to the browser window with absolute positioning and values from the browser edge (such as **left** and **top**).

In this chapter we look at ways to solve three of the most difficult alignment challenges: positioning images within text paragraphs, centering images within the browser window, and stretching images to fill the browser's entire viewport.

ALIGNING IMAGES IN RELATION TO THE TEXT

Images positioned within a text paragraph are generally small. You might insert only one image, or several in the same paragraph. What's significant in terms of alignment is whether the images are on the same line of text. Remember, if you used a layout that allows the line length to change, whether there are one or more images on a given line is out of your control.

One of the many CSS properties available in your web designer toolkit is **vertical-align**. When an image is placed within a text paragraph, you can use this CSS property to position it. There are five different positions you can set with the **vertical-align** property: **baseline**, `text-bottom`, `text-top`, `top`, `bottom`, and `middle`.

Baseline

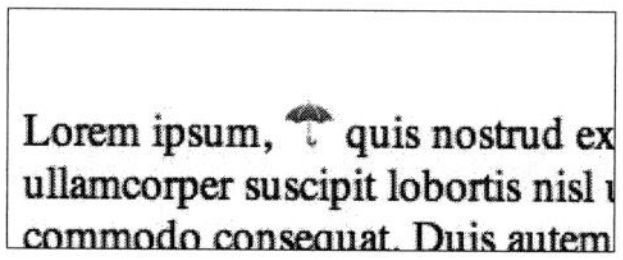

Lorem ipsum, ☂ quis nostrud ex
ullamcorper suscipit lobortis nisl
commodo conseguat. Duis autem

FIGURE 14.1 *The image rests on the baseline of the text.*

The first three positions are relative to the text, regardless of other images on the text line. For alignment options, consider the invisible horizontal lines associated with typography: the **baseline**, the **descender** line, and the **ascender** line. A line of text rests on a baseline: picture a line drawn at the base of most letters. Some letters, such as p, j, and q, have tails, or descenders, that drop below the baseline to the descender line. If a letter is taller than a lowercase x, such as b, l, or t, it has an ascender. More simply, the ascender line sits at the top of any capital letter.

The out of the box or default value for **vertical-align** is **baseline**. This means that an image is placed on the invisible line that the text "rests on" (**FIGURE 14.1**).

```
img {
  vertical-align: baseline;
}
```

LOOKING TO THE FUTURE

Other fascinating and admittedly easier ways to position images are in development, but they're not ready for use on sites at the time of this writing:

- Box Alignment—http://dev.w3.org/csswg/css3-align
- Flexible Box Layout—http://www.w3.org/TR/css3-flexbox

For a good review of FlexBox and other web design technologies, listen to the Non-Breaking Space Show's conversation with Tab Atkins, a web standards hacker at Google at http://nonbreakingspace.tv/tab-atkins.

Text-Bottom

The **text-bottom** value positions the bottom of the image at the descender line, the level where character descenders end (**FIGURE 14.2**).

```
img {
  vertical-align: text-bottom;
}
```

Of course, if the image is larger than the text line, it pushes down the text line it rests on (**FIGURE 14.3**).

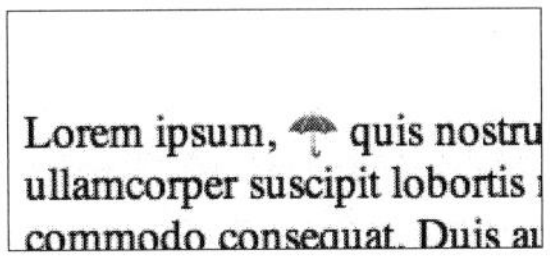

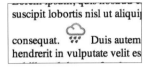

FIGURE 14.2 *The image rests at the same level as the descenders.*

FIGURE 14.3 *The text is pushed lower than the normal line spacing by an image that's taller than the height of one line.*

Text-Top

The opposite of placing an image with **text-bottom** is to place it using **text-top**. This value aligns the top of the image with the top of the ascender line (**FIGURE 14.4**).

```
img {
  vertical-align: text-top;
}
```

While **text-bottom** pushes down its own text line, if the image using **text-top** is larger than the text line, it pushes down the text below its own line (**FIGURE 14.5**).

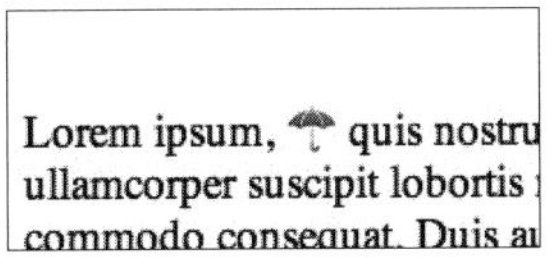

FIGURE 14.4 *The image is flush with the top of the text.*

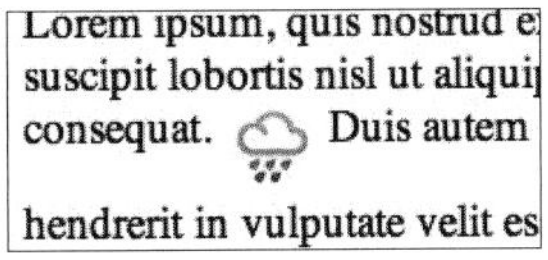

FIGURE 14.5 *When aligned text-top, the image pushes out the text below the line.*

Top and Bottom

Top and bottom are similar to their text-top and text-bottom counterparts with an exception. If there's another, larger image in the flow of the text, the image with this value will align to the top or bottom of the other image, rather than to the text (see **FIGURE 14.6** and **FIGURE 14.7**).

```
img {
  vertical-align: top;
}

img {
  vertical-align: bottom;
}
```

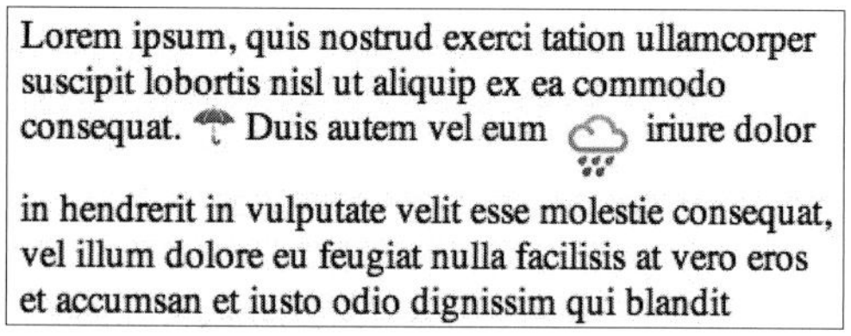

FIGURE 14.6 *The images are aligned to the top of the text/image line.*

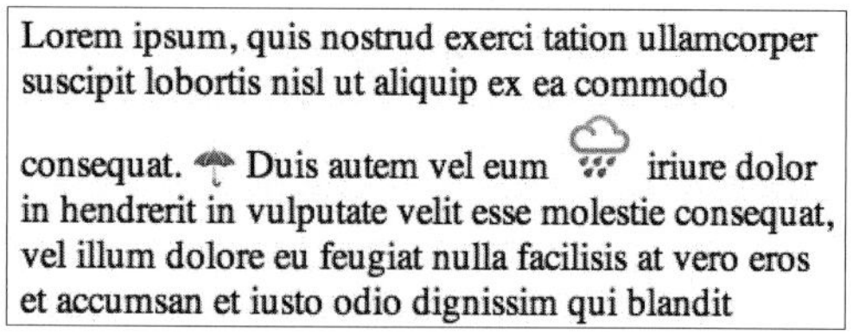

FIGURE 14.7 *The images are aligned to the bottom of the text/image line.*

Middle

The final value for the **vertical-align** property is **middle**. When it comes across this value, the browser determines the vertical center point of the text (**FIGURE 14.8**) and places the image accordingly.

```
img {
  vertical-align: middle;
}
```

Use this approach only with icons or small images, as images larger than the text introduce extra line spacing to the line above *and* below the image (**FIGURE 14.9**).

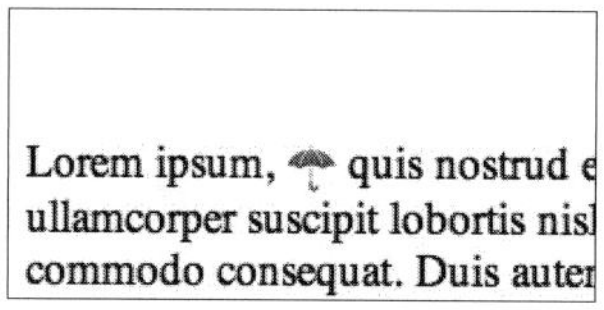

FIGURE 14.8 *The image is vertically centered with the text.*

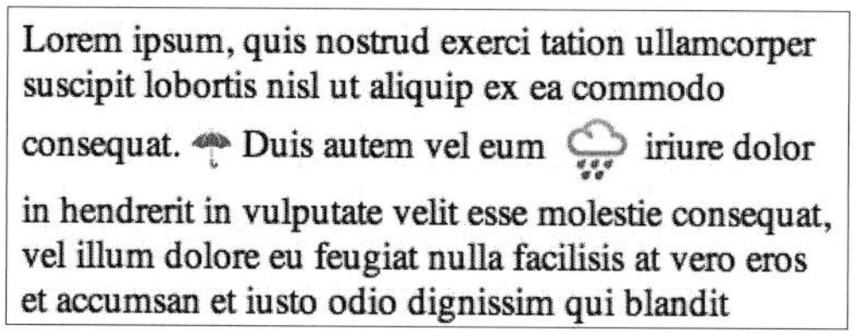

FIGURE 14.9 *The large icon creates more space above and below the line it rests in.*

CENTERING IMAGES IN THE WINDOW

Centering images both vertically and horizontally in the browser window is tricky. Your *approach* to centering an image within the browser window depends on the *technique* you want to use: positioning in the background with CSS, CSS positioning with negative margins, or CSS positioning with JavaScript. Each way has pros and cons.

In the Background with CSS

One way of displaying an image in the center of a page is to set the image as the background of the HTML element (**FIGURE 14.10**).

```css
html {
  width:100%;
  height:100%;
  background:url(logo.png) center center
  no-repeat;
}
```

It's critical to set the HTML element to 100%. Typically, a browser will only render a page *just* to the bottom of the content. So, when the viewer expands the browser's viewport to fill the monitor, the design expands only as far as the content.

For example, if you have a web page with only a small paragraph, and taking up less height than the image, the background image will not display properly (**FIGURE 14.11**).

By setting the width and height of the **html** element to 100% of the viewport, we instruct the browser to fill the entire window, not just the area with content.

A limitation of using the background to center an image is that it's not clickable and, therefore, cannot link to anything. There are a couple of solutions to center an image so that it can be turned into a link: CSS positioning with or without JavaScript.

FIGURE 14.10 *The image is centered through easy-to-set CSS background properties.*

FIGURE 14.11 *The background image is clipped to the height of the content in the browser.*

FIGURE 14.12 *The upper left corner of the image is centered, but what needs to be centered is the center of the image.*

FIGURE 14.13 *The image is now centered within the browser window, and is clickable.*

Just the CSS

To center a clickable image in the browser, use absolute positioning and set the offset properties at half of the browser height and width:

```
img {
    position: absolute;
    top: 50%;
    left: 50%;
}
```

Absolute positioning takes the image out of the normal flow of the document (as discussed in Chapter 2, "Styling with CSS"), but the 50% position doesn't quite center it (**FIGURE 14.12**). That's because the browser centers on the top left corner of the image.

To center an image, first set its width and height. Then use negative margins to pull the image to the left and top. These values should be half of the width and height so that the image's center matches with the center of the browser (**FIGURE 14.13**).

```
img {
    position: absolute;
    top: 50%;
    left: 50%;
    width: 600px;
    height: 336px;
    margin-left: -300px; /* Half of width */
    margin-top: -168px; /* Half of height */
}
```

No Need to Hardcode Numbers, Thanks to jQuery

If we were just dealing with only one image, we could set its width and height as well as half values for the the negative margins and that would be it.

But chances are that, as time passes, you'll need to update a centered image with another that has new dimensions. That means having to open up the CSS file, edit the dimensions, do more math, and so on.

To work around this doomsday scenario of math, we can offload the math onto something that likes it a lot: JavaScript. Specifically, jQuery. The first step is to set up the HTML as shown below. The results are shown in **FIGURE 14.14**.

```
<figure class="center">
 <img src="http://placekitten.com/400/400"
 width="400" height="400" />
</figure>
```

Use a bit of CSS for the basic absolute positioning.

```
.center {
 position: absolute;
}
```

Then, in your HTML document, insert a reference to jQuery along with this short snippet of code that does the math manipulation on the fly and updates the CSS for positioning (**FIGURE 14.15**):

```
<script src="http://code.jquery.com/
jquery-latest.min.js">
</script>
<script>
$(document).ready(function() {
 var $img = $('.center img');
 var h = $img.height();
 var w = $img.width();
 $img.css({
  marginTop: "-" + (h / 2) + "px",
  marginLeft: "-" + (h / 2) + "px"
 });
});
</script>
```

FIGURE 14.14 *The default rendering of the image.*

FIGURE 14.15 *The image is now centered and ready to take any width or height.*

> **! SET THE WIDTH AND HEIGHT**
>
> Be sure to set the **width** and **height** attributes in the **img** element, so that the JavaScript can access the dimensions of the image.

STRETCHING AN IMAGE ACROSS A BROWSER WINDOW

To make a bold impression, you can have an image take up the entire browser window. First, center the image as a background through CSS:

```
html {
  margin: 0;
  padding: 0;
  background: url(beach.jpg) no-repeat center
center fixed;
}
```

Then use the **background-size** property set to **cover** (**FIGURE 14.16**):

```
html {
  margin: 0;
  padding: 0;
  background: url(beach.jpg) no-repeat center
center fixed;
  background-size: cover;
}
```

The **cover** value tells the browser to fill the entire browser window with the background image. The browser will not distort the image in this stretching process. If the image doesn't match the proportion of the browser window, a portion of the background image might be cropped out by the viewport.

The **contain** value tells the browser to scale the image so that even though the image is stretched, the image isn't clipped as with **cover**. There will be areas of white space to the sides or top and bottom of an image as shown in **FIGURE 14.17**.

FIGURE 14.16 *The background image stretches to fill the entire space of the viewport.*

FIGURE 14.17 *The entire image is visible in the browser, but has white space at the top and bottom.*

Since raster formats like JPEG or PNG produce artifacts when displayed larger than their original size, it's a good idea to use SVG images, which are scalable (**FIGURE 14.18**).

```
html {
  margin: 0;
  padding: 0;
  background: url(example.svg) no-repeat center
center fixed;
  background-size: cover;
}
```

Of course, an image doesn't need to be as big as a browser window to make an impact on the overall design, but it might help.

IN CONCLUSION

Creating image-rich layouts means integrating images throughout your pages. Experiment with aligning them using relative or absolute positioning, and floats, depending on your needs. In this chapter we've covered three specific alignment situations that you might find challenging trying to do on your own. Now, explore how they can be used to fit into almost any area of your web design.

FIGURE 14.18 *Use the SVG file format to eliminate artifacts when enlarging an image like this beach illustration.*

CONCLUSION

We've covered a lot of ground in this book to help you become a great web designer. *Designing Web and Mobile Graphics* can't take the place of sweating the details to make every page look great, however.

To get better and faster, the best thing to do is to build web sites!

There's always something to figure out, like CSS property values, debugging browser issues, showing HTML elements, and so on. If you have a client project, great. What's even better is your idea for a project.

For example, Jessica Hische created a web page to help her mother understand how Twitter works (**FIGURE 1**) and a page describing her courtship and engagement to her husband (**FIGURE 2**). She did that in addition to her main website, which promotes her skills as a letterer.

Chris Coyier, the web designer behind CSS-Tricks.com, has built Quotes on Design (**FIGURE 3**) and a copy-and-paste HTML page (**FIGURE 4**).

Keep on learning, keep on building, and keep on launching new web projects.

My Twitter handle is @teleject. When you have a new, personal site up and ready, make sure to let me and others know about your latest creation.

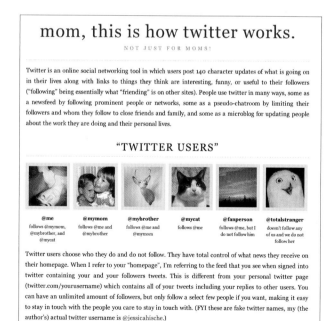

FIGURE 1 *Jessica Hische's funny and resourceful Twitter how-to.*

FIGURE 2 *Sharing the news about their love story.*

FIGURE 4 *Copy-and-paste sample HTML elements.*

FIGURE 3 *Chris Coyier's simply inspiring site for designers.*

INDEX